T0213193

Lecture Notes in Computer Science   10465

Commenced Publication in 1973
Founding and Former Series Editors:
Gerhard Goos, Juris Hartmanis, and Jan van Leeuwen

More information about this series at http://www.springer.com/series/7408

Flavio De Paoli · Stefan Schulte
Einar Broch Johnsen (Eds.)

Service-Oriented and Cloud Computing

6th IFIP WG 2.14 European Conference, ESOCC 2017
Oslo, Norway, September 27–29, 2017
Proceedings

 Springer

Editors
Flavio De Paoli
University of Milano-Bicocca
Milan
Italy

Einar Broch Johnsen
University of Oslo
Oslo
Norway

Stefan Schulte
Vienna University of Technology
Vienna
Austria

ISSN 0302-9743 ISSN 1611-3349 (electronic)
Lecture Notes in Computer Science
ISBN 978-3-319-67261-8 ISBN 978-3-319-67262-5 (eBook)
DOI 10.1007/978-3-319-67262-5

Library of Congress Control Number: 2017952388

LNCS Sublibrary: SL2 – Programming and Software Engineering

Printed on acid-free paper

This Springer imprint is published by Springer Nature
The registered company is Springer International Publishing AG
The registered company address is: Gewerbestrasse 11, 6330 Cham, Switzerland

Preface

These days, service-oriented computing and cloud computing have become pervasive in the software industry and the end-user market. We see services and the usage of cloud-based computational resources practically everywhere, regardless of particular application areas or target users. Service-oriented computing and cloud computing have gone a long way since their advent, but emerging technologies, aiming at the convergence of devices, networks, and the Internet of Things (IoT), sustain a very active research community aiming to develop these technologies further to build *smart* systems in research, business, and social contexts.

For the European research community, the European Conference on Service-Oriented and Cloud Computing (ESOCC) is the premier conference on advances in the state of the art and practice of service-oriented computing and cloud computing. The 6th event, ESOCC 2017, took place during September 27–29, 2017 at the University of Oslo, Norway, bringing together researchers and practitioners in the field.

ESOCC 2017 featured a number of events, most importantly the main research track, dedicated to the presentation of novel advances in the state of the art of service-oriented computing and cloud computing, and the industry track, dedicated to the presentation of applications and usage of services, concepts from service-oriented computing and cloud computing, and cloud-based computational resources in industry. Overall, 37 submissions were received, out of which 10 were accepted as full papers and another 6 as short papers. These papers (plus a keynote paper) are featured in these proceedings.

Each submission received at least three reviews by the members of the Program Committee (PC), with most submissions receiving four reviews. The review process was carried out in a "single blind" fashion. After the initial review phase, a discussion was initiated, which helped to further evaluate the strengths and weaknesses of the submissions. The program chairs thank the PC members and the additional reviewers for their accurate and extensive reviewing activities, which helped to improve the quality of the submissions and were also a big help to the authors of rejected papers.

This year, the conference featured a special track on the IoT, which aimed at showing how new requirements towards service-oriented computing and cloud computing arise because of the IoT. Vice versa, the second aim of this track was to show how the ESOCC community contributes to fulfilling the technical needs (and therefore the success) of the IoT.

As part of the main technical program, two inspiring keynotes were given by Stefan Tai (Full Professor and Head of Chair Information Systems Engineering at TU Berlin, Germany) and Hatay Tuna (Principal Software Architect, Azure Engineering, Microsoft). Stefan provided a talk on "Blockchain Insights", showing the potential of blockchain technologies to transform how organizations produce and capture value. Hatay gave insights on key experiences, patterns, and practices for "Design for Cloud".

Along with the main conference program, ESOCC featured a PhD symposium and an EU projects track, bringing together PhD students and EU project participants, respectively. In addition, three workshops were planned: REthinking SERvices CHallenges – Services Meet Data (IFIP WG SOS Workshop 2017), BPM@Cloud, and the 3rd International Workshop on Cloud Adoption and Migration (CloudWays). The proceedings are published separately.

The program chairs and the general chair would like to express their deep appreciation to all those who helped to make ESOCC 2017 a success. This includes the 55 PC members and the additional reviewers, the chairs and organizers of the PhD symposium, workshops, and EU projects track, as well as the many unnamed helpers who contributed in the background. We are especially grateful to the local organizing committee for their support, organizational efforts, and hospitality. Also, our thanks go to IFIP for supporting ESOCC 2017.

Finally, we thank all authors of research and industry papers, and those who presented their results, for contributing to this successful conference. With their work and dedication, ESOCC continues its tradition in advancing the field of service-oriented computing and cloud computing.

September 2017

Flavio De Paoli
Stefan Schulte
Einar Broch Johnsen

Organization

ESOCC 2017 was organized by the University of Oslo, Norway.

Organizing Committee

General Chair

Einar Broch Johnsen   University of Oslo, Norway

Program Chairs

Flavio De Paoli   University of Milano-Bicocca, Italy
Stefan Schulte   TU Wien, Austria

Industry Track Chairs

Alexander Lenk   BMW, Germany
Arne-Jørgen Berre   Sintef, Norway

Workshop Chairs

Zoltán Ádám Mann   University of Duisburg-Essen, Germany
Volker Stolz   Bergen University College, Norway

EU Projects Chair

Antonio Brogi   University of Pisa, Italy

Local Chair

Ingrid Chieh Yu   University of Oslo, Norway

Website Chair

Jacopo Mauro   University of Oslo, Norway

Steering Committee

Antonio Brogi   University of Pisa, Italy
Schahram Dustdar   TU Wien, Austria
Paul Grefen   Eindhoven University of Technology, The Netherlands
Kung-Kiu Lau   University of Manchester, UK
Winfried Lamersdorf   University of Hamburg, Germany
Frank Leymann   University of Stuttgart, Germany
Flavio De Paoli   University of Milano-Bicocca, Italy
Cesare Pautasso   University of Lugano, Switzerland

Ernesto Pimentel   University of Málaga, Spain
Ulf Schreier   University of Applied Sciences Furtwangen, Germany
Massimo Villari   University of Messina, Italy
John Erik Wittern   IBM Thomas J. Watson Research Center, USA
Gianluigi Zavattaro   University of Bologna, Italy
Olaf Zimmermann   HSR FHO Rapperswil, Switzerland
Wolf Zimmermann   Martin Luther University Halle-Wittenberg, Germany

Program Committee

Marco Aiello   University of Groningen, The Netherlands
Vasilios Andrikopoulos   University of Groningen, The Netherlands
Farhad Arbab   CWI, The Netherlands
Luciano Baresi   Politecnico di Milano, Italy
Frank de Boer   CWI, The Netherlands
Antonio Brogi   University of Pisa, Italy
Giacomo Cabri   University of Modena and Reggio Emilia, Italy
Roberto di Cosmo   Université Paris Diderot, France
Javier Cubo   University of Malaga, Spain
Juergen Dunkel   FH Hannover, Germany
Schahram Dustdar   TU Wien, Austria
Robert Engel   IBM Almaden, USA
Rik Eshuis   Eindhoven University of Technology, The Netherlands
David Eyers   University of Otago, New Zealand
George Feuerlicht   Prague University of Economics, Czech Republic
Marisol García-Valls   Universidad Carlos III de Madrid, Spain
Ilche Georgievski   University of Groningen, The Netherlands
Claude Godart   University of Lorraine, France
Paul Grefen   Eindhoven University of Technology, The Netherlands
Heerko Groefsema   University of Groningen, The Netherlands
Thomas Gschwind   IBM Zurich Research Lab, Switzerland
Reiner Haehnle   TU Darmstadt, Germany
Martin Henkel   Stockholm University, Sweden
Einar Broch Johnsen   University of Oslo, Norway
Birgitta Koenig-Ries   Universität Jena, Germany
Oliver Kopp   University of Stuttgart, Germany
Ernoe Kovacs   NEC Europe Network Labs, Germany
Peep Küngas   University of Tartu, Estonia
Patricia Lago   Vrije Universiteit Amsterdam, The Netherlands
Winfried Lamersdorf   University of Hamburg, Germany
Kung-Kiu Lau   University of Manchester, UK
Philipp Leitner   University of Zurich, Switzerland
Jörg Lenhard   Karlstad University, Sweden
Frank Leymann   University of Stuttgart, Germany
Welf Loewe   Linnaeus University, Sweden
Zoltán Ádám Mann   University of Duisburg-Essen, Germany

Roy Oberhauser	Aalen University, Germany
Guadalupe Ortiz	University of Cádiz, Spain
Claus Pahl	Free University of Bozen-Bolzano, Italy
Flavio De Paoli	University of Milano-Bicocca, Italy
Cesare Pautasso	University of Lugano, Switzerland
Ernesto Pimentel	University of Malaga, Spain
Pierluigi Plebani	Politecnico di Milano, Italy
Stefanie Rinderle-Ma	University of Vienna, Austria
Dumitru Roman	Sintef, Norway
Alessandro Rossini	Evry Cloud Services, Norway
Ulf Schreier	University of Applied Sciences Furtwangen, Germany
Stefan Schulte	TU Wien, Austria
Maarten van Steen	University of Twente, The Netherlands
Massimo Villari	University of Messina, Italy
Ingo Weber	Data61, Australia
Erik Wilde	CA Technologies, Switzerland
John Erik Wittern	IBM Thomas J. Watson Research Center, USA
Lai Xu	Bournemouth University, UK
Gianluigi Zavattaro	University of Bologna, Italy
Olaf Zimmermann	HSR FHO Rapperswil, Switzerland
Wolf Zimmermann	Martin Luther University Halle-Wittenberg, Germany
Christian Zirpins	University of Applied Sciences Karlsruhe, Germany

Additional Reviewers

Kristof Böhmer	University of Vienna, Austria
Richard Bubel	TU Darmstadt, Germany
Mehdi Fahmideh	University of New South Wales, Australia
Alireza Farhadi	Sharif University of Technology, Iran
Andrei Furda	Queensland University of Technology, Australia
Stijn de Gouw	CWI, The Netherlands
Philipp Hoenisch	Data61, Australia
Marc Hüffmeyer	University of Applied Sciences Furtwangen, Germany
Ahmad Ibrahim	University of Pisa, Italy
Georg Kaes	University of Vienna, Austria
Alexander Lazovik	University of Groningen, The Netherlands
Ivano Malavolta	Vrije Universiteit Amsterdam, The Netherlands
Matt McLarty	ca technologies, USA
Irakli Nadareishvili	Capital One, USA
Nikolay Nikolov	Sintef, Norway
Alfonso Garcia de Prado Fontela	University of Cádiz, Spain
Luca Rinaldi	University of Pisa, Italy
Adrian Rutle	Bergen University College, Norway

Brian Setz	University of Groningen, The Netherlands
Ang Sha	University of Groningen, The Netherlands
Mirco Stocker	HSR FHO Rapperswil, Switzerland
Oktay Turetken	Eindhoven University of Technology, The Netherlands
Bjørn Marius von Zernichow	Sintef, Norway

Contents

Keynote Paper

On or Off the Blockchain?
Insights on Off-Chaining Computation and Data

Jacob Eberhardt[✉] and Stefan Tai

Information Systems Engineering (ISE), TU Berlin, Berlin, Germany
{je,st}@ise.tu-berlin.de

Abstract. The potential for blockchains to fundamentally transform how organizations produce and capture value is huge and very real. Practical applications dealing with nearly any type of digital asset demonstrate this capacity. Blockchain-based application architectures benefit from a set of unique properties including immutability and transparency of cryptographically-secured and peer-recorded transactions, which have been agreed upon by network consensus. Blockchain-based applications, however, may also suffer from high computational and storage expenses, negatively impacting overall performance and scalability. In this paper, we report on lessons learned and insights gained from a set of experimental blockchain projects, focusing on off-chaining: How to move computation and data off-the-chain, without compromising the properties introduced and benefits gained by using blockchains in the first place.

1 Introduction

Blockchains are a combination of different computing and economics concepts, predominantly including peer-to-peer networks, asymmetric cryptography, consensus protocols, decentralized storage, decentralized computing and smart contracts, and incentive mechanisms. The synthesis of these concepts positions blockchains as a new technology and as a programmable platform and network at the same time. Blockchains introduce unique properties including immutability and transparency of cryptographically-secured and peer-recorded transactions, which have been agreed upon by network consensus. As such, the potential associated with blockchain to fundamentally transform how organizations produce and capture value is huge – and very real. While initially discussed especially in the financial services sector, there are practical applications today dealing with nearly any type of digital asset, ranging from asset provenance to peer-to-peer commerce. Establishing trustless interactions and business disintermediation remain major objectives when using blockchains.

Over the past two years, we have conducted a set of blockchain projects at the Information Systems Engineering research group at TU Berlin, mostly experimental projects that focus on a particular application challenge and which have been carried out in collaboration with industry partners. Further, we are

Published by Springer International Publishing AG 2017. All Rights Reserved
F. De Paoli et al. (Eds.): ESOCC 2017, LNCS 10465, pp. 3–15, 2017.
DOI: 10.1007/978-3-319-67262-5_1

conducting foundational research on blockchain technology and platforms, taking a distributed systems and data management perspective. In both settings, the question of on-chaining versus off-chaining is recurring: What exactly has to be on the chain and what can be off the chain, while retaining the overall properties and benefits associated with blockchains?

On-chain data – in the form of confirmed transactions organized in ordered blocks – and on-chain code – in the form of programs written in a general-purpose, Turing-complete language – require validation and consensus by network peers and result in append-only changes to the blockchain as a shared datastore that cannot be reversed. Transaction validation, consensus protocols, and decentralized program execution may, however, describe a communication and execution overhead. And they simply do take time. In addition, miners (that is, nodes that validate transactions and propose new blocks) typically charge fees, thereby incurring financial costs. Overall, scalability of the blockchain-based system may suffer. Bitcoin currently has a limit of 7 transactions per second; Ethereum has a limit of about 15 transactions per second. Furthermore, anything on the (public) blockchain is not inherently anonymous, but on the contrary purposely visible; privacy and confidentiality are not guaranteed for on-chain transactions.

The objective for off-chaining data and computation is to reduce or to overcome such limitations. By moving data and computation elsewhere off the blockchain, for example, to another datastore, server, or third party, the blockchain "footprint" obviously is reduced. However, the fundamental properties of blockchains and blockchain-based applications, may be compromised to different degrees when doing so. They may even be potentially prohibitively violated when using naive off-chaining approaches. After all, the system should remain "trustless" in the sense that no explicit trust is required.

In this paper, we report on first insights gained on off-chaining computation and data. We present five off-chaining patterns and discuss the context, principle idea, and implementation for each.

2   Blockchains and Smart Contracts

In a nutshell, blockchains are distributed peer-to-peer systems which implement a trustless shared public append-only transaction ledger [14].

Blockchains. Bitcoin, the first implementation of such a system, was proposed in 2008 by Satoshi Nakamoto [10]. The goal which led to the creation of the Bitcoin protocol was the design of a digital currency which allows the transfer of digital value fully peer-to-peer without relying on a trusted intermediary. To implement such a decentralized cryptocurrency, the system combines transactions secured by asymmetric cryptography with a consensus algorithm to decide on the transaction order within the network. Peers in the network can validate individual transactions by checking cryptographic signatures. In addition to that, however, a global order of the transactions has to be decided on to prevent double spending of digital funds. For that, as a main innovation of the Bitcoin system, the proof-of-work consensus protocol was developed which allocates the right to add transactions to the network in proportion to the computational effort spent to secure the network. For efficiency, multiple transactions are grouped into a block. These blocks are then ordered by consensus. Each block references its predecessor, which implies a chain data structure – the blockchain.

Extending Bitcoins idea of peer-to-peer value transfer, Ethereum, a trustless computing platform, was proposed in 2014 [9,16]. Ethereum adds a turing complete and stateful programming language to the blockchain idea, which enables the execution of complex code without trusting a server or central party. Trust is replaced by validating each program execution on every peer in the network and agreeing on an outcome.

Smart Contracts. These programs executed in a trustless and tamper-proof manner in the network are referred to as Smart Contracts. Note, that Smart Contracts need to be deterministic as otherwise peers could disagree on the results of valid executions. Hence, e.g., filesystem and network access are not permitted. While the term may imply a close connection to legal contracts, smart contracts have a much wider range of use cases and can be applied where automatically executed complex conditional logic is required. Hence, they can be imagined as self executing autonomous agents.

3   The Need for Off-Chaining Computation and Data

Over the last two years, we gained extensive experiences during proof-of-concept implementations of blockchain-based applications prototypes. We motivate off-chaining insights by discussing exemplary challenges for two of these applications. While all prototypes developed at TU Berlin have been realized on the Ethereum platform [9], we consider our findings to be representative for all of today's public blockchain implementations.

As a first application, we created a fair and manipulation-resistant chess game on the Ethereum platform [1].

Today, online gaming relies on a trusted intermediary which runs games and ensures players obey the rules. However, this intermediary needs to be trusted to not cheat or steal funds. To eliminate that trust, we implemented the chess logic as well as data structures required to persist the game state in a smart contract. Conceptually, that already solves the problem: Players send moves to the contract, which modifies game state persisted internally for valid moves. After a valid move, the contract checks end game conditions and pays out the winner if a condition is met. Checking end game conditions, however, is computationally expensive. All potential moves have to be calculated and verified to check the check mate condition. This is not possible in a smart contract as it violates the complexity upper bound for on-chain transactions.

Three things can be learned from that:

1. We need to find a way to perform the end-game check off chain, on the client side, without impacting the blockchain's trustlessness property.
2. As computations come with a fee, the end game check should be performed as rarely as possible. Hence, like in a physical chess game, we should have a player trigger the check instead of doing it after every valid move. In other words, we should move part of the control flow to the client side.
3. We have to expect to reach scalability limits of blockchains when creating applications. This emphasizes the need for research in and development of off-chaining techniques.

Another much more complex proof-of-concept was a decentralized service marketplace which enables trustless disintermediation between providers and consumers of service APIs. Using a cryptocurrency for payments, a consumer can buy time-constrained access to a service offered on the market place without involving a marketplace intermediary. Especially service discovery, one of the main building blocks of a service marketplace, posed a big challenge within the fully decentralized design: Data storage on blockchains is extremely expensive due to full replication in the peer-to-peer network. Nonetheless, a meaningful service discovery feature requires API descriptions to be stored. Simply pointing to an off-chain reference from a smart contract, e.g., a file hosted in a cloud storage system, is no alternative to on-chain storage. This approach would introduce trust in the storage system since the data stored could change while the reference remains the same. Additionally, since all data in a blockchain is stored on every node in the network, it is publicly visible. There is no obvious way for a service provider to hide some of his service descriptions from the public.

As a direct consequence of this public visibility, there is no way to perform computations on private data on-chain without revealing it. Assume a consumer wants to prove to a provider that he has access to another provider's API. That second provider could publicly provide the hashes of all tokes that give access to his service. Then, the consumer could simply hash his private access token and show the hash to the first provider, which could in turn verify it by comparing it to the published hashes. However, for this to be trustless, the consumer would need to perform the hash operation on-chain and with that reveal his private token. Simply computing the hash off-chain would not proof anything to the provider.

Again, we derive three challenges from these findings:

1. We need to find a way to store data off the chain without giving up its manipulation-resistance.
2. As all on-chain data is publicly visible, techniques for trustless but privacy-preserving off-chain storage should be developed.
3. Off-chain computations on private data which can be verified on-chain without revealing said data would augment the set of possible use cases.

In summary, off-chaining strategies are needed to address both, functional limitations of and high costs incurring from on-chain computation and storage.

4   Off-Chaining Patterns

We now introduce a set of off-chaining patterns identified, which can be used individually or in combination to move computation and data off the blockchain. Each pattern aims at maintaining the key properties of blockchains and includes techniques to ensure that they are not compromised to an unwanted degree.

4.1   Challenge Response Pattern

Context: A smart contract models a state machine with well-defined final states. State transitions are cheap to compute, but checking whether a given state is a final state is expensive.

Solution: Instead of checking whether a state is final or not in a smart contract on a blockchain, the same check is performed off-chain on the client side. A client can notify a smart contract when a final state has been reached. Other clients can prove claims wrong by providing a valid state transition. Using this pattern, the computation never has to be performed on-chain (Fig. 1).

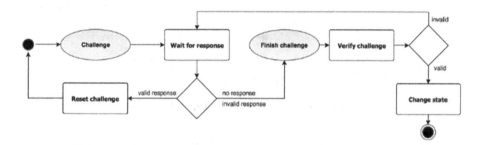

Fig. 1. Challenge response pattern

Example: The end game condition for chess is too expensive to check on-chain. The players, however, can easily check the condition off-chain. Hence, instead of checking the end game condition in a smart contract, a player simply claims check mate. If the claim was false, his opponent can simply prove him wrong by submitting a valid move. If the claim was true and the opponent cannot submit a valid move, the winner is paid out. Figure 2 gives an overview of the full challenge response protocol for chess also considering draws and timeouts. For a more detailed description, we refer to [1,2].

Discussion: This pattern allows computations to be off-chained efficiently in scenarios where smart contracts act as state-machines. Since it allows for complex operations to be moved completely off-chain and with that circumvents the complexity upper-bound for on-chain transactions, it can extend possible

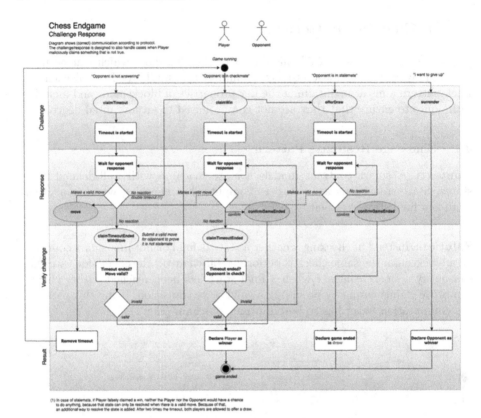

Fig. 2. Challenge response pattern applied for chess

use cases and potentially lead to cost savings. Note though, that the pattern increases the overall amount of on-chain transactions, which requires a careful calculation of costs. Also, increased availability of the parties involved in the smart contract implementing the pattern is required, since the use of timeouts is essential to ensure progress.

Implementation: This pattern does not require additional technologies besides smart contracts. For an exemplary implementation of this pattern, refer to [2].

4.2   Off-Chain Signatures Pattern

Context: Two network participants know that they will perform a set of transactions in the future. They want to reduce the cost of these transactions or want to hide them from other network participants.

Solution: Together, the two participants specify a smart contract including a function, which applies an external state given as argument to the contract state.

This function includes a signature check to ensure both participants agree with the state change. Only if valid signatures of both participants are supplied with a requested new state, the new state is applied. This contract is deployed to the blockchain and both participants optionally make a deposit.

Then, the participants perform transactions purely off-chain and peer-to-peer, without involving the blockchain: One participant computes a new state, wraps it in a transaction, signs it and sends it to his counterpart. The recipient then checks the new state, signs the transaction as well in case he agrees and sends it back to the sender.

This transaction, signed by both parties, can now be sent to the smart contract by a participant at any point in time. After validating both signatures, the contract updates its state accordingly.

Example: Participants A and B create a smart contract with a signature-locked state update function and deposit 50 units of cryptocurrency each. Now, A wants to transfer 10 units to B. For that, she creates a transaction locally, which includes a new state where A and B have balances of 40 and 60. She signs it and sends it to B, who signs it as well. Now, B can use the transaction to update the on-chain balance at any point in time. However, A and B could perform further off-chain value transfers without ever settling on-chain unless one side's deposit is used up. This application of the pattern for off-chain value transfer is often referred to as payment channel.

Discussion: This pattern allows efficient off-chain transactions without introducing trust into the system. The core insight is, that the guarantee to be able to settle a transaction is as good as actually executing the transaction on-chain. Signing a new state is analogous to writing a check in a traditional financial transaction. Using off-chain transactions can lead to significant cost savings as transaction fees only apply for on-chain settlement. Furthermore, the pattern can enhance privacy and confidentiality, as all transactions but the final settlement remain hidden from the network. From a blockchain network perspective, this pattern helps to take load off the system and with that enhances scalability.

There are many other applications besides simple value transfers. As shown in Fig. 3, we were able to move the core parts of the chess game off-chain by using this pattern. This not only helped to lower the cost of a game, but also to remove time dependence on block intervals.

Since initial deposits to the smart contracts are required in most cases, establishing contracts with many peers can lock a considerable amount of funds. Also, malicious participants could freeze funds by denying signatures. Hence, contracts should specify timeouts which trigger automatic settlement.

Implementation: Besides on-chain smart contracts, this pattern requires a peer-to-peer communication channel to exchange signed off-chain transactions. In the Ethereum ecosystem, for example, the Whisper Messaging Protocol [4] can

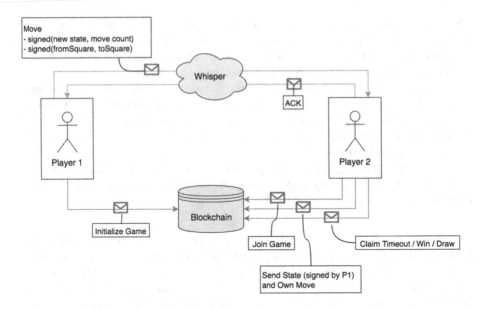

Fig. 3. Off- and on-chain interactions in the chess application

be used. There are various efforts to leverage this pattern to build off-chain value transfer networks for existing blockchains: The lightning network [12] provides an implementation for the Bitcoin ecosystem, while Raiden [5] targets the Ethereum network.

4.3   Content-Addressable Storage Pattern

Context: A large amount of data is associated with a smart contract. On-chain storage is too expensive.

Solution: Store the data off-chain in a content-addressable storage system and store the reference in the smart contract. Clients using the smart contract can retrieve the reference and based on that retrieve the data. Then, they can verify the data's correctness by recomputing its address from itself and comparing it to the reference stored in the smart contract.

Example: A smart contract encodes ownership of a piece of digital art. However, a piece of art would be very expensive to store on-chain due to its size. To solve this problem, the description is stored in a content-addressable storage system which stores files by their hashes. The file hash is also stored in the smart contract, serving as a reference to the artwork. Clients can then retrieve the hash of the externally stored piece of art from the contract and use it to query the storage system. The result can then simply be hashed to verify its correctness (Fig. 4).

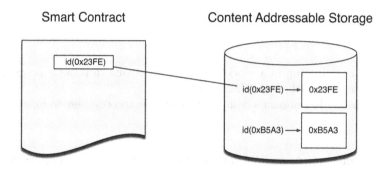

Fig. 4. Content-addressable storage pattern

Discussion: This pattern allows the trustless outsourcing of data to an off-chain storage system since a modification in the data would immediately change its address and with that invalidate its references.

By applying the pattern, an application's storage cost can be greatly reduced and files, which originally could not be stored on-chain in the first place, can now be referenced without introducing trust. Additionally, as the data retrieval is done on the client side from an external storage system, privacy features may be implemented by adding access control to that system. However, this requires careful considerations depending on the use case, since leaked data can immediately be confirmed to be authentic by recalculating its address.

While not in scope of this pattern, the required external content-addressable storage system itself has to be reliable and available. In case of unavailability or data-loss, the blockchain-based part of the application may also become unavailable.

In the future, this pattern could be extended to support trustless computation on data stored off-chain: First, content-addressed data referenced from a smart contract could be sent to the contract. Then, integrity could be verified on chain. In case of success, the smart contract could modify the data, update its reference to that new data and write it to an event. An untrusted external worker could then write that data back to the content-addressable storage system the inputs were retrieved from. While theoretically interesting, we did not yet observe this extension. Hence, it is not part of the pattern.

Implementation: As mentioned before, a content-addressable storage system is required to work in conjunction with smart contracts. Two such technologies, which address data by its hash and try to ensure availability and durability are the Interplanetary File System (IPFS) [7] and Swarm [15].

4.4   Delegated Computation Pattern

Context:

(a) A node participating in a blockchain network wants to prove a property of its private data without publishing it.
(b) A node wants to perform a computation that is too complex to be executed on-chain.

Solution: Outsource computation to an untrusted third party and, besides the result, generate a proof of correct execution. Instead of executing the computation itself, verify the proof of correct execution on-chain (Fig. 5).

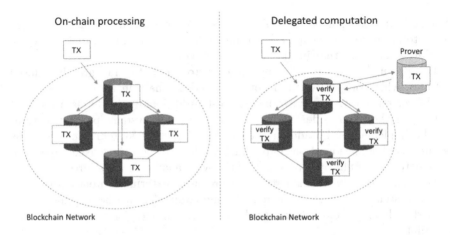

Fig. 5. On-chain processing vs. delegated computation pattern

Example: There is an on-chain list of hashes of ID-card information which refers to people who are allowed to call a smart contract function. Now, anyone listed can prove that he has an ID-card which authorizes him to call the contract function by hashing his card information locally and supplying the result including a proof of correctness. The proof does not require to reveal any of the information on the card.

Discussion: This pattern allows the trustless outsourcing of computation to untrusted parties. The third party, also called the prover, does not have to reveal any private inputs or intermediate results of the proof creation. The only information leaked is that the prover knows all the information necessary to correctly compute the output. For that, non-interactive zero-knowledge proofs, more specifically zero-knowledge Succinct Non-interactive ARgument of Knowledge (zkSNARKs), can be employed [8,11].

Unlike with regular computations on the blockchain, this pattern allows off-chained computations to hide information used during execution. Hence, not having to expose information but the result of a computation greatly enhances privacy. Furthermore, the proofs can be designed in a way that the verification cost is independent of the complexity of the off-chained computation. Thus, after a complexity threshold is reached, on-chain verification of a computation is cheaper than its on-chain execution. This result can be leveraged to increase a blockchain's throughput. Even operations exceeding the on-chain complexity limits for computations may still be executed off-chain using this patterns.

The state of the art non-interactive zero-knowledge proofs require a trusted setup phase to be performed before proofs can be generated. This can, depending on the use case, introduce undesirable trust in the overall system. Additionally, the proof generation for a computation causes an overhead over its non-verifiable execution. Yet, there is neither a high level language for the convenient specification of off-chain computations nor are there tools for simple on-chain verification of proofs. Therefore, while powerful and already used in practice, this pattern is currently only applied in rather specific scenarios, e.g., in zCash, which is a Bitcoin-based blockchain which implements privacy preserving transactions [6,13].

Implementation: For the verification of off-chain computations from smart contracts, the underlying blockchain needs to support the operations needed to check proofs. These can either be use case specific, or universal building blocks which can be used to verify any proof. While zCash directly added the verification logic for their specific computation to their protocol, Ethereum plans to add operations to support verification of arbitrary zkSNARKs with the Ethereum Improvement Proposals 196 and 197 [3].

4.5 Low Contract Footprint Pattern

Context: Changing a smart contract's state requires an on-chain transaction. To incentivize the processing of a transaction by the network, a fee has to be paid. This fee depends on the complexity of the smart contract function called as well as its use of storage.

Solution: To optimize fees, contracts should be designed in a way that minimizes the number and size of on-chain transactions. The following two techniques can be used to reduce the footprint.

- Do not check conditions on-chain after a state change. Let nodes perform the condition check locally and trigger an on-chain check in case of success.
- Optimize for writes, not reads. Reading from a smart contracts is a local off-chain operation and does not require an on-chain transaction. Minimize writes and store information free of redundancy. Compute derived data locally during reads.

Examples:

- In the service marketplace application, a service provider needs to make sure consumers are removed from the on-chain authorization list after the time period the consumer paid for is over. Instead of periodically triggering or linking the condition check to another contract function and risking frequent reevaluation, he tracks the access period locally and triggers the on-chain check after it has elapsed. This reduces the amount of on-chain evaluations to one.
- If the service provider wants to know the number of customers currently subscribed to his service, he should not add a counter to the smart contract. He can compute the number locally at any point from the authorization list. This saves storage space and counter update operations.

Discussion: This pattern may not initially seem like an off-chaining approach, as it does not explicitly take something off the chain. However, it prevents information to be stored or processed on-chain in the first place. Hence, this may be the least obvious, but the most employed and intuitive off-chaining pattern.

Implementation: No additional components or techniques are required besides smart contracts to implement this pattern.

5   Summary and Outlook

In this paper we motivated the need for off-chain approaches to overcome limitations in today's blockchain implementations and even more, to extend their functionality and to reduce usage costs. After deriving key challenges based on our experiences from implementing several blockchain-based applications, we presented five off-chaining patterns for moving computation and data off the blockchain, without compromising important blockchain properties, in particular, the trustlessness property.

We expect blockchain systems to further mature and improve with regards to scalability and privacy in the future by combining and implementing ideas like, for example, new consensus algorithms, sharding, or homomorphic encryption. However, we still consider off-chaining techniques to be key tools in blockchain-based application engineering as they introduce additional functionality and potentially significant cost benefits.

References

1. Chess on Ethereum. https://medium.com/@graycoding/lessons-learned-from-making-a-chess-game-for-ethereum-6917c01178b6. Accessed 26 June 2017
2. Ethereum Chess Proof-of-Concept Implementation. https://github.com/ise-ethereum/on-chain-chess. Accessed 26 June 2017

3. Ethereum Improvement Proposals (EIPs). https://github.com/ethereum/EIPs. Accessed 22 June 2017
4. Ethereum Whisper Protocol v5. https://github.com/ethereum/go-ethereum/wiki/Whisper. Accessed 27 June 2017
5. Raiden Network. http://raiden.network/. Accessed 12 May 2017
6. zCash. https://z.cash/. Accessed 20 June 2017
7. Benet, J.: IPFS - content addressed, versioned, P2P file system. CoRR abs/1407.3561 (2014). http://arxiv.org/abs/1407.3561
8. Bitansky, N., Canetti, R., Chiesa, A., Tromer, E.: From extractable collision resistance to succinct non-interactive arguments of knowledge, and back again. In: Proceedings of the 3rd Innovations in Theoretical Computer Science Conference, ITCS 2012, NY, USA, pp. 326–349 (2012). http://doi.acm.org/10.1145/2090236.2090263
9. Buterin, V.: Ethereum: a next-generation smart contract and decentralized application platform (2014). https://github.com/ethereum/wiki/wiki/%5BEnglish%5D-White-Paper
10. Nakamoto, S.: Bitcoin: a peer-to-peer electronic cash system (2008)
11. Parno, B., Howell, J., Gentry, C., Raykova, M.: Pinocchio: nearly practical verifiable computation. In: 2013 IEEE Symposium on Security and Privacy (SP), pp. 238–252. IEEE (2013)
12. Poon, J., Dryja, T.: The bitcoin lightning network: scalable off-chain instant payments (2015). https://lightning.network. Accessed 12 May 2017
13. Sasson, E.B., Chiesa, A., Garman, C., Green, M., Miers, I., Tromer, E., Virza, M.: Zerocash: decentralized anonymous payments from bitcoin. In: 2014 IEEE Symposium on Security and Privacy (SP), pp. 459–474. IEEE (2014)
14. Tai, S., Eberhardt, J., Klems, M.: Not ACID, not BASE, but SALT - a transaction processing perspective on blockchains. In: Proceedings of the 7th International Conference on Cloud Computing and Services Science, CLOSER, vol. 1, pp. 755–764. INSTICC, ScitePress (2017)
15. Trón, V., Fischer, A., Nagy, D.A., Felföldi, Z., Johnson, N.: Swap, swear and swindle - incentive system for swarm (2016)
16. Wood, G.: Ethereum: A secure decentralised generalised transaction ledger. Ethereum Project Yellow Paper (2014)

Microservices and Containers

Microservices Identification Through Interface Analysis

Luciano Baresi[1], Martin Garriga[1(✉)], and Alan De Renzis[2]

[1] Dipartimento di Elettronica, Informazione e Bioingegneria,
Politecnico di Milano, Milan, Italy
{luciano.baresi,martin.garriga}@polimi.it
[2] Faculty of Informatics, National University of Comahue, Neuquén, Argentina
alanderenzis@fi.uncoma.edu.ar

Abstract. The microservices architectural style is gaining more and more momentum for the development of applications as suites of small, autonomous, and conversational services, which are then easy to understand, deploy and scale. One of today's problems is finding the adequate granularity and cohesiveness of microservices, both when starting a new project and when thinking of transforming, evolving and scaling existing applications. To cope with these problems, the paper proposes a solution based on the semantic similarity of foreseen/available functionality described through OpenAPI specifications. By leveraging a reference vocabulary, our approach identifies potential candidate microservices, as fine-grained groups of cohesive operations (and associated resources). We compared our approach against a state-of-the-art tool, sampled microservices-based applications and decomposed a large dataset of Web APIs. Results show that our approach is able to find suitable decompositions in some 80% of the cases, while providing early insights about the right granularity and cohesiveness of obtained microservices.

Keywords: Microservices · Microservice architecture · Monolith decomposition

1 Introduction

Microservices is a novel architectural style that tries to overcome the shortcomings of centralized, monolithic architectures [1,2], in which the application logic is encapsulated in big deployable chunks. The most widely adopted definition of a microservices architecture is "an approach for developing a single application as a suite of small services, each running in its own process and communicating with lightweight mechanisms, often a RESTful API" [3]. In contrast to monoliths, microservices foster independent deployability and scalability, and can be developed using different technology stacks [4,5].

© IFIP International Federation for Information Processing 2017
Published by Springer International Publishing AG 2017. All Rights Reserved
F. De Paoli et al. (Eds.): ESOCC 2017, LNCS 10465, pp. 19–33, 2017.
DOI: 10.1007/978-3-319-67262-5_2

Although microservices can be seen as an evolution of Service-Oriented Architectures (SOA), they are inherently different regarding sharing and reuse [6]: given that service reuse has often been less than expected [7], instead of reusing existing microservices for new tasks or use cases, they should be small and independent enough to allow for rapidly developing a new one that can coexist, evolve or replace the previous one according to the business needs [1].

Several companies have recently migrated, or are considering migrating, their existing applications to microservices [8], and new microservice-native applications are being conceived. While the adoption of this architectural style should help one address the typical facets of a modern software system: for example, its distribution, coordination among parts, and operation, some aspects are still blurred [9,10]. One key issue is the definition of the right granularity level, that is, the trade-off between size and number of microservices [1].

The problem is not new: the literature has already addressed the *decomposition* problem—for identifying modules, packages, components, and "traditional" services—mainly by means of clustering techniques upon design artifacts [11] or source code [12]. However, the boundaries between software modules settled by these approaches were too flexible and allowed software to evolve into "big balls of mud" [13]. Microservices make these boundaries physical, and their unique characteristics in terms of distribution, granularity, and independent deployability, call for a new wave of techniques. Notwithstanding the existing body of knowledge, the elicitation of strong interface boundaries at the right level of granularity, along with proper tool support, remains an important challenge inherited from the early times of SOA [14]. The identification of "proper" microservices not only aims to partition the system to ease maintenance [7], but also defines how the system will be able to evolve and scale.

This paper borrows from the aforementioned experiences to introduce a novel approach to reason on microservices starting from an initial OpenAPI specification [15] (a language-agnostic, machine-readable interface for REST APIs) of the operations that the application should offer. This means that either the application, along with its interfaces, already exists and it must be re-engineered, or some design artifacts/specifications are available.

The process starts with mapping available OpenAPI specifications onto the entries of a reference vocabulary by means of a fitness function. In this paper, we use Schema.org[1] as reference, but any other shared vocabulary or even a domain-specific ontology would be appropriate. The fitness function is based on DISCO (DIStributionally related words using CO-occurrences, [16]), a pre-computed database of collocations and distributionally similar words that allows for computing the semantic similarity of terms according to their co-occurrences in large corpora of text. The goal is to provide a usable, automated solution to devise a decomposition—that is, a set of candidate microservices defined by groups of operations and their associated resources. The idea is to pair standardized (OpenAPI) specifications with homogeneous—because of the shared reference vocabulary—semantic characterizations. The reference vocabulary also

---

[1] http://Schema.org/docs/full.html.

act as a context that allows us to address large domains, in which certain concepts are used with different meanings across the system. The main properties driving the decomposition are granularity (a tradeoff between size and number of microservices), loose coupling (minimising inter-service calls) and high cohesion (keeping similar functionality together), while allowing the user to explore different alternatives by tunning the procedure.

In summary, the contribution of this work is an automated process for identifying candidate microservices by means of a lightweight, domain-agnostic semantic analysis of the concepts in the input specification with regard to a reference vocabulary.

The rest of this paper is organized as follows. Section 1.1 presents an example application to illustrate our approach. Section 2 introduces the main technologies used throughout the paper. Section 3 presents our approach for identifying microservices. Section 4 discusses the experimental validation. Section 5 surveys related work and Sect. 6 concludes the paper.

1.1   Example Application: Cargo Tracking

Figure 1 shows a simplified class diagram (domain model) of Cargo Tracking[2], a well-known example application [17] used to illustrate the approach. Each class defines a key concept and introduces a first set of attributes and operations.

The main focus of the application is to move a `Cargo` (identified by a `TrackingId`) between two `Locations` through a `RouteSpecification`. Once a `Cargo` becomes available, it is associated with one of the `Itineraries` (lists of `CarrierMovements`), selected from existing `Voyages`. `HandlingEvents` then trace the progress of the `Cargo` on the `Itinerary`. The `Delivery` of a `Cargo` informs about its state, estimated arrival time, and being on track.

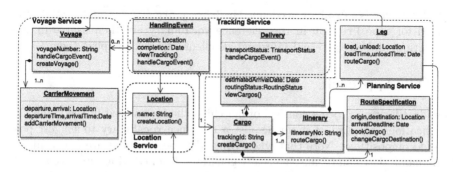

Fig. 1. Domain model and expected decomposition (dotted boxes) of the Cargo Tracking application.

---

[2] https://github.com/citerus/dddsample-core (Java implementation).

2 Background

DISCO [16] is a pre-computed database of collocations and distributionally similar words. The similarities are based on the statistical analysis of very large text collections (e.g., Wikipedia), through co-occurrence functions. For each word, DISCO indexes the first and second order vectors of related words.

The similarity between two words is then obtained by computing the similarity—based on co-occurrences—of the corresponding vectors. The highest the similarity value ($[0, 1]$) is, the closer the two words are. For example, if *bread* co-occurred with *bake, eat,* and *oven,* and *cake* also co-occurred with these three words, then *bread* and *cake* would be distributionally similar [16], and their similarity value would be 1 (if the vectors only comprised the three words).

OpenAPI, formerly known as Swagger[3], is a machine-readable, language-agnostic interface for RESTful APIs. Although OpenAPI can be seen as yet another attempt to define Web Service interfaces, it is just intended to describe RESTful APIs, and is supported by major industry partners such as Google, IBM, Microsoft, and PayPal. OpenAPI follows a JSON-based format[4] and is modular and extensible by means of the `$ref` keyword, with the goal of linking elements to concepts in a shared schema, or even a reference vocabulary. The elements/objects tagged with keyword `$ref` are then linked to a concept in a certain schema, which can be based on high level vocabularies, such as FOAF[5] or `Schema.org`. For example:

```
{"name":"Cargo",
 "description": "A cargo (product) identified by its TrackingId.",
   "schema": {
     "$ref": "schema.org.apis.apievangelist.com/api-commons/product/
               openapi-spec.json"
}}
```

says that `Cargo` is a `Product`, as defined in `Schema.org`. That is, all the attributes defined for type `Product` in the reference vocabulary are then usable in this description, and any external (automated) client can easily exploit them.

3 Our Approach

The identification process consists of matching the terms used in the OpenAPI specifications supplied as input against a reference vocabulary to suggest possible decompositions. Note that when OpenAPI specifications are not available beforehand, they can be automatically generated from existing interface specifications[6] The terms extracted from input artifacts are iteratively mapped on the

---

[3] http://swagger.io.

[4] Developers can thus exploit OpenAPI through the same tools and libraries used for JSON (e.g., Jackson).

[5] http://xmlns.com/foaf/spec/.

[6] E.g., the APIMatic tool (https://apimatic.io/transformer) accepts Swagger, WSDL, WADL and RAML among others.

concepts in the vocabulary by means of a fitness function based on the semantic similarity measure provided by DISCO. The best concept mappings are obtained through maximization of a co-occurrence matrix that contains all the possible pairs of terms and concepts.

Algorithm 1. Decomposition Algorithm

Data: OpenAPI specs, ref. vocabulary
Result: OpenAPI microservices' specifications
1 mappings ← ∅ ;
2 **foreach** *input specification* **do**
3 | map ← SemanticAssessment(specification,vocabulary);
4 | mappings ← mappings + map;
5 **end**
6 candidateMS ← GroupSimilar(mappings,vocabulary,level);
7 microserviceSpecs ← GenerateOpenApiSpecs(candidateMS, vocabulary);
8 **return** microserviceSpecs

Algorithm 1 summarizes the main steps of the decomposition algorithm. It receives a set of OpenAPI specifications and the reference vocabulary as input, and computes the best mappings between them through the DISCO-based semantic assessment algorithm (Line 3), further detailed later. This step generates a mapping between each operation in the input and a *reference concept* in the vocabulary, that is, the concept that most accurately describes the operation. The idea is that operations that share the same reference concept are highly cohesive, and should be grouped together (Line 6). Parameter level[7] determines the granularity of these groupings, that is, the level of interest in the hierarchy of concepts. For example, level=0 would only generate one candidate microservice, since everything would be grouped up to the root node of the vocabulary—Thing in Schema.org. The empirical assessment (Sect. 4), allowed us to set level to 2 to achieve a good compromise between the number of microservices and their granularity. Needless to say, the user can play with different values for level, identify different groupings, and analyze them.

Then, the suggested decomposition (Line 6) comprises one candidate microservice per identified reference concept. Each microservice is defined through its operations and their parameters, (public) complex types, and return values.

For example, if we started from the operations in Fig. 1 for the Cargo Tracking application, the process of Algorithm 1 would map Delivery and Handling onto DeliveryEvent (in Schema.org), and they would share the latter as reference concept. Delivery and Handling should then be part of the same candidate microservice, which could be named, for instance, EventTracker.

The OpenAPI specification of microservice EventTracker would then contain the operations defined within Delivery and Handling, and also a reference to the corresponding "shared" concept. The complete results for the case study are discussed in Sect. 4.

---

[7] Its values can range from 0 to the maximum depth of the vocabulary tree, which is 5 in Schema.org.

Algorithm 2 details the DISCO-based semantic assessment, called at Line 3 of the decomposition algorithm (Algorithm 1). It analyzes each operation of a specification artifact, along with the resources it defines (parameters, return value, complex types), with respect to the concepts in the shared vocabulary. The algorithm uses a robust term separator[8] [18] to identify and split words in the input terms (T) even when identifiers do not strictly follow any predefined naming convention (Line 3). The term separator also filters *stop words*[9], that is, meaningless words such as articles, pronouns, prepositions, digits, single alphabet characters, and possibly further domain- or context-specific words.

Then, the algorithm iteratively maps the set of input terms T onto all possible concepts C in the vocabulary by using DISCO (Line 5 to 8). For example, let us consider term `CargoTracking` and concept `DeliveryEvent`, with the following similarity scores:

	Cargo	Tracking
Delivery	0.3	0.1
Event	0.2	0.1

At a first glance, the best mappings are $(cargo, delivery)$ and $(cargo, event)$ with overall $score = (0.3 + 0.2)/2 = 0.25$. However, this mapping is not valid since it would consider word `Cargo` twice, but it would not use `Tracking`, and thus it would not be an acceptable mapping for the whole term. We must then find a suitable set of mappings that cover all the words in t and maximize the overall mapping score. When both t and c contain multiple words, finding the best mapping is not trivial, since it should consider all the words in t. This is done by applying the fitness function (Formula 1), followed by the Hungarian algorithm [19], a classical algorithm that solves the assignment problem in $O(n^3)$. As said, both t and c can be composed of multiple words (as `CargoTracking` and `DeliveryEvent`). $col(t_i, c_j)$ is the set of collocation scores for pairs of words $(t_i, c_j) \in (t, c)$, and N is the number of collocations between the different words in t and c that conform to the mapping (e.g., if t and c contain two words, then $N = 2$ since there can only be two possible valid mappings with two pairs each). Values range from 0 to 1, given the range of DISCO similarity function and the normalization factor N. The highest col is, the closest the two terms are. Note that although col ranges between 0 and 1, values are in general closer to 0, since $col = 1$ would mean that all the words appear together for all their occurrences in the DISCO corpus, which is highly unlikely in practice [16]. Scores are stored in a correlation matrix, where each column is a word in t and each row corresponds to a word in c linked to at least an element in t. Finally, the algorithm uses the matrix (Line 9) to identify the most adequate mappings.

$$score(t, c) = \sum (col(t_i, c_j))/N \tag{1}$$

---

[8] https://github.com/aderenzis/IdentifiersTermSeparator.
[9] http://www.webconfs.com/stop-words.php.

In the end, the concept in the reference vocabulary with the highest mapping score for a given input operation is elected as *reference concept*. The algorithm then returns a list with the best mapping for each operation in the input specification.

Back to the running example, for operation `CreateCargo` defined in `Cargo`, the concept in the vocabulary that shares the highest similarity according to DISCO is `Vehicle`, where: $(col(Create, Vehicle) = 0.07 + col(Cargo, Vehicle) = 0.61)/2 = 0.34$. Then, given the desired grouping granularity `Vehicle` can also become a `Product` in the vocabulary hierarchy. Since `Cargo` in Fig. 1 only shows one operation, it is grouped under `Product` as reference concept.

Algorithm 2. Semantic Assessment Algorithm

Data: OpenAPI specification, ref. vocabulary
Result: best mappings
1 bestMappings ← ∅ ;
2 **foreach** *operation in specification* **do**
3 | termsInput ← TermSeparation(operation);
4 | correlationMatrix ← [][];
5 | **foreach** *concept in vocabulary* **do**
6 | | termsContext ← TermSeparation(concept);
7 | | correlationMatrix ← DiscoCoOcurrrences(termsIput,termsContext);
8 | **end**
9 | bestMappings ← bestMappings + hungarianMax(correlationMatrix);
10 **end**
11 **return** bestMappings

---

4 Evaluation

This section presents the experiments we conducted to assess and validate the approach[10].

4.1 Decomposition of the Cargo Tracking Application

We performed the decomposition of the cargo tracking application (presented in Sect. 2), and compared our approach against Service Cutter [20], a state-of-the-art tool for microservice decomposition. The dotted boxes in Fig. 1 (Sect. 2) show the expected decomposition for the cargo tracking application (as defined in [20]). The input to our tool is an OpenAPI specification of the application that describes its different interfaces, operations, and resources. `Schema.org` is given as reference vocabulary. Figure 3 presents the candidate decomposition we obtained. As examples, we can take a closer look at some mappings. For interface `Voyage`, its operation `CreateVoyage` was mapped to the reference concept `Trip`, which is in turn an `Intangible` in `Schema.org`. Analogously, operation `RouteCargo` of interface `Leg` is also mapped to the reference concept `Trip`. Thus, these two operations will be grouped together in the candidate microservice `PlanningService`, along with all the other operations mapped

---

[10] Both the experimental prototype of the decomposition tool and the datasets used are available here: https://github.com/mgarriga/decomposer.

to `Trip` or other `Intangibles`. In turn, the remaining operation in `Voyage` is `HandleCargoEvent`, which is mapped to reference concept `Event`. This operation will be grouped under another candidate microservice named `EventTracker`, with the other operations also mapped to `Event` (or other concepts under `Event` in `Schema.org`), such as `ViewCargos` (from `Delivery`) and `ViewTrackings` (from `HandlingEvent`).

The input to Service Cutter is a set of specification artifacts, and a set of weighted coupling criteria, and the output is a graph where nodes represent candidate microservices, and weighted arcs indicate how cohesive and/or coupled two candidates are. Finally, a clustering algorithm provides the most suitable service cuts. Figure 2 depicts the best decomposition provided by Service Cutter, after manually prioritizing and fine-tuning the weights of coupling criteria to reflect the requirements of the application.

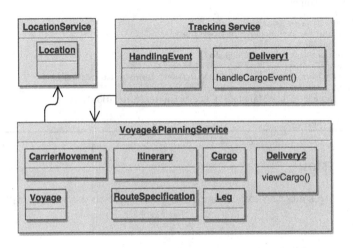

Fig. 2. Obtained decomposition with Service Cutter [20]

Our microservice decomposition process generated different candidate microservices than those obtained with Service Cutter. No approach returned the "expected" service decomposition, although it was defined manually in [20]. Thus, one can argue whether the expected decomposition is optimal, since it may be subjective, and biased by certain design decisions. From a comparative perspective, the main difference is service `Voyage&Planning` (Fig. 2) which in Service Cutter's decomposition encapsulates seven input artifacts, nine operations and two different business aspects. In contrast, our solution decomposes it in three different microservices (Fig. 3): `Trip`, `Planning` and `EventTracking`, all with a similar and finer granularity (three, four and five operations respectively). The only candidate microservice that could be too fine-grained is `Cargo`, which only encapsulates one operation.

From a comparative perspective, our approach requires as input the reference vocabulary and the OpenAPI descriptions of the interfaces (which can be

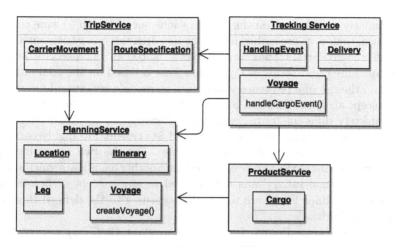

Fig. 3. Obtained decomposition with our approach

automatically generated from other descriptions). In turn, Service Cutter requires a detailed and exhaustive specification of the system, together with ad-hoc specification artifacts associated with coupling criteria [20]. The availability of such a broad range of documentation is, at least, arguable.

This section provided insights about the rationale of our approach and a comparison with a state-of-the-art-tool through a simple example. The experiments described in the next section use real-life microservice applications and a broader dataset of real-world Web APIs to help us better devise the feasibility of our approach.

4.2   Decomposition of Microservice Applications

The goal of the second experiment is to automatically devise adequate decompositions of two microservice-based applications[11]: Money Transfer, composed of four microservices (Customers, Accounts, Transfer, and Login) and Kanban Board, composed of three microservices (Boards, Tasks, and Authentication).

The original microservice architecture of each application acts as a gold standard to validate the results obtained with our approach. Again, we used the OpenAPI specifications as input—a single JSON per application, that acts as its "monolithic-like" description—and Schema.org as vocabulary.

Table 1 shows the decompositions for both applications. Each group of operations constitutes a different candidate microservice. Then, the rightmost column indicates if the mapping is adequate in the context of each decomposition, that is, whether the grouped operations corresponded to the same microservice in the original architecture.

---

[11] http://eventuate.io/exampleapps.html – from the curator of microservices.io [8].

Particularly, for MoneyTransfer, 8 operations out of 10 (80%) were correctly decomposed, that is, as prescribed in the original architecture. For example, operation `getAccountForCustomer` was correctly placed in microservice `Account` despite containing also terms of `Customer`. This is based on the co-occurrences criteria and the use of a reference vocabulary to provide contextual information to the concept analysis. This can be illustrated also by considering an operation with completely different terms, e.g., `getStatement`, which would be grouped into microservice `Account` since `Account` and `Statement` are highly correlated according to DISCO (0.48 as similarity value). For the two remaining operations, `getCustomersByEmail` was placed in another candidate microservice, while `transactionsHistory` was not mapped to any concept of `Schema.org`, since the relationships found are too weak (according to the defined threshold) to devise a similarity.

In turn, for KanbanBoard, 10 operations out of 13 (77%) were correctly decomposed. As for the three remaining operations, they were grouped together in another candidate microservice. Obtained results suggest that our approach is able to detect correct candidate microservices for around 80% of an application's functionality, given that the expected decomposition (gold standard) was known beforehand.

Table 1. Obtained decomposition for MoneyTransfer and KanbanBoard.

Application	Cand. microservice	Operation	Suitable?
Money Transfer	Customer	`createCustomer,getCustomer,` `getCurrentUser`	Yes
	Account	`getAccountsForCustomer` `addToAccount,createAccount`	Yes
	Login	`doAuthorization`	Yes
	MoneyTransfer	`moneyTransfer`	Yes
	Other	`getCustomersByEmail`	No
	N/A	`transactionsHistory`	No
		Total	8/10
Kanban Board	Task	`listAllTasks,saveTask,update-` `Task,deleteTask,backlogTask,` `completeTask,getTaskHistory`	Yes
	Auth	`doAuthentication`	Yes
	Board	`listAllBoards,getBoard`	Yes
	Other	`readAction,scheduleAction,resumeAction`	No
		Total	10/13

4.3   Decomposition of a Large Dataset of Real-World APIs

The goal of this experiment is to decompose a dataset of real-world APIs and analyze the potential applicability/utility of our approach. Moreover, this is helpful to profile the decomposition process and find its optimal configuration, according to expected decompositions defined by software engineers. We used a dataset of OpenAPI specifications from APIs.Guru[12], currently the largest repository of publicly available, real-world OpenAPI specifications. From all the APIs available in the repository (550 in total), we focused on specifications with at least two operations, which is the minimal condition to be potentially decomposable, and less than fifty operations, which avoids the noise introduced by too large APIs. We ended up with a dataset of 452 OpenAPI specifications defining a total of 6634 endpoints, which are equivalent to the notion of operations in this paper.

From this dataset, we randomly selected 5 samples of 14 services, that were delivered to five different software engineers (both PhD. students and researchers in software engineering with industry experience). Then the engineers manually defined the decompositions for these services. Note that the engineers were unaware of the rationale behind our approach, to avoid biasing their answers. We configured different similarity *thresholds over the fitness function* (Formula 1) *and different values for the grouping level* (Algorithm 1) and executed the decomposition over the sample services, comparing our candidate microservices with those suggested by the developers. The results were measured in terms of *precision* and *recall*, according to the expected and achieved decompositions. Figure 4 shows the precision/recall curve that considers an average of the different samples and different configurations for the aforementioned values *threshold* and *level*. The tiny x on the curve represents the optimal compromise between precision/recall among all the tested configurations, where *precision* $= 0.8$ and *recall* $= 0.8$.

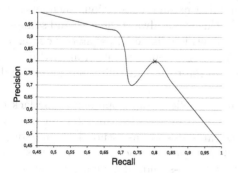

Fig. 4. Precision/Recall curve for the APIs.Guru dataset.

Table 2. APIs.Guru dataset and number of concepts mapped in Schema.org.

Operations	Services	Avg. concepts
2...5	115	1.47
6...10	106	2.56
11...20	120	4.18
21...30	54	6.25
31...40	34	7.79
41...50	23	8.26
Tot.: 452	Avg.: 3.8

After this profiling and configuration step, we executed the decomposition algorithm with the whole dataset of 452 OpenAPI specifications as input. Table 2 shows the number of operations per service and the average concepts mapped

---

[12] https://apis.guru/openapi-directory/.

in `Schema.org`. Input APIs were decomposed in 3.8 candidate microservices on average. Although it is not possible to analyze each suggested decomposition individually, this value can be considered close enough to the expected range for this dataset, since the previous step of manual decomposition generated 3.2 microservices per API on average. It could be also interesting to analyze whether the obtained decompositions minimize the number of inter-service calls for sample use cases, but this is outside the scope of this experiment.

This experiment shows that the OpenAPI specifications in the repository are good candidates for decomposition. The original dataset of 452 APIs potentially contains 1735 microservices, which would be cohesive and fine-grained, according to our decomposition approach. This also suggests the applicability/utility of our approach to decompose real-world service APIs, particularly in scenarios where these APIs define a high number of operations, which can then be cumbersome to understand and analyze.

4.4 Possible Limitations

These experiments, and some others not reported here, helped us identify some possible limitations of our solution. In certain cases, we noticed that the input artifacts may be mapped to too few concepts of the shared vocabulary, and thus the decomposition would generate coarse-grained microservices. If it is the case, one should think of: (a) using a domain-specific vocabulary to reduce the ambiguity of terms, (b) fine-tuning parameter `level` to analyze different decompositions, and (c) augmenting obtained results with manual improvements to get a more appropriate decomposition.

Our approach relies on well-defined and described interfaces that provide meaningful names, and follow programming naming conventions such as camel casing and hyphenation. Unfortunately, this is not always the case and some situations are difficult to cope with (e.g., identifiers like `op1`, `param` or `response`). This can be mitigated by the heuristics in the term separation algorithm, and by applying state-of-the-art techniques to improve readability and understandability of interfaces [18].

To conclude, a limitation that is not specific to our approach is the lack of a comprehensive, well-known dataset of microservices to run experiments and replicate/compare the results. Although an industry case study in a large organization is important for validation of a single approach [21], an open-source large dataset of microservices can act as a gold-standard for current and future research in the field. Due to this limitation, we performed our validation upon case studies, example applications, and a large dataset of traditional Web APIs.

5   Related Work

The approach presented in this paper can be seen from a clustering perspective, since candidate microservices are devised by grouping operations according to their shared reference concepts. Clustering techniques have been broadly applied in the SOA field, for Web Service discovery [22,23] and composition [24]. Traditional flat clustering techniques, such as k-means, are straightforward to apply but their results in the context of traditional Web Services [23] and microservices [20] report a below-average performance. More complex techniques, such as Hierarchical Agglomerative Clustering (HAC, [25]), have proven to be more effective than traditional flat clustering at the cost of lower efficiency but, to the best of our knowledge, these techniques have not been applied to the field of microservices, thus further research in this direction is required to determine their suitability.

Moving to other decomposition approaches for microservices, the Service Cutter tool and framework [20] and the comparison with our approach are already discussed in Sect. 4.1. In the same direction, the work in [21] describes a technique to identify microservices based on dependency graphs among the different tiers of the application (client, server, database). This is a white-box approach, in which interfaces between components in different tiers are analyzed to generate the dependency graph, and then code inspection is performed to devise in detail the boundaries of candidate microservices. The authors claim that the approach is successful since in the case study (a large banking application), candidate microservices were identified and suggested for all subsystems. The authors assume the availability of white-box information (i.e., source code), which is not always the case. Additionally, for complex domains such as banking, it is suggested to start the decomposition gradually and at the edges (where the system is more dynamic and its external interfaces are explicit) [2].

The Enterprise Services Architecture Model Integration (ESAMI) [26] supports the systematic manual integration of microservices by exploiting an ad-hoc architectural reference model [27], and correlation matrices to identify similarities. In contrast, we generalize the idea of reference model, which can be any high-level shared vocabulary or even a domain-specific ontology. We also provide automated support for the identification of microservices.

From the deployment point of view, [28] addresses decomposition in microservices as a suitable means for cloud migration, being the first cloud-native novel architectural style. An industry case study shows applicability scenarios and migration patterns. In this case, the target microservices in the architecture are defined a priori and in a manual way, since the focus is on the deployment of the solution while our approach focuses on its design. Also [29] presents a microservices-based architecture from a deployment point of view. They do not fully migrate the application to microservices at application-level, but preserved the monolithic structure of the application and replicated certain components. This work considers microservices as a way to scale the development process itself rather than the application's functionality, as our solution does.

6   Conclusions and Future Work

This paper proposes a novel approach to support the identification of microservices and the specification of the resulting artifacts both during the initial phases of the design of a new system and while re-architecting existing applications. The specification artifacts of available operations are mapped onto the entries of a reference vocabulary to highlight their similarities and thus their willingness of being part of different microservices. Then, identified microservices are rendered using OpenAPI, which allows for standardization and fine-grained reuse. Conducted experiments show that our approach found suitable decompositions in some 80% of the cases, while providing early insights about the right granularity and cohesiveness of obtained microservices.

Our future work comprises the addition of non-functional aspects that can affect the decomposition (response time, resource allocation or cost) and the support to "smart" deployment and execution through our deployment framework EcoWare [30].

References

1. Hassan, S., Bahsoon, R.: Microservices and their design trade-offs: a self-adaptive roadmap. In: IEEE International Conference on Services Computing (SCC), pp. 813–818. IEEE (2016)
2. Fowler, M.: Monolith first (2015). http://martinfowler.com/bli-ki/MonolithFirst.html
3. Lewis, J., Fowler, M.: Microservices: a definition of this new architectural term (2014). http://martinfowler.com/articles/microservices.html
4. Balalaie, A., Heydarnoori, A., Jamshidi, P.: Microservices architecture enables devops: migration to a cloud-native architecture. IEEE Softw. **33**(3), 42–52 (2016)
5. Garriga, M.: Towards a microservices taxonomy. In: Microservices: Science and Engineering Workshop, Co-located with Software Engineering and Formal Methods (SEFM), Trento, Italy (2017, accepted for publication)
6. Richards, M.: Microservices vs. service-oriented architecture. (2015)
7. Wilde, N., Gonen, B., El-Sheikh, E., Zimmermann, A.: Approaches to the evolution of SOA systems. In: El-Sheikh, E., Zimmermann, A., Jain, L.C. (eds.) Emerging Trends in the Evolution of Service-Oriented and Enterprise Architectures. ISRL, vol. 111, pp. 5–21. Springer, Cham (2016). doi:10.1007/978-3-319-40564-3_2
8. Richardson, C.: Microservices architecture (2014). http://micro-services.io/
9. George, F.: Challenges in implementing microservices (2015). http://gotocon.com/dl/goto-amsterdam-2015/slides/FredGeorgeChallengesInImplementingMicroServices.pdf
10. Zimmermann, O.: Do microservices pass the same old architecture test? Or: Soa is not dead-long live (micro-) services. In: Microservices Workshop at SATURN Conference, SEI (2015)
11. Browning, T.R.: Applying the design structure matrix to system decomposition and integration problems: a review and new directions. IEEE Trans. Eng. Manag. **48**(3), 292–306 (2001)
12. Kuhn, A., Ducasse, S., Gorba, T.: Semantic clustering: identifying topics in source code. Inf. Softw. Technol. **49**(3), 230–243 (2007). 12th Working Conference on Reverse Engineering
13. Chen, L.: Continuous delivery: overcoming adoption challenges. J. Syst. Softw. **128**, 72–86 (2017)

14. Pautasso, C., Zimmermann, O., Leymann, F.: Restful web services vs. "Big" web services: making the right architectural decision. In: 17th International Conference on World Wide Web, pp. 805–814. ACM Press (2008)

15. OpenAPI Consortium: The OpenAPI Initiative (OAI) (2016). https://www.openapis.org/

16. Kolb, P.: Experiments on the difference between semantic similarity and relatedness. In: Proceedings of the 17th Nordic Conference on Computational Linguistics - NODALIDA 2009. Link University Electronic Press, May 2009

17. Evans, E.: Domain-Driven Design: Tackling Complexity in the Heart of Software. Addison-Wesley Professional, Reading (2004)

18. Renzis, A.D., Garriga, M., Flores, A., Cechich, A., Mateos, C., Zunino, A.: A domain independent readability metric for web service descriptions. Comput. Stand. Interfaces **50**, 124–141 (2017)

19. Kuhn, H.W.: The Hungarian method for the assignment problem. Naval Res. Logistic Q. **2**, 83–97 (1955)

20. Gysel, M., Kölbener, L., Giersche, W., Zimmermann, O.: Service Cutter: a systematic approach to service decomposition. In: Aiello, M., Johnsen, E.B., Dustdar, S., Georgievski, I. (eds.) ESOCC 2016. LNCS, vol. 9846, pp. 185–200. Springer, Cham (2016). doi:10.1007/978-3-319-44482-6_12

21. Levcovitz, A., Terra, R., Valente, M.T.: Towards a technique for extracting microservices from monolithic enterprise systems. In: 3rd Brazilian Workshop on Software Visualization, Evolution and Maintenance (VEM), pp. 97–104 (2015)

22. Nayak, R., Lee, B.: Web service discovery with additional semantics and clustering. In: IEEE/WIC/ACM International Conference on Web Intelligence, pp. 555–558. IEEE, Silicon Valley (2007)

23. Cong, Z., Fernandez, A., Billhardt, H., Lujak, M.: Service discovery acceleration with hierarchical clustering. Inf. Syst. Front. **17**(4), 799–808 (2015)

24. Alrifai, M., Skoutas, D., Risse, T.: Selecting skyline services for QoS-based web service composition. In: Proceedings of the 19th International Conference on World Wide Web, pp. 11–20. ACM (2010)

25. Murtagh, F., Legendre, P.: Ward's hierarchical agglomerative clustering method: which algorithms implement ward's criterion? J. Classif. **31**(3), 274–295 (2014)

26. Bogner, J., Zimmermann, A.: Towards integrating microservices with adaptable enterprise architecture. In: 2016 IEEE 20th International Enterprise Distributed Object Computing Workshop (EDOCW), pp. 1–6, September 2016

27. Zimmermann, A., Sandkuhl, K., Pretz, M., Falkenthal, M., Jugel, D., Wissotzki, M.: Towards an integrated service-oriented reference enterprise architecture. In: Proceedings of the 2013 International Workshop on Ecosystem Architectures, pp. 26–30. ACM (2013)

28. Balalaie, A., Heydarnoori, A., Jamshidi, P.: Migrating to cloud-native architectures using microservices: an experience report. In: Celesti, A., Leitner, P. (eds.) ESOCC Workshops 2015. CCIS, vol. 567, pp. 201–215. Springer, Cham (2016). doi:10.1007/978-3-319-33313-7_15

29. Toffetti, G., Brunner, S., Blöchlinger, M., Spillner, J., Bohnert, T.M.: Self-managing cloud-native applications: design, implementation, and experience. Future Gener. Comput. Syst. **72**, 165–179 (2017)

30. Baresi, L., Guinea, S., Leva, A., Quattrocchi, G.: A discrete-time feedback controller for containerized cloud applications. In: Proceedings of the 2016 24th ACM SIGSOFT International Symposium on Foundations of Software Engineering, FSE 2016, pp. 217–228. ACM, New York (2016)

A Performance Survey of Lightweight Virtualization Techniques

Max Plauth[✉], Lena Feinbube, and Andreas Polze

Operating Systems and Middleware Group, Hasso Plattner Institute for Software
Systems Engineering, University of Potsdam, Potsdam, Germany
{max.plauth,lena.feinbube,andreas.polze}@hpi.uni-potsdam.de

Abstract. The increasing prevalence of the microservice paradigm creates a new demand for low-overhead virtualization techniques. Complementing containerization, unikernels are emerging as alternative approaches. With both techniques undergoing rapid improvements, the current landscape of lightweight virtualization approaches presents a confusing scenery, complicating the task of choosing a suited technology for an intended purpose. This work provides a comprehensive performance comparison covering containers, unikernels, whole-system virtualization, native hardware, and combinations thereof. Representing common workloads in microservice-based applications, we assess application performance using HTTP servers and a key-value store. With the microservice deployment paradigm in mind, we evaluate further characteristics such as startup time, image size, network latency, and memory footprint.

1 Introduction

With the increasing pervasiveness of the cloud computing paradigm for all sorts of applications, low-overhead virtualization techniques are becoming indispensable. In particular, the microservice architectural paradigm, where small encapsulated services are developed, operated and maintained by separate teams, require easy-to-use and disposable machine images. Ideally, such infrastructure should allow for fast provisioning and efficient operation.

Approaches to lightweight virtualization roughly fall into the categories of *container virtualization* and *unikernels*. Both have been gaining notable momentum recently (see [9,21] and Fig. 1). As more and more virtualization techniques are being introduced and discussed, making a choice between them is getting harder. Published performance measurements thus far either have a strong focus on throughput and execution time [2,6,27,31] – not analyzing startup latency and other system metrics in depth – or focus on highlighting the strengths of one particular approach without comparing it to a broad range of alternative unikernels and container technologies [3,6,9,16,19,27].

We close this gap by presenting an extensive performance analysis of lightweight virtualization strategies, which takes into account a broad spectrum both of investigated technologies and measured metrics. Our evaluation includes

© IFIP International Federation for Information Processing 2017
Published by Springer International Publishing AG 2017. All Rights Reserved
F. De Paoli et al. (Eds.): ESOCC 2017, LNCS 10465, pp. 34–48, 2017.
DOI: 10.1007/978-3-319-67262-5_3

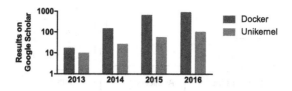

Fig. 1. The relevance of *Docker* and *unikernels* in the research community is indicated by the number of results on Google Scholar (as of May 15, 2017).

containers (*Docker, LXD*), unikernels (*Rumprun, OSv* and *MirageOS*), whole-system virtualization, native hardware, and certain combinations thereof. While previous work has laid a strong focus on *high performance computing* (HPC) applications (see Sect. 3), our goal is to evaluate metrics that are applicable to cloud applications. For this purpose, we measure application throughput performance using HTTP servers and a key-value store. Additionally, we provide further metrics, such as startup time, image size, network latency, and memory footprint. To facilitate full repeatability of our results, all test setups used throughout this paper have been made available online[1].

The remainder of the paper is organized as follows: Sect. 2 provides background about the employed virtualization approaches. Section 3 reviews related work that deals with quantifying the performance impact of lightweight virtualization approaches. Afterwards, Sect. 4 refines the scope of this work. Section 5 then documents the benchmark procedure yielding the results presented in Sect. 6. Finally, Sect. 7 concludes this work with final remarks.

2   Background

"Traditional", whole-system virtualization introduces performance and memory overhead, incurred by the hypervisor or *virtual machine manager* (VMM). This problem has been addressed by introducing *paravirtualization* (PV) and *hardware-assisted virtualization* (HVM). Still, the additional layer of indirection necessitates further context switches, which hurt I/O performance [9]. Even though techniques such as *kernel samepage merging* (KSM) [1] have managed to reduce memory demands, they do not provide an ultimate remedy as they dilute the level of isolation among virtual machines [12].

This work focuses on lightweight virtualization approaches, which, addressing both issues, have gained notable momentum both in the research community and in industry. Figure 2 illustrates how these approaches aim at supporting the deployment of applications or operating system images while eluding the overhead incurred by running a full-blown operating system on top of a hypervisor. With *containers* and *unikernels* constituting the two major families of lightweight virtualization approaches, the main characteristics and two representatives of each family are introduced hereafter.

---

[1] https://github.com/plauth/lightweight-vm-performance.

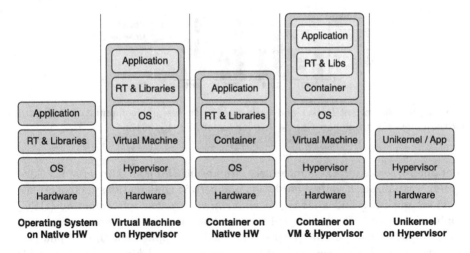

Fig. 2. Illustrated comparison of the software stack complexity of various deployment strategies, including native setups, virtual machines, containers, containers within virtual machines and unikernels.

2.1 Container (OS-Level Virtualization)

Containers are based on the observation that the entire kernel induces overly much resource overhead for merely isolating and packaging small applications. Here, we distinguish two classes of container virtualization approaches: application and OS-oriented containers. For application-oriented containers, single applications constitute the units of deployment. For OS-oriented containers, the entire user space of the operating system is reproduced. Currently, with *LXD*, the latter approach is becoming more prominent again, as it allows for the creation of *virtual machine* (VM)-like behavior without the overhead of a hypervisor. In the following paragraphs, we discuss the containerization technologies under investigation.

Docker. Among the application-oriented containers, the open source project *Docker* [7] currently is the most popular approach. It relies on Linux kernel features, such as namespaces and control groups, to isolate independent containers running on the same instance of the operating system. A *Docker* container encapsulates an application as well as its software dependencies; it can be run on different Linux machines with the *Docker engine*.

Apart from providing basic isolation and closer-to-native performance than whole-system virtualization, *Docker* containerization has the advantages that pre-built *Docker* containers can be shared easily, and that the technology can be integrated into various popular *Infrastructure as a Service* (IaaS) solutions such as *Amazon web services* (AWS).

LXD. The Linux-based container solution *LXD* [5] builds up upon the *LXC* (Linux container) [4] interface to Linux containerization features. *LXD* uses the *LXC* library for providing low-overhead operating system containers. In addition to advanced container creation and management features, *LXD* offers integration into the OpenStack Nova compute component [29].

2.2   Unikernel (Hypervisor Virtualization)

Unikernels are a new take on the library operating system concept, providing merely a thin layer of protection and multiplexing facilities for hardware resources whereas hardware support is left to employed libraries and the application itself. Whereas library operating systems (e.g., Exokernel [8]) had to struggle with having to support real hardware, unikernels avoid this burden by targeting only virtual hardware interfaces provided by *hypervisors* or VMMs [20]. With the absence of many abstraction mechanisms present in traditional operating systems, the unikernel community claims to achieve a higher degree of whole-system optimization while reducing startup times and the VM footprint [19,21].

Rumprun. The *Rumprun* unikernel is based on the *rump kernel* project, which is a strongly modularized version of the *NetBSD* kernel that was built to demonstrate the *anykernel* concept [14]. With the goal of simplified driver development in mind, the *anykernel* concept boils down to enabling a combination of monolithic kernels, where drivers are executed in the kernel, and microkernel-oriented user space drivers that can be executed on top of a rump kernel. One of the major features of the *Rumprun* unikernel is that it supports running existing and unmodified POSIX software [15], as long as it does not require calls to `fork()` or `exec()`.

OSv. The *OSv* unikernel has been designed specifically to replace general-purpose operating systems such as Linux in cloud-based VMs. Similarly to *Rumprun*, *OSv* supports running existing and unmodified POSIX software, as long as certain limitations are considered [16]. However, *OSv* provides additional APIs for exploiting capabilities of the underlying hypervisor, such as a zero copy API intended to replace the socket API to provide more efficient means of communication among *OSv*-based VMs.

MirageOS. Being developed from scratch, the *MirageOS* unikernel resembles a puristic, clean-slated approach. *MirageOS* builds up on top of the *Mini-OS* kernel from the *Xen* project and only supports software written in the *OCaml* programming language [21]. Denying any compatibility with existing POSIX-compatible software, the static type system and the strong runtime safety capabilities of *OCaml* lead to a high level of software robustness [20].

3   Related Work

An overview of publications about performance measurements of lightweight virtualization techniques from the last few years are presented in Table 1. Previous research has measured selected performance properties of lightweight virtualization techniques, mostly in comparison with a traditional whole-system virtualization approach. However, we are not aware of any comprehensive analysis of up-to-date container versus unikernel technologies.

Felter et al. [9] have presented a comprehensive performance comparison between *Docker* containers and the *KVM* hypervisor [17]. Their results from various compute-intensive as well as I/O-intensive programs indicate that *"Docker equals or exceeds KVM performance in every case tested"*. For I/O-intensive workloads, both technologies introduce significant overhead, while the CPU and memory performance is hardly affected. Mao et al. [22] have studied the startup time of virtual machines for the major cloud providers Amazon EC2, Windows Azure, and Rackspace. Among different influencing factors, the image size was shown to have a significant impact on the startup performance. Kivity et al. [16] focus on the performance of *OSv* in comparison to whole-system virtualization with *KVM*. Both micro- and macro-benchmarks indicate that *OSv* offers better throughput, especially for memory-intensive workloads.

Table 1. Related work on performance measurements of lightweight virtualization approaches. Studies printed in gray indicate a HPC context.

Metrics	Docker	LXC	Open VZ	Rump-run	OSv	Mirage OS	KVM	Xen	others
	Container			Unikernel			Virtualization		
app. performance	[9, 25] [6]	[2, 31]	[27, 31]		[3, 16]	[3, 19]	[3, 9, 16] [2, 27]	[3] [27, 31]	[25] [31]
startup time	[25]				[19]	[13]		[22]	[25]
image size								[22]	
network latency	[9, 25]	[2]	[27]		[3, 16]	[3, 19]	[3, 9, 16] [2, 27]	[3] [2, 27]	[25]

4   Scope of this Work

Here, we present an extensive performance evaluation of containers (*Docker, LXD*), unikernels (*Rumprun, OSv* and *MirageOS*), and whole-system virtualization. Related work has focused on subsets of the approaches we consider, but we are not aware of any comprehensive analysis of up-to-date container versus unikernel technologies.

This paper extends our work published in [26], providing commensurable network stack parameters for all tested approaches and measurements for additional properties such as *startup time*, *image size*, and *network latency*. Furthermore, *Xen* and *MirageOS* have been included as additional *hypervisor* and *unikernel* approaches. Startup time is a relevant metric in scenarios, where the infrastructure is booted on demand to process certain requests. Requirements regarding the infrastructure and runtime environment are getting more ad hoc, may change spontaneously, and call for rapid just-in-time deployment and reactive approaches. Such scenarios are becoming more common with the microservice development pattern.

Our research questions are the following:

- How fast are containers, unikernels, and whole-system virtualization when running different workloads? Are the results from related work confirmed in our test cases?
- What is the most suitable virtualization technology for on-demand provisioning scenarios?
- What is the impact of the virtualization technology on general system properties such as *image size*, *network latency* and *memory footprint*?

5 Benchmark Procedure

This section provides a description of the benchmark methodologies applied within this work. All tests were performed on an HPE ProLiant m710p server cartridge [11] with the detailed specifications denoted in Table 2. Where applicable, all approaches were evaluated using *Xen*, *KVM* and native hardware to evaluate the performance impact of the employed virtualization approach. For container-based approaches, we also distinguish between native and virtualized hosts, where the latter represent the common practice for deploying containers on top of IaaS-based virtual machines. All configuration files, custom benchmarking utilities as well as modifications to existing utilities are provided online (see Footnote 1).

Table 2. Specifications of the test systems.

Server model	HPE ProLiant m710p Server cartridge
Processor	Intel Xeon E3-1284L v4 (Broadwell)
Memory	4 × 8GB PC3L-12800 (SODIMM)
NIC	Mellanox Connect-X3 Pro (Dual 10GbE)
Operating system	Ubuntu Linux 16.04.1 LTS

5.1 General Properties

Startup Time. To avoid potential confounding variables, startup time is measured irrespectively from the application type. Referring to the test procedure suggested by Nickoloff [25], our test set-up is composed of a minimal application which sends a UDP packet containing a single character to a predefined host and a counterpart application listening for said UDP packet. The listening application is executed on the virtualization host and issues the startup command for the corresponding *container* or *unikernel* VM and measures the time until the UDP packet is received.

Image Size. In practice, image size strongly influences startup time [22], as images have to be transported over potentially slow networks. Hence, the eventual image sizes are reported for all examined technologies. To avoid skewed readouts caused by sparse image files, the actual disk utilization is retrieved using the du command line utility.

Network Latency. Since network latency may be a decisive factor in latency-sensitive use cases such as *network function virtualization* (NFV) [23], the network round-trip time is measured between a dedicated host and the test object using the ping command line utility.

Memory Footprint. Reducing the memory footprint is one of the main objectives of lightweight virtualization approaches. For native and *LXD*-based execution, memory consumption was measured using the htop command line utility. In the case of *Docker*, the docker ps command line facility was used to retrieve memory consumption measurements. As the memory footprint of VMs and *unikernels* is defined statically at the time of their instantiation, VM-sizing must be chosen carefully. Hence, we identified the least amount of memory that did not degrade performance by testing different values in steps of 8 MiB.

5.2 Application Performance

Representing common workloads of cloud-hosted applications, we picked HTTP servers and key-value stores as exemplary applications. As these I/O-intensive use cases involve a large number of both concurrent clients and requests, the network stack considerably contributes to the overall application performance. Hence, in order to eliminate an unfavorable default configuration of the network stack as a confounding variable, we modified the configuration on Linux, *Rumprun* and *OSv*. Since many best practices guides cover the subject of tuning network performance on Linux, we employed the recommendations from [30], resulting in the configuration denoted in Table 3.

Based on this model, we modified the configuration parameters of both *Rumprun* and *OSv* to correspond to the Linux-based settings [28]. The resulting

Table 3. Optimized settings for the *Linux* network stack.

Path	Parameter	Value
/etc/sysctl.conf	fs.file-max	20000
/etc/sysctl.conf	net.core.somaxconn	1024
/etc/sysctl.conf	net.ipv4.ip_local_port_range	1024 65535
/etc/sysctl.conf	net.ipv4.tcp_tw_reuse	1
/etc/sysctl.conf	net.ipv4.tcp_keepalive_time	60
/etc/sysctl.conf	net.ipv4.tcp_keepalive_intvl	60
/etc/security/limits.conf	nofile (soft/hard)	20000

configuration for *Rumprun* is specified in Table 4, and the corresponding configuration for *OSv* is documented in Table 5. Currently, there is no mechanism in *Rumprun* to permanently modify the values of the *ulimit* parameter. As a workaround, the *Rumprun* sysproxy facility has be activated by passing the parameter `-e RUMPRUN_SYSPROXY=tcp://0:12345` to the `rumprun` command-line utility upon start. Using the `rumpctrl` utility, the configuration values of the *ulimit* parameter have to be changed remotely, as exemplified in Listing 1.1.

```
1 export RUMP_SERVER=tcp://[IP]:12345
2 . rumpctrl.sh
3 sysctl -w proc.0.rlimit.descriptors.soft=200000
4 sysctl -w proc.0.rlimit.descriptors.hard=200000
5 sysctl -w proc.1.rlimit.descriptors.soft=200000
6 sysctl -w proc.1.rlimit.descriptors.hard=200000
7 sysctl -w proc.2.rlimit.descriptors.hard=200000
8 sysctl -w proc.2.rlimit.descriptors.soft=200000
9 rumpctrl_unload
```

Listing 1.1. The *ulimit* values of *Rumprun* have to be changed remotely using the *sysproxy* facility and the associated `rumpctrl` utility.

Table 4. Optimized settings for the *Rumprun* network stack.

Path	Parameter	Value
./sys/conf/param.c	MAXFILES	20000
./sys/netinet/in.h	IPPORT_ANONMIN	1024
./sys/netinet/in.h	IPPORT_ANONMAX	65535
./sys/netinet/tcp_timer.h	TCPTV_KEEP_INIT	30*PR_SLOWHZ
./sys/netinet/tcp_timer.h	TCPTV_KEEPINTV	30*PR_SLOWHZ
./sys/sys/socket.h	SOMAXCONN	1024

Table 5. Optimized settings for the *OSv* network stack.

Path	Parameter	Value
./include/osv/file.h	FDMAX	0x30D40
./libc/libc.cc	RLIMIT_NOFILE	20000
./bsd/sys/netinet/in.h	IPPORT_EPHEMERALFIRST	1024
./bsd/sys/netinet/in.h	IPPORT_EPHEMERALLAST	65535
./bsd/sys/netinet/in.h	IPPORT_HIFIRSTAUTO	1024
./bsd/sys/netinet/in.h	IPPORT_HILASTAUTO	65535
./bsd/sys/netinet/tcp_timer.h	TCPTV_KEEP_INIT	60*hz
./bsd/sys/netinet/tcp_timer.h	TCPTV_KEEPINTV	60*hz
./bsd/sys/sys/socket.h	SOMAXCONN	1024
./include/api/sys/socket.h	SOMAXCONN	1024

Static HTTP Server. We use the *Nginx* HTTP server (version 1.8.0) to evaluate the HTTP performance for static content, as it is available on all tested platforms with the exception of *OSv* and *MirageOS*. As no port of *Nginx* exists for *MirageOS*, we had to trade in the aspect of full commensurability with *Nginx* and use the *conduit server* code example [24] in order not to exclude *MirageOS* from the HTTP server discipline. Regarding *OSv* however, we refrain from running HTTP benchmarks due to the lacking availability of an adequate HTTP server implementation.

Our measurement procedure employs the benchmarking tool *weighttp* [18] and the *abc* wrapper utility [10] for automated benchmark runs and varying connection count parameters. The *abc* utility has been slightly modified to report standard deviation values in addition to average throughput values for repeated measurements. The benchmark utility is executed on a dedicated host to avoid unsolicited interactions between the HTTP server and the benchmark utility. As static content, we use our institute website's *favicon*[2]. We measured the HTTP performance ranging from 0 to 1000 concurrent connections, with range steps of 100 and *TCP keepalive* being enabled throughout all measurements.

Key-Value Store. In our second application benchmark discipline, we use *Redis* (version 3.0.1) as a key-value store. Except for *MirageOS*, *Redis* is available on all tested platforms. In order to rule out disk performance as a potential bottleneck, we disabled any persistence mechanisms in the configuration files and operate *Redis* in a cache-only mode of operation. For executing performance benchmarks, we use the *redis-benchmark* utility, which is included in the *Redis* distribution. The benchmark utility is executed on a separate host to represent real-world client-server conditions more accurately and to avoid unsolicited interactions between the benchmark utility and the *Redis* server. We measured

---

[2] http://hpi.de/favicon.ico.

the performance of GET and SET operations ranging from 0 to 1000 concurrent connections, with range steps of 100 and both *TCP keepalive* and pipelining being enabled throughout all measurements. The CSV-formatted output of *redis-benchmark* was aggregated to yield average values and standard deviation using a simple python script.

6   Results and Discussion

Here, we provide and discuss the results obtained from the benchmark procedure elaborated in Sect. 5. All values are expressed as mean$\pm$SD (n $= 30$).

6.1   General Properties

Startup Time. The measurements presented in Fig. 3(a) illustrate that both unikernels and containers can achieve much faster startup times compared to whole-system virtualization using *Ubuntu* Linux. The distinct differences between *LXD* and *Docker* demonstrate, that a large portion of the startup time of a Linux system is not caused by the kernel itself, but that it can be traced back to the services launched upon startup.

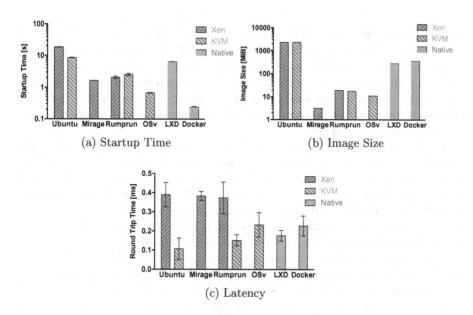

Fig. 3. A logarithmic scale is used to accommodate a wide range of values. (a) Startup time in seconds as measured using the procedure documented in [25]. (b) Image size in MiB as reported by the *du* utility. (c) Round-trip time in milliseconds as measured from a dedicated host.

Image Size. The results presented in Fig. 3(b) indicate that container approaches undercut the image size of whole-system virtualization roughly by an order of magnitude, whereas unikernels reduce image sizes by one (*Rumprun* and *OSv*) or two (*MirageOS*) additional orders of magnitudes compared to containers. The substantial reduction of image sizes can lead to a considerable advantage in IaaS scenarios, where image size often correlates with instantiation time [22].

Network Latency. The measurements presented in Fig. 3(c) indicate similar response times for *Rumprun*, *OSv*, and the container-based approaches. However, the choice of the hypervisor strongly affects the round-trip time performance. Even though para-virtualized network devices were used for both *Xen* and *KVM*, the latter yields much faster round-trip times for all tested guest systems.

6.2   Application Performance

For a statistically meaningful evaluation, an ANOVA and a post-hoc comparison using the Tukey method were applied. For the hypervisor-based approaches using both *Xen* and *KVM*, the choice of the hypervisor had no statistically significant effect on application performance. Hence, only the results for *KVM* are plotted to avoid visual clutter.

Static HTTP Server. The ANOVA test revealed a significant impact of the lightweight virtualization technique on the HTTP server performance ($p < 0.0001$, $F(9, 2970) = 3921$). Containers introduce a significant amount of overhead compared to native execution ($p < 0.0001$), both in native (see Fig. 4(a)) and virtualized environments (see Fig. 4(b)). A likely cause for this overhead is that all traffic has to go through a NAT in common configurations for both container-based approaches.

On the side of unikernels, *MirageOS* is running out of competition, as the employed *conduit server* can not be compared with a heavily optimized HTTP-server such as *Nginx*. For *Rumprun* however, it is surprising to see a similar performance compared to containers. Only for 600 concurrent clients and more, slight but statistically significant performance improvements can be observed for *Rumprun* compared to containers ($p < 0.0001$). With HTTP-servers heavily relying on the performance of the operating systems network stack, it can be assumed that the Linux networking stack has undergone massive optimization efforts that the *NetBSD* network stack can hardly compete with. To verify this hypothesis, we performed the same HTTP benchmark procedure using *NetBSD 7.0.1* in a virtual machine. Here, *Rumprun* performed distinctly better than *NetBSD* (data not shown), which indicates the potential of the unikernel-concept. With further optimizations of the network stack, *Rumprun* might achieve similar or even better performance than a regular Linux-based virtual machine.

In terms of memory footprint, unikernels manage to undercut the demands of a full-blown Linux instance (see Fig. 5(a)). However, containers still can get by with the least amount of memory. The major advantage of containers remains the possibility of dynamic memory allocation, whereas virtual machines are restricted to predefining the amount of allocated memory at the time of instantiation. Still, *MirageOS* demonstrates that a puristic approach can yield distinctly reduced memory footprints, even though sophisticated porting efforts are necessary.

Key-Value Store. The ANOVA test revealed a significant performance impact of the lightweight virtualization technique ($p < 0.0001$, $F(7, 7920) = 4099$). As illustrated in Fig. 6, the key-value store exhibits similar results regarding container-based approaches and whole-system virtualization: Regardless of native or virtualized deployments, containers come with a significant amount of overhead ($p < 0.0001$). In contrast, *Rumprun* and *OSv* offer slight but nevertheless significant performance improvements compared to Linux under many conditions. Regarding memory consumption (see 5(b)), containers still offer the highest degree

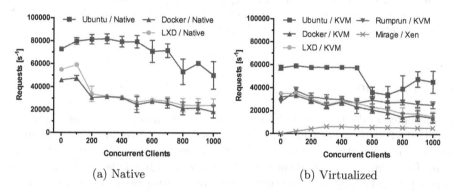

(a) Native   (b) Virtualized

Fig. 4. Throughput of *Nginx* (1.8.0) was evaluated on native hardware (a) and in virtualized environments. (b) For MirageOS, the *conduit server* was used. Throughput was measured using *weighttttp* and the modified *abc wrapper* utility.

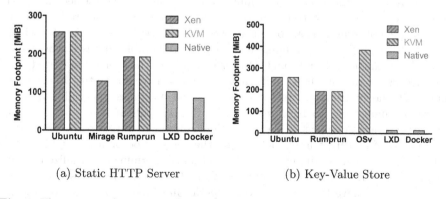

(a) Static HTTP Server   (b) Key-Value Store

Fig. 5. The memory footprints of the static HTTP server scenario (a) and the Key-Value Store scenario (b) were measured for each virtualization technique.

of flexibility. While *Rumprun* still undercuts the memory footprint of Linux, *OSv* required distinctly more memory in order to withstand the benchmark.

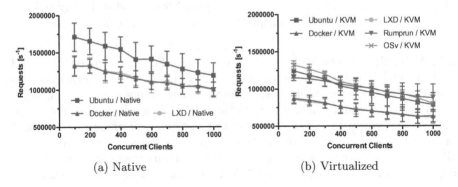

(a) Native   (b) Virtualized

Fig. 6. Throughput of *Redis* (version 3.0.1) was evaluated on native hardware (a) and in virtualized environments. (b) The plotted values show the throughput for GET requests as retrieved through the *redis-benchmark* utility.

7 Conclusion

Performance evaluations of lightweight virtualization techniques thus far have mostly dealt with application performance and neglected relevant system properties such as startup latency, image size, network latency and memory footprint. Furthermore, many of these studies focused on highlighting the strengths of one particular approach without comparing it to a broad range of alternative technologies. To take remedial action, we present an extensive performance evaluation of containers, unikernels, and whole-system virtualization, focusing on metrics that are applicable to cloud applications.

Regarding application throughput, most unikernels performed at least equally well as or even better than containers. We also demonstrated that containers are not spared from overhead regarding network performance, which is why virtual machines or unikernels may be preferable in cases where raw throughput matters. Even though *Docker* can achieve the shortest startup times considering the raw numbers, unikernels are competitive due to tiny image sizes and much shorter startup times than full virtual machines, especially in cases where the image has to be transferred to the compute host first. These are just some aspects demonstrating that, while containers have already reached a sound level of maturity, unikernels are on the verge of becoming a viable alternative. Even though we did not see unikernels outperforming a virtualized Linux instance, our brief comparison between *NetBSD* and *Rumprun* also suggested that unikernels have the potential of outperforming their full-grown operating system relatives.

Acknowledgments. We would like to thank Vincent Schwarzer for engaging our interest in *unikernels* in the course of his master's thesis [28]. Furthermore, we thank the HPI Future SOC Lab for granting us access to the hardware resources used in this paper.

This paper has received funding from the European Union's Horizon 2020 research and innovation program 2014–2018 under grant agreement No. 644866.

Disclaimer
This paper reflects only the authors' views and the European Commission is not responsible for any use that may be made of the information it contains.

References

1. Arcangeli, A., Eidus, I., Wright, C.: Increasing memory density by using KSM. In: Proceedings of the Linux Symposium, pp. 19–28. Citeseer (2009)
2. Beserra, D., Moreno, E.D., Endo, P.T., Barreto, J., Sadok, D., Fernandes, S.: Performance analysis of LXC for HPC environments. In: 2015 Ninth International Conference on Complex, Intelligent, and Software Intensive Systems (CISIS), pp. 358–363, July 2015
3. Briggs, I., Day, M., Guo, Y., Marheine, P., Eide, E.: A Performance Evaluation of Unikernels, Prepared for CS6480, Advanced Computer Networking, Fall 2014 (2015). http://media.taricorp.net/performance-evaluation-unikernels.pdf
4. Canonical, Ltd.: LXC. https://linuxcontainers.org/lxc/introduction/. Accessed 15 July 2017
5. Canonical Ltd.: LXD. https://linuxcontainers.org/lxd/introduction/. Accessed 15 July 2017
6. Di Tommaso, P., Palumbo, E., Chatzou, M., Prieto, P., Heuer, M.L., Notredame, C.: The impact of Docker containers on the performance of genomic pipelines. Peer J. **3**, e1273 (2015)
7. Docker Inc.: Docker. https://www.docker.com/. Accessed 15 July 2017
8. Engler, D.R., Kaashoek, M.F., O'Toole Jr., J.: Exokernel: an operating system architecture for application-level resource management. In: Proceedings of the Fifteenth ACM Symposium on Operating Systems Principles, SOSP 1995, pp. 251–266. ACM, New York (1995)
9. Felter, W., Ferreira, A., Rajamony, R., Rubio, J.: An updated performance comparison of virtual machines and Linux containers. In: 2015 IEEE International Symposium on Performance Analysis of Systems and Software, pp. 171–172, March 2015
10. ApacheBench - G-Wan, ab.c: http://gwan.com/source/ab.c. Accessed 15 July 2017
11. Hewlett Packard Enterprise: HPE ProLiant m710p Server Cartridge QuickSpecs (2015). https://goo.gl/0dV579
12. Irazoqui, G., Inci, M.S., Eisenbarth, T., Sunar, B.: Wait a minute! A fast, cross-VM attack on AES. In: Stavrou, A., Bos, H., Portokalidis, G. (eds.) RAID 2014. LNCS, vol. 8688, pp. 299–319. Springer, Cham (2014). doi:10.1007/978-3-319-11379-1_15
13. Jones, M., Arcand, B., Bergeron, B., Bestor, D., Byun, C., Milechin, L., Gadepally, V., Hubbell, M., Kepner, J., Michaleas, P., et al.: Scalability of VM Provisioning systems. arXiv preprint (2016). arXiv:1606.05794
14. Kantee, A.: Flexible operating system internals: the design and implementation of the any kernel and rump kernels. Ph.D. thesis, Aalto University, Finland (2012)

15. Kantee, A.: The rise and fall of the operating system, login: the USENIX magazine, pp. 6–9 (2015)
16. Kivity, A., Laor, D., Costa, G., Enberg, P., HarEl, N., Marti, D., Zolotarov, V.: OSv–optimizing the operating system for virtual machines. In: 2014 USENIX Annual Technical Conference, pp. 61–72 (2014)
17. KVM project: KVM. http://www.linux-kvm.org/page/Main. Accessed 15 July 2017
18. Lighty labs: weighttp. https://redmine.lighttpd.net/projects/weighttp/. Accessed 15 July 2017
19. Madhavapeddy, A., Leonard, T., Skjegstad, M., Gazagnaire, T., Sheets, D., Scott, D., Mortier, R., Chaudhry, A., Singh, B., Ludlam, J., et al.: Jitsu: just-in-time summoning of unikernels. In: 12th USENIX Symposium on Networked Systems Design and Implementation, pp. 559–573 (2015)
20. Madhavapeddy, A., Mortier, R., Rotsos, C., Scott, D., Singh, B., Gazagnaire, T., Smith, S., Hand, S., Crowcroft, J.: Unikernels: library operating systems for the cloud. In: Proceedings of the 18th International Conference on Architectural Support for Programming Languages and Operating Systems, pp. 461–472. ACM, New York (2013)
21. Madhavapeddy, A., Scott, D.J.: Unikernels: the rise of the virtual library operating system. Commun. ACM **57**(1), 61–69 (2014)
22. Mao, M., Humphrey, M.: A performance study on the VM startup time in the cloud. In: 2012 IEEE Fifth International Conference on Cloud Computing, pp. 423–430. IEEE (2012)
23. Martins, J., Ahmed, M., Raiciu, C., Olteanu, V., Honda, M., Bifulco, R., Huici, F.: ClickOS and the art of network function virtualization. In: Proceedings of the 11th USENIX Conference on Networked Systems Design and Implementation, pp. 459–473. USENIX Association (2014)
24. MirageOS: Conduit Server Code Example. https://github.com/mirage/mirage-skeleton/tree/master/conduit_server
25. Nickoloff, J.: Evaluating container platforms at scale. https://medium.com/on-docker/evaluating-container-platforms-at-scale-5e7b44d93f2c
26. Plauth, M., Feinbube, L., Polze, A.: A performance evaluation of lightweight approaches to virtualization. In: 8th International Conference on Cloud Computing, GRIDs, and Virtualization, IARIA, February 2017
27. Regola, N., Ducom, J.C.: Recommendations for virtualization technologies in high performance computing. In: 2010 IEEE Second International Conference on Cloud Computing Technology and Science, pp. 409–416. IEEE (2010)
28. Schwarzer, V.: Evaluierung von Unikernel-Betriebssystemen für Cloud-Computing. Masters thesis (in german), Hasso Plattner Institute for Software Systems Engineering, University of Potsdam (2016)
29. The OpenStack project: Nova. https://github.com/openstack/nova. Accessed 15 July 2017
30. Veal, B., Foong, A.: Performance scalability of a multi-core web server. In: Proceedings of the 3rd ACM/IEEE Symposium on Architecture for Networking and Communications Systems, pp. 57–66. ACM (2007)
31. Xavier, M.G., Neves, M.V., Rossi, F.D., Ferreto, T.C., Lange, T., Rose, C.: Performance evaluation of container-based virtualization for high performance computing environments. In: 2013 21st Euromicro International Conference on Parallel, Distributed, and Network-Based Processing, pp. 233–240 (2013)

Low-Level Exploitation Mitigation
by Diverse Microservices

Christian Otterstad$^{(\boxtimes)}$ and Tetiana Yarygina

Department of Informatics, University of Bergen, Bergen, Norway
{christian.otterstad,tetiana.yarygina}@uib.no

Abstract. This paper discusses a combination of isolatable microservices and software diversity as a mitigation technique against low-level exploitation; the effectiveness and benefits of such an architecture are substantiated. We argue that the core security benefit of microservices with diversity is increased control flow isolation. Additionally, a new microservices mitigation technique leveraging a security monitor service is introduced to further exploit the architectural benefits inherent to microservice architectures.

Keywords: Security · Software diversity · Design patterns · Robustness

1 Introduction

Microservices is a recent trend in software design. A microservice architecture simplifies the development of complex horizontally scalable systems that are highly flexible, modular, and language-agnostic. We define a microservice as a small specialized autonomous service communicating over a network boundary. By extension, a microservice system is a distributed software system consisting of a set of microservices communicating to perform some computation as an aggregated result of their collective operation. For further information, we refer the reader to the comprehensive study of microservice principles by Zimmermann [1] who identified commonalities in the popular microservice definitions and concluded that microservices represent a development- and deployment-level variant of the service-oriented architecture (SOA).

Although microservice architectures constitute an important trend in software design with major implications in software engineering, surveys such as the one conducted by Dragoni et al. [2] have highlighted a general lack of research in the area of microservice security. In Newman's book [3] on microservice design, a subset of security traits for improving the security of microservice networks is discussed. The idea of combining microservices with secure containers and compiler extensions to build critical software has been investigated in a recent study by Fetzer [4]. The paper by Lysne et al. [5] briefly introduces the notion of microservice networks to mitigate vendor-malware and other forms of attacks, without any further elaboration or working examples.

© IFIP International Federation for Information Processing 2017
Published by Springer International Publishing AG 2017. All Rights Reserved
F. De Paoli et al. (Eds.): ESOCC 2017, LNCS 10465, pp. 49–56, 2017.
DOI: 10.1007/978-3-319-67262-5_4

Herein, we expand and elaborate on the generalized notion of mitigating low-level exploitation. To our knowledge, we are the first to demonstrate the benefits of using a microservice architecture to defend against remote low-level exploitation. Unlike a deployment monolith, a microservice architecture facilitates strong process isolation partly because the services run on different physical machines. The paper also introduces a security monitor service that further leverages the architectural benefits of a microservice network, including added software diversity, to enable anti-fragility to low-level exploitation.

2   Microservice Architecture and Its Security Merits

2.1   Model Overview

In general, an attacker wants to gain access to an asset controlled by a defender, extending up to full access to the targeted system. It is assumed that the external attacker is able to carry out the following types of exploits: an initial exploit (E_{init}), a virtual machine or sandbox escape exploit (E_{VM}), and a lateral exploit (E_{lat}). E_{init} is used to gain a shell on a microservice node, E_{VM} enables the attacker to escape from a sandbox, while E_{lat} is an exploit type that abuses the trusted relationship between microservice nodes in cases where additional attack surface is needed and E_{init} is not sufficient.

Figure 1 illustrates a generic attack on the system model. The attacker initially obtains access using E_{init} and then proceeds to escape the sandbox using E_{VM}. Once the attacker has executed the latter exploit, full control over all nodes hosted by the same hypervisor is obtained. However, the attacker does not control the whole network. To extend the control further, the process must basically be repeated. However, the same exploit E_{init_1} may not work against VM_{n_1}—a node hosted by a different machine n, which cannot be reached through the hypervisor. Therefore, the attacker will have to resort to either using a different exploit E_{init_2}, or, depending on the available attack surface and overall exploitability, a lateral exploit E_{lat_1} to utilize the now exposed trusted relationship between the nodes.

2.2   Security Considerations

There are two distinct types of microservices in the context of interaction: microservices that allow both external and internal interaction and microservices that only allow internal interaction. Internal interaction is communication between two microservices within the system boundary. External interaction is interaction between an external host and a microservice that is part of the system. A microservice that only allows external interaction is effectively defined as a monolithic program.

However, regardless of the type of microservice and of the granularity at which microservices are implemented, every microservice must contain functionality for network interaction. The code the user can externally interact with is the most obvious attack vector. The microservices must assume that any input

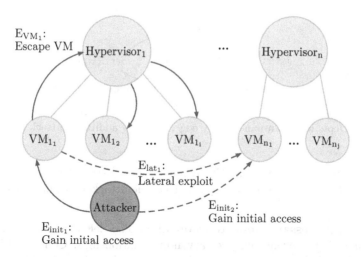

Fig. 1. Attacking a microservice architecture with diverse microservices running in a virtualized environments on networked machines.

encountered is hostile. Not only are the microservices communicating over an insecure network, but some of the nodes in the network may be compromised. Therefore, even properly authenticated nodes should not trust the subsequent input to be sane or properly formatted by its peer(s).

Microservice systems employ several design patterns [6,7] to facilitate the basic operation of the overall system—some of which affect the security of the microservice network. The *API Gateway* pattern is the entry point for all clients. A system without an API Gateway or equivalent would need to expose the required services to external users—hence increasing the initial attack surface. *Circuit breaker* prevents cascading failures by changing the component behavior based on the number of failed calls made. *Service Discovery* is a centralized scheme allowing services to discover other services. An attacker can exploit the service discovery to determine the internal structure and communication patterns between services.

A *robust system* is basically what is commonly referred to as a hardened system. Robustness is a property we use to denote how much effort is required to successfully perform a low-level exploit against the system. The following discussion covers some security considerations specific to enhancing the robustness of microservice networks and moving towards anti-fragility [8].

Maximizing API security. Exposed network interfaces must be minimal, have strong input validation, and be of the highest type in the Chomsky hierarchy [9]. These are well-known design traits for a secure system, and they apply equally to both monolithic designs and microservice designs. If there is any way to accomplish the same functionality while exposing the server to less computation on

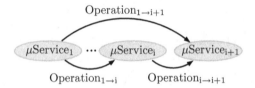

Fig. 2. Depiction of an unnecessary edge, exposing additional attack surface.

external input, this is advisable. The defender should strive to minimize the set and depth of possible control flow paths that the attacker can influence at any step.

Avoiding unnecessary node relationships. The defender must employ an architecture that prevents unnecessary node relationships. Consider Fig. 2. If μService$_1$ can reach μService$_{i+1}$ through μService$_i$, then there should not be any edge between μService$_1$ and μService$_{i+1}$. Adding the extra edge may increase the attack surface for the involved nodes. While taking a shortcut of this type to obtain information or perform functions directly might result in better performance and less complexity, doing so would violate the trade-off of increased security for less performance and higher complexity. If a microservice network forms a dense graph, then most likely the design of such a system and/or its decomposition into microservices is incorrect.

Asymmetric node strength. To optimize the robustness of the network to low-level exploitation, the more secure nodes should be placed at critical network segments, such as entry points and nodes guarding the more valuable assets, as shown in Fig. 3. A more priced asset could be functionality that allows making a transaction as compared to merely viewing the list of already performed transactions. The payment functionality could use most of the budget for hardening whereas viewing an account is considered less severe and should not be as prioritized. Examples of hardening are given in the next section. High diversity as a mechanism for hardening microservices is also discussed in the next section. Such changes can be done a priori, in contrast to tactical choices based on real world statistics.

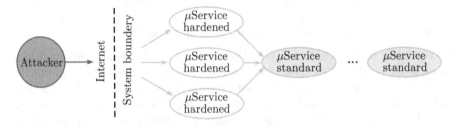

Fig. 3. The use of asymmetric node strength to defend against low-level attacks.

3   The Security Monitor Service

3.1   Security Through Diversity

The purpose of diversity in this security context is to make an exploit less statistically likely to succeed and to make the attack scale less effectively, thus, providing the defender with time to react to the attack. The most common (as of 2017) examples of diversity in computer systems are the use of different programming languages, hardware architectures, cloud providers, operating systems, hypervisors, compilers or compiler arguments, and ASLR (Address Space Layout Randomization) versions that enable identical programs to possess diversity. It has previously been argued that there are inherent benefits to software diversity in the context of mitigation of attacks [10,11].

Minimal diversity has previously been defined [12] as "when failure of one of the versions is always accompanied by failure of the other". This definition is also applicable in the context of exploitation. If there is so little diversity that the exact same exploit works equally well on both versions, then the diversity is of no benefit to the defender. However, diversity still serves a purpose in terms of redundancy against other types of failures, but not against targeted attacks.

It should be stressed again that a microservice system has inherent diversity, simply as a consequence of microservices implementing different functionality. Different bugs are assumed to be associated with different functionality. However, this may not be true in all cases—two microservices with different functionality could employ a common library with an exploitable vulnerability.

3.2   Introducing the Security Monitor Service

Normally, a system will only get patched after developers have identified issues and rolled out the changes. Although this improves the system over time it can introduce a large attack window due to the inherent latency of the process. A microservice network may automate some of the issues that arise, specifically by introducing a security monitor system. The security monitor can identify nodes that exhibit unusual behavior, trigger IDS detections, or in the case of an N-version programmed system simply report inconsistent data compared to its siblings. Anomalous behavior may result in the monitor taking explicit, autonomous action, as explained later in this section.

A simple example would be an N-version programmed system with a set of nodes that perform the same task using compiler derived diversity [13]. Similarly to the N-variant system suggested by Cox et al., we propose a security monitor scheme to exploit the fact that the defender retains part of the control flow of the overall system [11]. If a particular node issues erroneous data, the security monitor can detect it by comparing the output against the healthy nodes. The erroneous node is then isolated and the security monitor notes the compiler arguments that resulted in this defective machine code. The security monitor is not concerned with the root cause of the program error, but the compiler arguments used to derive the code are assumed to be faulty and should not be reused for the particular code in question.

Consider the case of removing an infection as indicated in Fig. 4. The security monitor detects invalid data being sent from a service. The security monitor's presence on the host system is more privileged than the service itself. Hence, the security monitor is able to forcibly destroy the environment for the service, permute, and restore it. If the permutation step was skipped, the attacker could simply replay the exploit. The security monitor should proceed to flag the event as an anomaly to allow a human to examine the faulty binary to identify the underlying cause—which is likely only masked by the permutation. The security monitor may choose to no longer trust the hosting machine for the infected service, i.e. informing the assumed clean services to blacklist the malicious nodes as well as wipe and restore the system in an attempt to deal with a rootkit on the hosting machine. In addition, the security monitor can decide to destroy, permute, and restore all immediately adjacent services.

Another option is to start a new node and ignore, but record the I/O of the infected node, as well as monitor it through the host system. The defender would be able to learn information about the attacker—in particular, exploitation attempts—as the attacker is likely to continue to interact with the system. Such a honeypot strategy could be implemented to varying degrees of sophistication, all requests could be ignored, or some could be simulated, such that the attacker would continue to interact with the simulated environment, but not be able to gain any valuable asset or do damage. In the case of multiple infected nodes, a segment of the system could be isolated. Regardless, the defender should then also migrate away any other services running on the same infected host(s). There is always the risk that the attacker could escape the VM and take control over the whole system.

A simple policy for a security monitor service would be to detect an intrusion, e.g. by using an IDS, kill the service environment, rebuild the environment, and

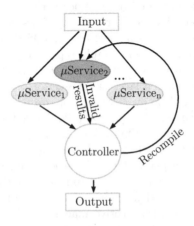

Fig. 4. A security monitor dealing with an infection in an N-version system.

finally restart the service. In this generalized procedure, the defender can either host the security monitor as a normal process with normal user privileges, in a container environment, or in a virtual machine. Regardless, the policy should be the same. It is important to destroy the whole environment, otherwise the risk of the attacker persisting increases dramatically. Even when destroying the environment the risk is only made smaller. If no containers are used, all processes should be removed and ideally the system (and firmware) restored from a trusted image—although even in this case advanced rootkits may persist. If containers or virtual machines are used, the entire container or virtual machine must be rebuilt. The recompilation step ensures that diversity is added, which hopefully removes the issue. Such an approach reduces the overhead in terms of cost and time in terms of enabling the system to react to certain types of attacks. The security monitor scheme essentially allows the system to autonomously discover certain security related issues and react to them. Manual interaction is still required to resolve the root cause of the issue. However, at the same time, the microservice architecture ensures that more effort is required to compromise the overall system, which makes the system more secure.

The security monitor system can be multi-layered. A local security monitor may reside in each execution context for each service. However, an additional external security monitor is also possible. An external security monitor would enable more complex evaluations and actions being taken as a result of the state of the overall system, as compared to merely a single node.

3.3   Evaluating the Security Monitor Service

In terms of the overall system architecture, the security monitor service becomes a part of the infrastructure similarly to logging, monitoring, and discovery services that are needed for any reasonably sized microservice system to function properly. In contrast to these basic services, the security monitor attempts to mitigate attacks autonomously, making the overall system more resilient to low-level exploitation.

A more privileged mode that offers an attack surface is an ideal target. Indeed, the security monitor is such a target itself. IDS systems and anti-malware solutions have previously become a viable attack surface which raises the question whether such systems do more harm than good [14]. An IDS is always a trade-off, to prevent it from exposing the system to more risk rather than protecting it, the security monitor should adhere to the aforementioned principles from Sect. 2.2 of least privilege, minimal attack surface, and have any grammar be of the highest type in the Chomsky hierarchy [9].

4   Conclusion

We have examined how the increased isolation of microservices coupled with software diversity can mitigate the impact of low-level exploitation. Microservices, when coupled with some method of achieving diversification, appears to offer added robustness over monolithic solutions. Key design rules and examples were presented to substantiate this claim.

We claim that the slow turnaround time for issues to be detected, fixed, and finally deployed by human operators can be made more autonomous and with lower latency if we introduce an automated security monitor to resolve the issues. One of the open questions that still remain is determining to what extent arbitrary programs can benefit from hardening and diversification. It is particularly important to consider the cost as most security enhancing features introduce overhead in terms of performance, compatibility, or usability, the mitigations suggested herein being no different.

References

1. Zimmermann, O.: Microservices tenets: agile approach to service development and deployment. Comput. Sci. Res. Dev. **32**(3–4), 301–310 (2017)
2. Dragoni, N., Giallorenzo, S., Lluch-Lafuente, A., Mazzara, M., Montesi, F., Mustafin, R., Safina, L.: Microservices: yesterday, today, and tomorrow. CoRR abs/1606.04036 (2016). http://arxiv.org/abs/1606.04036
3. Newman, S.: Building Microservices. O'Reilly Media, Sebastopol (2015)
4. Fetzer, C.: Building critical applications using microservices. IEEE Secur. Priv. **14**(6), 86–89 (2016)
5. Lysne, O., Hole, K.J., Otterstad, C., Ytrehus, Ø., Aarseth, R., Tellnes, J.: Vendor malware: detection limits and mitigation. Computer **49**(8), 62–69 (2016)
6. Richardson, C., Smith, F.: Microservices from Design to Deployment. NGINX, Inc. (2016)
7. Montesi, F., Weber, J.: Circuit breakers, discovery, and API gateways in microservices. CoRR abs/1609.05830 (2016). http://arxiv.org/abs/1609.05830
8. Hole, K.J.: Anti-fragile ICT Systems. Simula SpringerBriefs on Computing. Springer, Heidelberg (2016). doi:10.1007/978-3-319-30070-2
9. Sassaman, L., Patterson, M.L., Bratus, S., Shubina, A.: The halting problems of network stack insecurity. Login **36**(6), 22–32 (2011)
10. Homescu, A., Jackson, T., Crane, S., Brunthaler, S., Larsen, P., Franz, M.: Large-scale automated software diversity - program evolution redux. IEEE Trans. Dependable Secure Comput. **14**, 158–171 (2015)
11. Cox, B., Evans, D., Filipi, A., Rowanhill, J., Hu, W., Davidson, J., Knight, J., Nguyen-Tuong, A., Hiser, J.: N-variant systems a secretless framework for security through diversity (2006)
12. Partridge, D., Krzanowski, W.: Software diversity: practical statistics for its measurement and exploitation. Inf. Softw. Technol. **39**(10), 707–717 (1997)
13. Jackson, T., Salamat, B., Homescu, A., Manivannan, K., Wagner, G., Gal, A., Brunthaler, S., Wimmer, C., Franz, M.: Compiler-generated software diversity. In: Jajodia, S., Ghosh, A., Swarup, V., Wang, C., Wang, X. (eds.) Moving Target Defense. Advances in Information Security, vol. 54, pp. 77–98. Springer, New York (2011)
14. Ormandy, T.: Fireeye exploitation: project zero's vulnerability of the beast. https://googleprojectzero.blogspot.no/2015/12/fireeye-exploitation-project-zeros.html. Accessed 7 Feb 2017

Security

A Formal Approach for the Verification of AWS IAM Access Control Policies

Ehtesham Zahoor[1]([✉]), Zubaria Asma[1], and Olivier Perrin[2]

[1] Secure Networks and Distributed Systems Lab (SENDS),
National University of Computer and Emerging Sciences, Islamabad, Pakistan
ehtesham.zahoor@nu.edu.pk, zubaria.asma@gmail.com
[2] Université de Lorraine, LORIA, BP 239,
54506 Vandoeuvre-lès-Nancy Cedex, France
olivier.perrin@loria.fr

Abstract. Cloud computing offers elastic, scalable and on-demand network access to a shared pool of computing resources, such as storage, computation and others. Resources can be rapidly and elastically provisioned and the users pay for what they use. One of the major challenges in Cloud computing adoption is security and in this paper we address one important security aspect, the Cloud authorization. We have provided a formal Attribute Based Access Control (ABAC) model, that is based on Event-Calculus and is able to model and verify Amazon Web Services (AWS) Identity and Access Management (IAM) policies. The proposed approach is expressive and extensible. We have provided generic Event-Calculus modes and provided tool support to automatically convert JSON based IAM policies in Event-Calculus. We have also presented performance evaluation results on actual IAM policies to justify the scalability and practicality of the approach.

Keywords: AWS cloud · IAM · Access control · Verification · Event-Calculus

1 Introduction

Information security has been in the mainstream of computing. In the last decade, advancements in the domain of Cloud computing have further amplified the need to protect digital information. Cloud computing offers elastic, scalable and on-demand network access to a shared pool of computing resources such as storage, computation and communication. Resources can be rapidly and elastically provisioned and the users pay for what they use. These benefits and offerings from different Cloud providers have improved its adoption as businesses are seeking new opportunities to reduce hardware and management costs by offloading their capabilities to the Cloud. One of the major challenges in Cloud computing adoption is security for Cloud users.

© IFIP International Federation for Information Processing 2017
Published by Springer International Publishing AG 2017. All Rights Reserved
F. De Paoli et al. (Eds.): ESOCC 2017, LNCS 10465, pp. 59–74, 2017.
DOI: 10.1007/978-3-319-67262-5_5

The security policy of an organization helps to better prepare for and address security challenges. It is a high-level specification of how to implement security principles and technologies. For instance, the Authentication policy of an organization specifies which users are allowed to use its services. In this paper we address the issues related to one important class of security policies, called the Access Control or Authorization policies. There is an important distinction between the authentication and authorization policies of an organization. When a user attempts to access some resource, the first step is to determine and validate the identity of the user using some authentication measures such as login credentials. These credentials are then matched with the organization's authentication policy to identify the validity of user. Once a user has been authenticated, the authorization process involves determining what rights a user has. The authorization process allows to determine who can access what resources, under what conditions, and for what purpose. The authorization process can be based on temporal aspects and may involve delegation. While the Cloud based authentication has been a highly active research direction, Cloud authorization has remained relatively less explored. In this paper, we have provided a formal attribute based access control model, that is based on Event-Calculus and is able to model and verify authorization policies. Specifically our contributions include:

A formal authorization model: In contrast to traditional XML (or JSON in case of AWS IAM) based authorization policy specification languages, our approach is formal and based on Event-Calculus, a logical language for specification of and reasoning about events and their effects.

AWS IAM policies verification: We have applied our approach to model and verify AWS IAM policies. We have categorized conflicts as either Intra or Inter-Policy conflicts. To best of our knowledge there exists no approach that attempts to model and verify IAM policies.

ABAC based approach: Our approach is based on Attribute Based Access Control (ABAC) and it is by design a generic approach to handle other authorization models. For instance, AWS IAM is based on Role Based Access Control (RBAC) and our proposed approach allows it to be modeled and verified by considering Role as an attribute.

Extensible approach: The proposed approach can be extended to model other Authorization services provided by Cloud providers. For instance, OpenStack provides Role-Based Access Control for networks (Neutron) and user management. Our approach can be used to formally verify and reason about them.

Tool support and performance evaluation: We have provided generic Event-Calculus models and provided tool support to automatically convert JSON based IAM policies in Event-Calculus. We have also presented performance evaluation results on actual IAM policies to justify the scalability and practicality of the approach.

2   Background and Related Work

The term Access Control in the context of Cloud computing research has attracted interest in two broad subdomains. A number of approaches have addressed the security issues related to the data storage on the Cloud based storage services. In this context Attribute-Based Encryption (ABE) [1] has been proposed which implements attribute-based access control by encrypting data based on attributes. In such a scheme, only authorized users having same set of attributes can decrypt the data. A number of approaches have been proposed to address different related aspects such as introduction of attribute hierarchies [2], handling of the attributes revocation problem [3], P2P storage Cloud [4] and attribute-based keyword search scheme with user revocation [5].

The other subdomain for the research related to access control includes the policy languages for specifying authorization policies. For Cloud based applications or resources, authorization should not only be performed based on the content, but also by the context and is prone to performance, bandwidth, attributes availability and other requirements. The authorization process and policies can be considered from the enterprise or federation point of view, using approaches such as XACML, or from a user point of view (e.g. OAuth or Lockr). In general, access control and authorization has remained an active research area and a basic approach is to assign access policy directly to end users. This approach however does not scale with the increase in number of users. A number of approaches thus consider the Role Based Access Control (RBAC) model and its variations [6]. In RBAC users are assigned roles and the access policy is associated with these roles. Task based access control (TBAC) extends the traditional model by considering task based contextual information. Even though RBAC is a well defined model and still being used extensively, for instance AWS IAM is RBAC, it suffers from *role explosion* as too many roles (may even surpass the number of users) may need to be managed [7]. Some approaches have investigated the use and challenges for RBAC in a distributed environment [8–11].

In contrast to RBAC models, the Attribute based Access Control (ABAC) model is based on the attributes [12]. The resources, subjects and environment have attributes and the policy rule is a boolean function on these attributes. ABAC model can be considered more generic and provides more flexibility and expressiveness than RBAC models. ABAC can subsume RBAC as a role itself can be an attribute in an ABAC model. XACML (eXtensible Access Control Markup Language) is a XML-based language based on the ABAC model. XACML is verbose and based on XML and this makes it difficult to analyze and verify the consistency of a set of policies. A number of approaches to provide formal semantics of XACML have been proposed [13–15]. Further, a number of approaches have been proposed that build upon XACML for its usage in collaborative and distributed environments. These include [16] in which the authors propose a distributed device access control architecture called *MPABAC*. In [17] the authors have developed a formal policy language *BelLog* that can express both delegation and composition operators. Some access control policies are user-centric, that is when the user determines the access for their resources. The most prominent approach being the OAuth [18] which allows users to share their personal resources with other sites without giving them their credentials. User-Managed Access (UMA)[1] is another user centric approach and it provides services for authorization, monitoring and changing data sharing. Lockr [19] is an access control system based on social relationships.

Formal methods are being used at Amazon to verify and validate their distributed systems since last few years [20]. They have used *TLA+*, a formal specification language based on basic set theory and predicates, and *PlusCal*, closer to a C-style programming language and even more expressive than *TLA+* to model and verify AWS services such as *S3*, *DynamoDB* and *EBS*. However, the AWS IAM Policies are not formally verified and although AWS does provide a *PolicySimulator*, its scope and usage is limited as it does not attempt to verify the consistency of policies. In this work we have used the Event-Calculus, a logic programming formalism, to model and verify AWS IAM policies. Our approach builds upon our previous work in handling temporal, trust and delegation aspects in distributed environments [21,22]. In this work, we have thoroughly updated the models and instead of trust and/or temporal aspects considered AWS IAM policies verification. We have provided generic models, tool support and the performance is evaluated on actual AWS IAM polciies. To best of our knowledge there exists no approach, other than limited AWS Policy Simulator, that attempts to model and verify IAM policies.

3   AWS IAM Policies Specification

The Identity and Access Management (IAM) service provided by Amazon Web Services (AWS) is an example of RBAC model. The service provides both authentication and authorization. IAM has a notion of policy which is a high level representation of the actions a user is allowed to perform on resources, Fig. 1.

```
1    {
2        "Version": "2012-10-17",
3        "Statement": [
4            {
5                "Effect":  "Allow",
6                "Action":  ["ec2:*"],
7                "Resource":["*"]
8            },
9            {
10               "Effect": "Deny",
11               "Action": ["ec2:*"],
12               "Resource": ["*"]
13           }
14       ]
15   }
```

Fig. 1. An example AWS IAM policy with two statements

---

[1] http://docs.kantarainitiative.org/uma/draft-uma-core.html.

The policies are high level description that explicitly lists permissions. Each *policy* has a set of *statements* and on a broad level a *statement* specifies the following:

- **Service and Resources:** You can specify to which AWS service this policy applies; such as *Amazon EC2* or *Amazon S3*. Then for each service you can further specify to what specific resource this statement refers. Resources are specified using Amazon Resource Name (ARN).
- **Actions:** You can further specify to what specific action(s) this statement applies. The set of actions are service-dependent and each AWS service has its own actions, for instance the *CreateKeyPair* action is associated with *Amazon EC2* service. You can select all actions using the Policy Generator or use a wildcard (*) in the JSON document.
- **Effect:** You need to specify if the effect of the statement is either *Allow* or *Deny*. For instance you can specify that a statement allows some action on some resource of an AWS service.
- **Conditions:** You can optionally further constrain a statement by providing conditions which are specified by providing a *condition* (for instance *StringEquals*), a *key* (for instance *aws:userid*) and a *value*.

Each policy document is stored in JSON format, see Fig. 1, and contains a set of statements, each at least having the elements mentioned above. A policy may contain other elements such as *statement ID (sid)* and policy version. Once a policy has been created, it can be assigned directly to IAM Users. This basic form of access control model can be termed as User Based Access Control as discussed in Sect. 2. This approach would not scale and would be hard to manage with the increase in number of users. Alternatively, AWS allows to assign a policy to IAM Groups, a collection of users. For example, you can create an IAM Group named, *Administrators*, assign it a policy giving complete access. You can then add and remove users from this group as the need arises. Such an access control model is termed as Role Based Access Control (RBAC). However, one major limitation associated with RBAC based models is Role Explosion. It may be feasible when the number of roles (IAM groups) is small but for large organizations the number of roles may eventually surpass the number of users. This is because of various reasons such as the scale of services provided by AWS, most having numerous resources such as number of Buckets in *S3*. In addition, a large number of actions can be performed on these services and their resources. Principle of least privilege would force policy designer to create numerous roles and it would make it difficult for this model to scale.

Then there are other limitations regarding policy specification and its verification as provided by AWS IAM. The conflicts in policy specification can be broadly categorized into intra-policy and inter-policy conflicts. Intra-policy conflicts are within a single policy while the inter-policy conflicts are when multiple policies are combined and attached to a single user or group. If we closely look at the policy specification in Fig. 1, we can see that the two statements are conflicting; one allows for the access to EC2 while the other denies it. During policy specification, AWS does provide an option to validate the policy but it only checks if the policy is syntacticly correct and does not provide such conflict detection.

4   Proposed Approach

The proposed approach for AWS IAM Policies modeling is based on Attribute Based Access Control (ABAC) model and this choice is both to address the scalability and role explosion limitations associated with the IAM RBAC model, as discussed in previous section. In contrast to RBAC model, the ABAC model is based on the attributes [12]. The resources, subjects and environment have attributes and the policy rule is a boolean function on these attributes. ABAC model can be considered more generic and provides more flexibility and expressiveness than RBAC models. ABAC can subsume RBAC as a role itself can be an attribute in an ABAC model. The proposed models build on our previous work on providing a formal approach to XACML [21]. The proposed policies specification approach is based on Event-Calculus modeling formalism.

The choice of Event-Calculus is motivated by several reasons. Space limitations restrict us to provide an exhaustive comparison of all temporal languages, however based on our analysis we do believe that Event-Calculus has many interesting properties to model access control policies. First, Event-Calculus integrates an explicit time structure, in contrast to Situation Calculus, and is independent of any sequence of events (possibly concurrent). A second advantage of using Event-Calculus (over Linear Temporal Logic for instance) is that Event-Calculus supports the possibility to express quantitative time constraints (unlike LTL, except considering extensions and with limitations – see extensions of CTL/LTL). Then, considering policies that could include intervals (for instance, an access policy is set from 8 pm to 7 am), the ability of Event-Calculus to handle intervals (e.g. Allen's intervals) is definitely interesting. Third, as underlined in [23], techniques based on LTL are not fully suitable for continuous support, whereas in our context, as events occur, the Event-Calculus models are able to detect possible violations of the policies as soon as an event is detected. It allows us for a number of reasoning tasks that can be broadly categorized into deductive, abductive, and inductive tasks. In relation to TLA+ we believe that the security policies are more event-driven and thus Event-Calculus is a better choice. Fourth, using Event-Calculus provides the ability to express constraints not only upon actions, but also on data. Last, Event-Calculus is very interesting as the same logical representation can be used for verification at both design time (static analysis) and runtime (dynamic analysis and monitoring).

4.1   Event-Calculus

Event-Calculus is a logic programming language [24], first proposed by Robert Kowalski and Marek Sergot in 1986. The event-calculus represents the effect of *Actions* on *Fluents*. Event-Calculus has a set of *events* (or actions) that trigger the change, $\mathcal{A}$, a set of *fluents* that represent anything whose value is subject to change over time, $\mathcal{F}$, a set of time points $\mathcal{T}$, and a set of objects related to the particular context $\mathcal{X}$. Some basic event calculus predicates used for modeling the proposed framework are:

- *Initiates*(*e*, *f*, *t*) - fluent *f* holds after timepoint *t* if event *e* happens at *t*.
- *Happens*(*e*, *t*) specifies that event *e* happens at timepoint *t*.
- *HoldsAt*(*f*, *t*) is true iff fluent *f* holds at timepoint *t*.

The Event-Calculus models are presented using the discrete Event-Calculus language [25] and we will only present the simplified models that represent the core aspects, intentionally leaving out the supporting axioms[2]. All the variables (such as *stmt*, *time*,...) are universally quantified. Due to space limitations, some names are either abbreviated. In addition, we have shortened representation of some events and fluents such as *AllowPolicy* and *DenyPoliy*, are written as *Allow/DenyPolicy*.

4.2 Statements Specification

The *statements* (abbreviated as stmt in our models) allow to specify one specific access rule. Each statement has a *Target*, an *Effect* and the associated *Conditions*. This would seem different from the IAM policy model where statements contain other elements such as *Actions* and *Resources*. This approach is at the heart of our ABAC model as we treat all the information needed as to be composed of name-value attributes. For instance, the *Resource*, the *Action*, the *Group* of the user and other such information is considered as attributes having names and values. It thus allows for adding new attributes for target specification if needed. We start our Event-Calculus modeling approach by first presenting the Event-Calculus model for specifying statements and then using *DECReasoner*[3] to reason about a statement.

```
Statements Model 1 (Meta-model for IAM Statements)
;Sorts for attributes name/values
sort stmt, atname, atvalue        predicate AtHasValue (atname, atvalue)
;Fluents for Stmts evaluation
fluent StmtTargetHolds(stmt), StmtConditionHolds(stmt)
fluent StmtEffectIsPermit(stmt), StmtIsPermitted/Denied/NotApplicable(stmt)
;Events for Stmts evaluation
event (Mis)Match(stmt), Approve/DenyStmt(stmt), StmtDsntApply(stmt)

;These axioms link fluents with events
Initiates (Match(stmt), StmtTargetHolds(stmt), time).
Initiates(Approve/DenyStmt(stmt), StmtIsPermitted/Denied(stmt), time).
Initiates(StmtDsntApply(stmt), StmtIsNotApplicable(stmt), time).

;Conditions on events occurrence
Happens(ApproveStmt(stmt), time) -> HoldsAt(StmtTargetHolds(stmt), time) &
HoldsAt(StmtCondHolds(stmt), time) & HoldsAt(StmtEffectIsPermit(stmt), time).
Happens(StmtDsntApply(stmt), time) -> !HoldsAt(StmtTargetHolds(stmt), time).

;Initial state of the Fluents
!HoldsAt(StmtIsPermitted/Denied/NotApplicable(stmt),0).
;The goal for the reasoner
HoldsAt(StmtTargetHolds(stmt),1) | !HoldsAt(StmtTargetHolds(stmt),1).
HoldsAt(StmtIsPermitted/Denied/NotApplicable(stmt),2).
```

---

[2] Complete models can be found at https://members.loria.fr/operrin/files/esocc.txt.
[3] http://decreasoner.sourceforge.net/.

In the Event-Calculus model above, we first define some sorts, such as *stmt*, *atname* and *atvalue*, which can be considered as types of which individual variables can be instantiated. We use the sort named *stmt* to represent individual statements. Similarly the sorts *atname* and *atvalue* would be used to model attribute names and value respectively. We have then defined a predicate *AtHasValue* which specifies name-value pairs for attributes.

The core part of the model above concerns definition of fluents and events to model the state of a statement being evaluated. A fluent is anything whose value is subject to change over time and we have thus defined fluents such as *StmtIsPermitted/Denied/NotApplicable*. A statement is neither *Approved*, *Denied* or *NotApplicable* by default so the fluents are initialized such that they do not hold at the start. We then define some events which can happen and whose occurrence would change the fluent state. To link an event with fluent state, we use Event-Calculus initiates axioms and for instance, if the event *ApproveStmt* happens at time t, the fluent *StmtIsPermitted* would hold at timepoint $t + 1$. Then we have defined some constraints on events occurrence; for instance *ApproveStmt* event can only happen at time t, if the fluents *StmtTargetHolds*, *StmtCondHolds* and *StmtEffectIsPermit* holds. Finally we specify the initial conditions for the fluents and the goal for the reasoner. The *Match/Mismatch* events occurrence decide if the fluent *StmtTargetHolds* holds or not. If the *StmtTargetHolds* doesn't hold, we consider the statement to be not applicable, *StmtIsNotApplicable*. If the statement does apply, that is fluent *StmtTargetHolds* holds, it would decide if the statement is permitted or denied based on its conditions and effects.

The model above has been intentionally made generic and can be considered as a meta-model. We can put this model in a file and include the file for the specification of any specific statement. As an example on how to use the generic model, we model the IAM policy statement, as shown in Fig. 1, which allows any action on any EC2 resource.

Statements Model 2 (AWS IAM statement specification)

```
load includes/stmts/... ;generic model
atname Object, Action
atvalue AnyEC2resource, AnyAction
AtHasValue(Object,AnyEC2resource). AtHasValue(Action,AnyAction).
stmt StmtAllow

;Specifying when the statement target holds
Happens(Match(stmt),time) & AtHasValue(Object, atvalue1) & AtHasValue(Action,
atvalue2) -> atvalue1 = AnyEC2resource & atvalue2 = AnyAction.

HoldsAt(StmtEffectIsPermit(StmtAllow),0).
HoldsAt(StmtConditionHolds(StmtAllow),0).
```

In the model above, we instantiate the generic model for a specific IAM statement. We first thus include the generic model files and then specify attribute names/values and link them using a predicate *AtHasValue*. We name the statement (by creating an instance of sort *stmt*) as *StmtAllow*. Then we define a conditional axiom that the event *Match* can only happen if the attribute name value pairs match (we define the same for *Mismtach* event but is not shown due to space limitations). If we invoke the Event-Calculus reasoner, called *DECReasoner*, for the Event-Calculus based specification, it returns a solution as shown below.

Solution 1 (Statement evaluation using DECReasoner)

55 variables and 163 clauses
relsat solver
1 model
—

model 1:
0
StmtConditionHolds(StmtAllow).
StmtEffectIsPermit(StmtAllow).
Happens(Match(StmtAllow), 0).
1
+StmtTargetHolds(StmtAllow).
Happens(ApproveStmt(StmtAllow), 1).
2
+StmtIsPermitted(StmtAllow).

The solution returned by *DECReasoner* is shown above. In order to reason about Event-Calculus models, *DECReasoner* first encodes the problem in a Satisfiability (SAT) problem and then invokes the SAT solver, to reason about the models. The solution shows that the encoded SAT problem has 55 variables and 163 clauses. Then for each time-point, the solution shows which events happen at that time-point and what fluents hold true at that time-points. In case a fluent starts to hold true at time-point t (after an event happens at time-point $t-1$) it is shown with a plus(+) sign. The solution above shows that as the attributes' values are intentionally same as the ones specified in the statement, the statement target thus holds. If we change any of the attributes like the *Resource* has any other value, the *DECReasoner* will provide a model which shows that the event mismatch would happen and the statement does not apply to it, modeled by the fluent *StmtIsNotApplicable(stmt)*.

Once the target of the statement holds, it is then evaluated based on associated *Condition* and *Effect*. The statement Effect is to either *Permit* or *Deny* and the rule Condition can be considered as a set of predicates, based on the functional and the non functional constraints, that specify what conditions we need to check for the statement. In the statement above, we intentionally considered statement effect to be *Permit* modeled by fluent *StmtEffectIsPermit(StmtAllow)*, and the condition to hold, modeled by fluent *StmtConditionHolds(StmtAllow)*.

5   Intra-policy Conflicts

For the proposed approach, individual statements can be grouped into a policy, similar to the IAM policy. The proposed modeling approach is generic and thus allows for easily aggregating statements. In order to discuss the Event-Calculus models related to policies, let us consider that another statement named *StmtDeny* exists which is similar to the *StmtAllow* but having effect as Deny (space limitations restrict us to detail the model). The proposed policy Event-Calculus model is shown in the model below:

Policy Model 1 (Meta-model for IAM Policies)

sort policy   predicate PolicyHasStmt(policy, stmt)
;Fluents for Policy State/Evaluation
fluent PolicyIsPermitted/Denied/NotApplicable/Invalid(policy)

;Events for Policy State Change
event PolicyDoesntApply(policy), Approve/Deny/InvalidatePolicy(policy)
;Initiates Axioms for Events/Fluents
Initiates(PolicyDoesntApply(policy), PolicyIsNotApplicable(policy), time).
Initiates(Approve/DenyPolicy(policy), PolicyIsPermitted/Denied(policy), time).
Initiates(InvalidatePolicy(policy), PolicyIsInvalid(policy), time).

;Policy is invalid if the outcome of stmts is conflicting
Happens(InvalidatePolicy(policy), time) -> {stmt1, stmt2}PolicyHasStmt(policy, stmt1)
& PolicyHasStmt(policy, stmt2)
& HoldsAt(StmtIsPermitted(stmt1), time) & HoldsAt(StmtIsDenied(stmt2), time) .
;Initial conditions for fluents
!HoldsAt(PolicyIsPermitted/Denied/NotApplicable/Invalid(policy)(policy),0).

5.1 Statements Combining Algorithms

The proposed approach does not only allow for conflict detection but rather is generic to model other combination algorithms. For instance, the *Permit Overrides* would permit a Policy in case of conflicting outcome of statements and *Deny Overrides* (the only option currently provided by AWS IAM) would deny a policy in case of any statement being Denied. The choice of expressive Event-Calculus allows a number of other combining algorithms based on temporal, cardinality (for instance decision is based on majority x out of y statements), trust and other aspects. Space limitations restrict us to detail them further.

Policy Model 2 (Meta-model for IAM Policies - Combining Algorithms)

;Permit if even one of the stmts is permitted - permit overrides
Happens(ApprovePolicy(policy), time) -> {stmt} PolicyHasStmt(policy, stmt) &
HoldsAt(StmtIsPermitted(stmt), time).
;Deny if all of the stmts are denied
Happens(DenyPolicy(policy), time) & PolicyHasStmt(policy, stmt) ->
HoldsAt(StmtIsDenied(stmt), time).

5.2 Instantiated Policy Model

In order to see an example of intra-policy conflicts identification, we instantiate the generic Policy model shown above to model the policy shown in Fig. 1.

Policy Model 3 (AWS IAM Policy Specification)

;Load generic models for statements/policies and instantiated statements
load includes/stmts/...   load includes/policy/...
load includes/stmts/defined/StmtAllow/StmtDeny.e

policy AmazonEC2FullAccess
PolicyHasStmt(AmazonEC2FullAccess, StmtAllow/StmtDeny).
;Goal: Decide if the policy is permitted/denied/NotApplicable/Invalid
HoldsAt(PolicyIsPermitted | Denied | Invalid...(policy),3).

In the model above, we have already defined two statements, *StmtAllow* and *StmtDeny* and we add them to a policy using the predicate *PolicyHasStmt*.

The result returned by the *DECReasoner* is shown below. As both the statements concern the attributes event *Match* happens for both statements. As the effect of one statement is *Permit* and other is *Deny*, so at time-point 2, one gets permitted and other gets denied (as shown by fluents *StmtIsDenied* and *StmtIsPermitted*). Then at time-point 2, event *InvalidatePolicy* happens and the policy is considered invalid.

Solution 2 (Policy evaluation result by DECReasoner)

```
0
StmtConditionHolds(StmtAllow).
StmtConditionHolds(StmtDeny). StmtEffectIsPermit(StmtAllow).
Happens(Match(StmtAllow), 0). Happens(Match(StmtDeny), 0).
1
+StmtTargetHolds(StmtAllow). +StmtTargetHolds(StmtDeny).
Happens(ApproveStmt(StmtAllow), 1). Happens(DenyStmt(StmtDeny), 1).
2
+StmtIsDenied(StmtDeny). +StmtIsPermitted(StmtAllow).
Happens(InvalidatePolicy(AmazonEC2FullAccess), 2).
3
+PolicyIsInvalid(AmazonEC2FullAccess).
```

The proposed intra-policy conflicts verification approach provides a number of benefits. First the proposed models are intentionally made generic and thus it is easy to model policies and statements, without going into concrete details of Event-Calculus. In addition it has allowed us to provide tool support for automatically converting AWS IAM policies into Event-Calculus models. The proposed models scale well and even with 100 statements within a policy, the time taken by *DECReasoner* to encode the problem into a SAT problem is 1.1 s and solution by relsat solver takes 0.1 s. We detail the performance evaluation results in Sect. 7.

6   Inter-policy Conflicts

In order to model and verify inter policy conflicts, we group multiple policies in a *PolicySet*. Just as a policy groups multiple statements, a *PolicySet* groups multiple policies. The Event-Calculus models are shown below; due to space limitations we discuss only the instantiated model and corresponding outcome. We model the case where there are two policies, one having only one statement to allow access to EC2 resources (the policy is thus permitted) and the second policy has again only one statement to deny access to EC2 resources (the policy is thus denied). To verify any conflict, we group them in a *PolicySet* as shown below.

PolicySet Model 1 (Instantiated model for grouping policies)

```
policyset EC2PolicySet
PolicySetHasPolicy(EC2PolicySet, AmazonEC2Allow/DenyAccess).
;Goal: Decide if the policySet is permitted/denied/NotApplicable/Invalid
HoldsAt(PolicySetIsPermitted | Denied | Invalid...(policyset),4).
```

The result returned by the *DECReasoner* is shown below. It can be seen that as both the policies evaluated to different decisions at time-point 3, event

InvalidatePolicySet happens and makes the policy set invalid, as represented by the fluent *PolicySetIsInvalid*.

Solution 3 (PolicySet evaluation by DECReasoner)

```
0
StmtConditionHolds(StmtAllow/StmtDeny).
StmtEffectIsPermit(StmtAllow). Happens(Match(StmtAllow/StmtDeny), 0).
1
+StmtTargetHolds(StmtAllow). +StmtTargetHolds(StmtDeny).
Happens(ApproveStmt(StmtAllow), 1). Happens(DenyStmt(StmtDeny), 1).
2
+StmtIsDenied(StmtDeny). +StmtIsPermitted(StmtAllow).
Happens(Approve/DenyPolicy(AmazonEC2Allow/DenyAccess), 2).
3
+PolicyIsDenied(AmazonEC2DenyAccess).
+PolicyIsPermitted(AmazonEC2AllowAccess).
Happens(InvalidatePolicySet(EC2PolicySet), 3).
4
+PolicySetIsInvalid(EC2PolicySet).
```

The proposed inter-policy conflicts verification approach provides a number of benefits. First the proposed models are intentionally made generic and thus it is easy to model policies, and adding them to a *PolicySet* for the verification, without going into concrete details of Event-Calculus. In addition it has allowed us to provide tool support for automatically converting AWS IAM policies into Event-Calculus models.

7   Implementation and Performance Evaluation

In order to justify the practicality of our approach and to abstract the details of Event-Calculus models, we have developed a Web application[4] to automate the verification process. Our Web application uses AWS access keys and AWS SDK to fetch IAM Users, Groups and their attached policies. The application then allows to first select the IAM Users or Groups and then the Policies that need to be evaluated, Fig. 2-A/B. For the verification process, our application automatically generates the Event-Calculus models for the selected AWS policies, invokes the *DECReasoner* and returns the results, Fig. 2-C. Space limitations restrict us to discuss the implementation details further.

In order to test the scalability of the proposed approach, we need to scale and verify policies for both intra and inter-policy conflicts. For the Inter-Policy conflicts, we have increased the number of policies assigned to a IAM Group/User and measured the time taken by *DECreasoner* to encode the problem in a SAT problem and the time taken by the *relsat* solver. Instead of merely duplicating a policy to test scalability, we have used the actual AWS Managed IAM policies provided by the AWS. However for the Intra-Policy conflicts, we have manually added statements to a policy as AWS managed policies does not contain a large number of statements as needed to test the scalability of the approach.

---

[4] Implementation details available at https://members.loria.fr/operrin/files/esocc.txt.

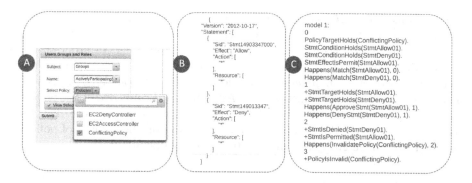

Fig. 2. Automatic conversion from IAM policies to Event-Calculus Models

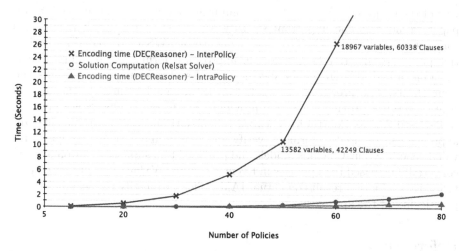

Fig. 3. Performance evaluation results

The performance evaluation test were conducted on a Amazon EC2 m4.2 x large instance having 8 vCPUs and 32 GiB memory running Ubuntu Server 16.04 LTS. Further, we have used modified and improved *DECreasoner* version as we proposed in [26]. The performance evaluation results are shown in Fig. 3, with Y-axis showing the time-taken in seconds while the X-axis showing the increase in the problem size. In general, the solution computation by *relsat* solver is very efficient even with the most complicated models. The Event-Calculus to SAT encoding process in general does not scale well but we have intentionally modeled policies in a way that the axioms do not use a large number of universally quantified free variables. Thus the SAT encoding also scales reasonably well. The encoding results can be further improved by using incremental encoding or by further improving *DECReasoner* code. For intra policy, the proposed models scale well and even with 100 statements within a policy,

the time taken by *DECReasoner* to encode the problem into a SAT problem is
1.1 s and solution by relsat solver takes 0.1 s.

The performance evaluation results are very encouraging. In order to test
the scalability of our approach we intentionally added a number of policies and
statements. However, in practice it would be rare to encounter policies with
hundreds of statements; for instance the AWS managed (provided) IAM policies
have mostly a single statement and in rare cases policies have more then ten
statements. Similarly, AWS imposes some limitations on the number of policies
attached to a single group (maximum 10 policies can be attached).

8 Conclusion

One of the major challenges in Cloud computing adoption is security and in this
paper we address one important security aspect, the Cloud authorization. In
contrast to traditional XML (or JSON in case of AWS IAM) based authorization policy specification languages, our approach is formal and based on Event-
Calculus, a logical language for specification of and reasoning about events and
their effects. The proposed approach can be extended to model other authorization services provided by Cloud providers. For instance, OpenStack provides
Role-Based Access Control for networks (Neutron) and user management. Our
approach can be used to formally verify and reason about them. We have provided generic Event-Calculus models and provided tool support to automatically
convert JSON based IAM policies in Event-Calculus. We have also presented performance evaluation results on actual IAM policies to justify the scalability and
practicality of the approach.

References

1. Yu, S., Wang, C., Ren, K., Lou, W.: Achieving secure, scalable, and fine-grained
   data access control in cloud computing. In: INFOCOM 2010, pp. 534–542
2. Zhu, Y., Huang, D., Hu, C., Wang, X.: From RBAC to ABAC: constructing flexible
   data access control for cloud storage services. IEEE Trans. Serv. Comput. **8**(4),
   601–616 (2015)
3. Yang, K., Jia, X.: Expressive, efficient, and revocable data access control for multi-
   authority cloud storage. IEEE Trans. Parallel Distrib. Syst. **25**(7), 1735–1744
   (2014)
4. He, H., Li, R., Dong, X., Zhang, Z.: Secure, efficient and fine-grained data access
   control mechanism for P2P storage cloud. IEEE Trans. Cloud Comput. **2**(4), 471–
   484 (2014)
5. Sun, W., Yu, S., Lou, W., Hou, Y.T., Li, H.: Protecting your right: verifiable
   attribute-based keyword search with fine-grained owner-enforced search authorization in the cloud. IEEE Trans. Parallel Distrib. Syst. **27**(4), 1187–1198 (2016)
6. Park, J.S., Sandhu, R.S., Ahn, G.J.: Role-based access control on the web. ACM
   Trans. Inf. Syst. Secur. **4**(1), 37–71 (2001)

7. Elliott, A., Knight, S.: Role explosion: acknowledging the problem. In: Proceedings of the 2010 International Conference on Software Engineering Research and Practice, SERP, 12–15 July 2010, Las Vegas, Nevada, USA, 2 Volumes, pp. 349–355 (2010)

8. Freudenthal, E., Pesin, T., Port, L., Keenan, E., Karamcheti, V.: DRBAC: distributed role-based access control for dynamic coalition environments. In: ICDCS, pp. 411–420 (2002)

9. Wu, T., Pei, X., Lu, Y., Chen, C., Gao, L.: A distributed collaborative product design environment based on semantic norm model and role-based access control. J. Netw. Comput. Appl. **36**(6), 1431–1440 (2013)

10. Ruan, C., Varadharajan, V.: Dynamic delegation framework for role based access control in distributed data management systems. Distrib. Parallel Databases **32**(2), 245–269 (2014)

11. Lee, H.K., Luedemann, H.: Lightweight decentralized authorization model for inter-domain collaborations. In: SWS, pp. 83–89 (2007)

12. Hu, V.C., Ferraiolo, D., Kuhn, R., Schnitzer, A., Sandlin, K., Miller, R., Scarfone, K.: Guide to attribute based access control (ABAC) definition and considerations. NIST Spec. Publ. **800**, 162 (2014)

13. Bryans, J.: Reasoning about XACML policies using csp. In: SWS, pp. 28–35 (2005)

14. Nguyen, T.N., Le Thi, K.T., Dang, A.T., Van, H.D.S., Dang, T.K.: Towards a flexible framework to support a generalized extension of XACML for spatio-temporal RBAC model with reasoning ability. In: Murgante, B., Misra, S., Carlini, M., Torre, C.M., Nguyen, H.-Q., Taniar, D., Apduhan, B.O., Gervasi, O. (eds.) ICCSA 2013. LNCS, vol. 7975, pp. 437–451. Springer, Heidelberg (2013). doi:10.1007/978-3-642-39640-3_32

15. Kolovski, V., Hendler, J.A., Parsia, B.: Analyzing web access control policies. In: WWW, pp. 677–686 (2007)

16. Liang, F., Guo, H., Yi, S., Zhang, X., Ma, S.: An attributes-based access control architecture within large-scale device collaboration systems using XACML. In: Yang, Y., Ma, M. (eds.) Green Communications and Networks. Lecture Notes in Electrical Engineering, pp. 1051–1059. Springer, Dordrecht (2012)

17. Tsankov, P., Marinovic, S., Dashti, M.T., Basin, D.: Decentralized composite access control. In: Abadi, M., Kremer, S. (eds.) POST 2014. LNCS, vol. 8414, pp. 245–264. Springer, Heidelberg (2014). doi:10.1007/978-3-642-54792-8_14

18. Hardt, D.: The oauth 2.0 authorization framework (2012)

19. Tootoonchian, A., Saroiu, S., Ganjali, Y., Wolman, A.: Lockr: better privacy for social networks. In: CoNEXT (2009)

20. Newcombe, C., Rath, T., Zhang, F., Munteanu, B., Brooker, M., Deardeuff, M.: How amazon web services uses formal methods. Commun. ACM **58**(4), 66–73 (2015)

21. Zahoor, E., Perrin, O., Bouchami, A.: CATT: a cloud based authorization framework with trust and temporal aspects. In: 10th IEEE International Conference on Collaborative Computing: Networking, Applications and Worksharing, CollaborateCom 2014, Miami, Florida, USA, 22–25 October 2014, pp. 285–294 (2014)

22. Bouchami, A., Perrin, O., Zahoor, E.: Trust-based formal delegation framework for enterprise social networks. In: 2015 IEEE TrustCom/BigDataSE/ISPA, Helsinki, Finland, 20–22 August 2015, vol. 1, pp. 127–134 (2015)

23. Montali, M., Maggi, F.M., Chesani, F., Mello, P., van der Aalst, W.M.P.: Monitoring business constraints with the event calculus. ACM Trans. Intell. Syst. Technol. **5**(1), 17:1–17:30 (2014)

24. Kowalski, R.A., Sergot, M.J.: A logic-based calculus of events. New Gener. Comput. **4**(1), 67–95 (1986)
25. Mueller, E.T.: Commonsense Reasoning. Morgan Kaufmann Publishers Inc., San Diego (2006)
26. Zahoor, E., Perrin, O., Godart, C.: An event-based reasoning approach to web services monitoring. In: ICWS (2011)

Foundations for Designing, Defining, Validating and Executing Access Control Policies in Cloud Environments

Simeon Veloudis, Iraklis Paraskakis$^{(\boxtimes)}$, and Christos Petsos

South East European Research Centre (SEERC), The University of Sheffield,
International Faculty CITY College, Thessaloniki, Greece
{sveloudis,iparaskakis,chpetsos}@seerc.org

Abstract. By embracing cloud computing enterprises are able to boost their agility and productivity whilst realising significant cost savings. However, due to security and privacy concerns, many enterprises are reluctant to migrate their data and operations to the cloud. One way to alleviate these concerns is to devise access control policies that infuse suitable security controls into cloud services. Nevertheless, the complexity inherent in such policies, stemming from the dynamic nature of cloud environments, calls for a framework that provides *assurances* with respect to the *effectiveness* of the policies. In this respect, this work proposes a class of constraints, the so-called *well-formedness constraints*, that provide such assurances by empowering stakeholders to harness the *attributes* of the policies. Both the policies and the constraints are expressed *ontologically* hence enabling automated reasoning about the abidance of the policies with the constraints.

Keywords: Foundation framework for policies · Designing policies · Defining policies policy governance · Access control · Policy governance · Ontologies · Description logics

1 Introduction

Cloud computing enables enterprises to realise significant cost savings, whilst boosting their agility and productivity. Nevertheless, due to security and privacy concerns, many enterprises are reluctant to relinquish control of—oftentimes critical—corporate assets by migrating their data and applications to third-party cloud providers [1]. One way to alleviate these concerns, hence bolster the adoption of cloud computing, is to infuse adequate *access control policies* into the applications through which critical assets are accessed in the cloud [2]. Nevertheless, the inherently dynamic nature of cloud environments calls for policies that are able to incorporate a potentially complex body of *contextual knowledge* pertaining to access requests [3]. As an example, consider a policy whereby a particular entity (s) is allowed to read a sensitive data object (o) only when: (i) o resides in a data centre in the EU; (ii) s resides in a specific geographical area (say the city of Athens), or the request originates from a particular subnet; (iii) the request is received during a prescribed time interval.

© IFIP International Federation for Information Processing 2017
Published by Springer International Publishing AG 2017. All Rights Reserved
F. De Paoli et al. (Eds.): ESOCC 2017, LNCS 10465, pp. 75–82, 2017.
DOI: 10.1007/978-3-319-67262-5_6

We argue that, for stakeholders to entrust such complex access control policies with the protection of their sensitive assets, a framework that provides assurances about the *effectiveness* of the policies is required [2]. In particular, a framework is required that assists developers in infusing effective access control policies into the applications through which sensitive assets are accessed in the cloud. Our work, conducted as part of the PaaSword project [4], provides such a framework. More specifically, it offers a generic *security-by-design* solution—essentially a PaaS offering—that provides assurances about the effectiveness of *context-aware* access control policies by facilitating their *governance*. To this end, it draws upon a *semantic representation* of policies, one that *ontologically* captures the various knowledge artefacts that are encoded in the policies. Such a representation disentangles the expression of policies from the actual code of the applications into which they are infused hence enabling automated reasoning about their *correctness*.

This paper proposes an approach to such reasoning. In particular, it proposes a set of *ontologically-expressed constraints*, the so-called *well-formedness constraints*, that articulate all those *knowledge artefacts* that *must*, *may* or *must not* be embodied in an access control policy. These constraints give rise to a *higher-level ontology*, one that specifies an allowable *form*, or *structure*, by which access control policies must abide. Evidently, well-formedness constraints empower stakeholders to harness the knowledge artefacts embodied in access control policies that protect their sensitive assets. In other words, they empower stakeholders to infuse into these policies their business logic and overall stance towards security. In this respect, well-formedness constraints assist developers in devising policies that are appropriate for the stakeholders' needs, hence for the assets that they protect.

The rest of this paper is structured as follows. Section 2 presents an ontological representation for access control policies and well-formedness constrains. Section 3 outlines a mechanism that reasons about the satisfaction of well-formedness constraints. Section 4 discusses related work and Sect. 5 outlines conclusions.

2 Constraining Access Control Policies

As already discussed, the dynamic nature of cloud environments calls for access control policies that are able to incorporate the *contextual knowledge* pertaining to access requests. *Attribute-based Access Control* (*ABAC*) policies [5], due to their inherent generality stemming from their inherent reliance on the generic concept of an *attribute*, are particularly suitable for capturing such knowledge [3] and are thus adopted in our work. This section outlines an OWL-based representation for ABAC policies and *well-formedness constraints*; as already mentioned, the latter harness the attributes embodied in the former.

2.1 A Model for ABAC Rules and Policies

Following the XACML standard [6], an ABAC policy comprises one or more ABAC *rules*. Upon receipt of an access request, a rule-combining algorithm [6] is executed in order to select which one of these rules, if any, will be applied in order to arrive at a 'permit' or a 'deny' decision. It follows that, for each access request, an ABAC policy resolves to at most one of its constituent rules (a policy that does not resolve to any of its constituent rules is considered 'Not Applicable' or 'Indeterminate' [6]).

An ABAC rule comprises an *antecedent* and a *consequent*. The latter specifies the rule's *decision*, which according to the XACML standard, invariably resolves to either a *'permit'* or a *'deny'*. The former articulates a *(pre-)condition* (or *'target'* in the XACML jargon) that must be satisfied in order for the rule to be *enforceable*. More specifically, it incorporates a set of relevant knowledge artefacts, its *attributes*, whose values need to be taken into account when deciding whether to permit, or deny, a request. These attributes are drawn from an underlying Context Model (CM)—an extensible ontological framework that includes interrelated concepts suitable for capturing attributes and the properties thereof. A simplified view of the CM that is used in this work, one which includes only concepts and properties considered in this paper, is depicted in Fig. 1 (for more details on the CM, the interested reader is referred to [7]).

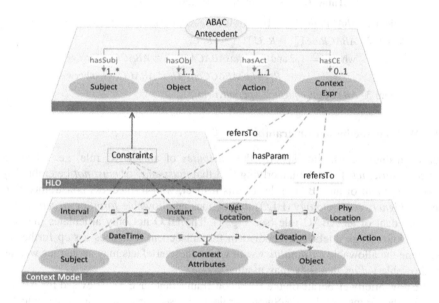

Fig. 1. HLO constraints

Ontologically, ABAC policies are represented as instances of the concept *ABACPolicy*, and ABAC rules as instances of the concept *ABACRule*; ABAC policies are associated with their constituent rules through the object property *hasABACRule*. The antecedent and consequent of an ABAC rule are represented, respectively, as instances of the concepts *ABACAnt* and *ABACCons*; an ABAC rule is associated with its antecedent and consequent via the properties *hasABACAnt* and *hasABACCons* respectively. In addition, the following *restrictions* apply. Firstly, an ABAC policy is invariably associated with *at least one* ABAC rule; secondly, an ABAC rule is invariably associated with *exactly one* antecedent and *exactly one* consequent; thirdly, the consequent of an ABAC rule always resolves to either a 'permit' or a 'deny' decision (represented respectively by the individuals *permit* and *deny*). All three restrictions are ontologically captured in terms of *terminological (TBox) axioms* expressed in the $\mathcal{SROJQ}$ Description Logic (DL) [8]. These axioms are presented in Table 1. The first demands that each ABAC policy, i.e. each instance of the concept *ABACPolicy*, is also an instance of the (abstract) class that comprises all those individuals that have *at least one* association through the property *hasABACRule* with an individual from the concept *ABACRule*. The second demands that each ABAC rule, i.e. each instance of *ABACRule*, is also an instance of the class that comprises all those individuals that have *exactly one* association through each of the properties *hasABACAnt* and *hasABACCons* with individuals from the concepts *ABACAnt* and *ABACCons* respectively. Finally, the third axiom demands that the class *ABACCons* comprises solely the individuals *permit* and *deny*.

Table 1. ABAC policy model restriction axioms

Axiom 1	$ABACPolicy \sqsubseteq\ \leq 1hasABACRule.ABACRule$
Axiom 2	$ABACRule \sqsubseteq (\geq R_i.C_i) \sqcap (\leq 1R_i.C_i)$
	where $i = 1, 2$ and $R_i \equiv hasABACAnt, C_i \equiv ABACAnt$, for $i = 1$
	$R_i \equiv hasABACCons, C_i \equiv ABACCons$, otherwise
Axiom 3	$ABACConsequent \equiv \{permit, deny\}$

2.2   Well-Formedness Constraints

Well-formedness constraints specify the *attributes* of an ABAC rule, i.e. all those *knowledge artefacts* from the underlying CM that *must, may* or *must not* be embodied in the antecedent of an ABAC rule. In this respect, well-formedness constraints give rise to a *higher-level ontology* (HLO) that defines an allowable *form*, or *structure*, for the antecedent of an ABAC rule (see Fig. 1). The HLO not only articulates the permissible knowledge artefacts embodied in the antecedent, but goes a step further to determine the allowable *cardinalities* with which these artefacts may appear, as well as the allowable *values* that they may assume.

We now briefly elaborate on the HLO constraints that have been devised for ABAC rules in the frame of the PaaSword project. These constraints are ontologically expressed in terms of $\mathcal{SROJQ}$ TBox axioms which restrict the class *ABACAnt*. It is to be noted here that these constraints are *malleable* in the sense that they can be altered to express alternate structures for the antecedent of ABAC rules—i.e. structures that potentially reflect more accurately the application-specific needs of an organisation adopting the PaaSword framework. This malleability is of utmost significance for it empowers stakeholders to infuse into access control policies their business logic and overall stance towards security.

The first constraint states that each ABAC rule *must* embody *exactly one* protected asset. Ontologically, this is captured through a TBox axiom that demands that the antecedent of an ABAC rule, i.e. each instance of the concept *ABACAnt*, is associated with *exactly one* individual from the class *Object* of the CM, and that this association should be realised through the object property *hasObj*. Table 2 provides a formal expression of this axiom, as well as of the rest of the axioms outlined in this section. Similarly, the second axiom states that each ABAC rule must be associated, through the property *hasAct*, with *exactly one* action from the class *Action* (i.e. with exactly one action to be performed on the protected asset); the third axiom states that each ABAC rule must be associated with *at least one* subject from the class *Subject* (i.e. with at least one entity requesting access to the protected asset), and the fourth axiom demands that each ABAC rule *may* refer, via the property *hasCE* to *at most one context expression*— i.e. to at most one expression that constrains the values of the contextual attributes that pertain to an access request. Context expressions take the form of instances of the class *ContextExpr* (see Fig. 1) and are further discussed below.

Table 2. HLO axioms

Axiom 1	$ABACAnt \sqsubseteq (\leq 1 hasObj.Object) \sqcap (\geq 1 hasObj.Object)$
Axiom 2	$ABACAnt \sqsubseteq (\leq 1 hasAct.Action) \sqcap (\geq 1 hasAct.Action)$
Axiom 3	$ABACAnt \sqsubseteq \leq 1 hasSubj.Subject$
Axiom 4	$ABACAnt \sqsubseteq \geq 1 hasCE.ContextExpr$

A context expression (CE) is a propositional logic expression that is attached to the antecedent of an ABAC rule and articulates the *contextual conditions* that must hold in order to permit, or deny, a request. These contextual conditions may refer to the subject and/or object of a request, or to the request itself. In other words, a CE captures the body of contextual knowledge that must be taken into account when deciding upon a request. Ontologically, a CE is represented as an instance of the class *ContextExpr* (see Fig. 1). The various attributes that it binds, i.e. its *parameters*, are represented as instances of the CM—in particular, as instances of the classes encompassed by the *ContextAttributes* concept. These parameters are associated with their encompassing CE through the object property *hasParam* and may be combined through the usual propositional logic connectives. A CE invariably enjoys at least one association with a parameter; ontologically, this is captured by an axiom analogous to Axiom 3 of Table 2. Moreover, a CE may be defined recursively, in terms of one or more other CEs; this is captured by including the class *ContextExpr* in both the domain and the range of the property *hasParam*. Finally, a context expression is attached to the entity that it refers to through the object property *refersTo*.

The HLO may encompass constraints that restrict the allowable forms that a CE can assume when attached to a particular ABAC rule. These constraints restrict the *cardinalities* with which certain knowledge artefacts from the class *ContextAttributes* may appear in a CE, as well as the allowable *ranges of values* that these artefacts may assume. As an example, consider an HLO constraint that demands that *any* CE attached to an ABAC rule should invariably incorporate at least one parameter that confines the whereabouts of the subject *s* of a request to the physical location identified as *Athens*, or to the network location identified by the subnet 123.0.0.0/8. Ontologically, this constraint takes the form:

$$ContextExpression \sqsubseteq (\leq 1 refersTo.\{s\}) \sqcap ((\leq 1 hasParam.\{Athens\})$$
$$\sqcup (\leq 1 hasParam.\{123.0.0.0/8\})) \tag{1}$$

3 Reasoning About the Correctness of ABAC Policies

Reasoning about the correctness of an ABAC rule, hence about the correctness of an ABAC policy that resolves to that rule, involves reasoning about the abidance of the rule by the HLO constraints. Below, we outline how this reasoning is performed by a mechanism that we have developed as part of the PaaSword project. As an example, suppose the following set of $\mathcal{SROIQ}$ axioms that articulate the attribute values associated with an ABAC rule; we shall term such an axiom-set a *knowledge base* (KB) [9].

$$\mathcal{R} \equiv \{ABACRule(r), ABACAnt(a), Object(o), Subject(s),$$
$$ContextExpr(e), PhyLocation(Athens), hasABACAnt(r,a),$$
$$hasABACCons(r, permit), hasObj(a,o), hasSubj(a,s), \tag{2}$$
$$hasCE(a,e), hasParam(e, Athens), refersTo(e,s)\}$$

According to $\mathcal{R}$, the antecedent a of the ABAC rule r is associated with the object o, the subject s and the context expression e; e is further associated with the (physical) location parameter *Athens* which refers to s.

Two seminal assumptions underpinning OWL are the Open-World Assumption (OWA) and the non-Unique Name Assumption (non-UNA). Nevertheless, these assumptions render the use of OWL cumbersome when reasoning about *constraint satisfaction*. Consider, for example, the KB $\mathcal{R}$ above. $\mathcal{R}$ fails to specify the *action* that is to be performed upon the object o. However, according to the OWA, this does not mean that the rule r described by $\mathcal{R}$ does not have such an action associated with its antecedent: it merely means that this association is not specified in $\mathcal{R}$. In order to overcome this obstacle, we adopt the approach proposed in [9] and dispense with the OWA and the non-UNA, effectively enabling *closed-world reasoning* when checking the abidance of ABAC rules by HLO constraints. This reasoning is based on an extended semantics of OWL, namely the Integrity Constraint semantics [9]; an outline of how such reasoning is performed is in order.

Each HLO axiom is translated into a *query*, one that is posed to the KB under validation with the aim of discovering any individuals that *violate* the axiom: if the query returns an empty set of individuals, the axiom is considered to hold; otherwise, it is considered to be violated. The query is, in fact, an assertion axiom that uses variables in place of individuals and expresses the *negation* of the HLO axiom that it translates. As an example, consider Axiom 2 of Table 2. This axiom is translated into a query that attempts to discover in $\mathcal{R}$ any individuals that belong to the class *ABACAnt* and which either enjoy no associations (through the property *hasAct*) with instances of the class

Action, or enjoy two or more such associations with distinct instances of *Action*. Formally:

$$ABACAnt(x) \land (\textbf{not}(hasAct(x,y) \land Action(y)) \lor$$
$$(hasAct(x,y) \land hasAct(x,z) \land Action(y) \land Action(z) \land \textbf{not}(y = z))$$

(3)

These queries are termed in [9] *Distinguished Conjunctive Queries* with Negation as Failure (DCQ$^{\textbf{not}}$). DCQ$^{\textbf{not}}$ are posed to the KB under validation as SPARQL queries [10]. SPARQL queries are executed in the Pellet reasoner [11] (however, any other OWL reasoner could have been used instead). In [9], a set of translation rules for turning a $\mathcal{SROIQ}$ axiom into a DCQ$^{\textbf{not}}$, hence into a SPARQL query, is presented.

4 Related Work

A number of approaches have been proposed for the semantic representation of policies [12–14]. These generally rely on OWL [15] for capturing the various knowledge artefacts that underpin the definition of a policy. In [12] KaoS is presented—a generic framework offering: (i) a human interface layer for the expression of policies; (ii) a policy management layer that is capable of resolving conflicting policies; (iii) a monitoring and enforcement layer that encodes policies in a programmatic format suitable for enforcing them. KaoS lacks any mechanism for automatically checking the correctness, hence the effectiveness, of policies.

In [13] Rei is proposed: a framework for specifying, analyzing and reasoning about policies. Similar to our work, a policy comprises a list of rules that take the form of OWL properties; it also comprises a context that defines the underlying policy domain. Rei resorts to the use of constructs adopted from rule-based programming languages for the definition of policy rules. This essentially prevents Rei from exploiting the full inferencing potential of OWL as policy rules are expressed in a formalism that is alien to OWL. In addition, it does not provide any mechanism for reasoning about the effectiveness of policies.

In [14] the authors propose POLICYTAB for facilitating trust negotiation in Semantic Web environments. POLICYTAB adopts ontologies for the representation of policies that guide a trust negotiation process ultimately aiming at granting, or denying, access to sensitive Web resources. These policies essentially specify the credentials that an entity must possess in order to carry out an action on a sensitive resource that is under the ownership of another entity. Nevertheless, no attempt is made to semantically model the context associated with access requests, rendering POLICYTAB inadequate for the dynamic nature of cloud environments.

5 Conclusions

We have presented an approach to reasoning about the correctness, hence the effectiveness, of access control policies in dynamic cloud environments. The correctness is judged on the basis of *ontologically-expressed* constraints, the so-called *HLO constraints.* The reasoning is based on an extended semantics of OWL, one that dispenses with the OWA and the non-UNA, allowing the transformation of the constraints into queries that are posed to the KBs that represent the rules under validation.

Acknowledgements. The research leading to these results has received funding from the European Union's Horizon 2020 research and innovation programme under grant agreement No 644814.

References

1. Cloud Security Alliance: What's Hindering the Adoption of Cloud Computing in Europe? Cloud Security Alliance (2015). https://blog.cloudsecurityalliance.org/2015/09/15/whats-hindering-the-adoption-of-cloud-computing-in-europe/. Accessed 6 May 2017
2. Veloudis, S., Paraskakis, I.: Defining an ontological framework for modelling policies in cloud environments. In: CloudCom 2016 – Proceedings of the 8th IEEE International Conference on Cloud Computing Technology and Science, pp. 277—284. IEEE Computer Society, Los Alamitos (2016)
3. Veloudis, S., Paraskakis, I., Petsos, C., Verginadis, Y., Patiniotakis, I., Mentzas, G.: An ontological template for context expressions in attribute-based access control policies. In: CLOSER 2017 – Proceedings of the 7th International Conference on Cloud Computing and Services Science, pp. 123–134. Scitepress (2017)
4. PaaSword project. http://www.paasword.eu/. Accessed 6 May 2017
5. Hu, V.C., Ferraiolo, D., Kuhn, R., Schnitzer, A., Sandlin, K., Miller R., Scarfone, K.: Guide to Attribute Based Access Control (ABAC), Definition and Considerations. NIST (2014)
6. eXtensible Access Control Markup Language (XACML) Version 3.0. 22 January 2013. OASIS   Standard.   http://docs.oasis-open.org/xacml/3.0/xacml-3.0-core-spec-os-en.html. Accessed 6 May 2017
7. PaaSword Deliverable 2.1. https://www.paasword.eu/deliverables/. Accessed 6 May 2017
8. Horrocks, I., Kutz, O., Sattler, U.: The even more irresistible *SROIQ*. In: Doherty, P., Mylopoulos, J., Welty, C.A. (eds.) Proceedings of the 10th International Conference on Principles of Knowledge Representation and Reasoning (KR 2006), pp. 57–67. AAAI Press (2006)
9. Tao, J., Sirin, E., Bao, J., McGuinness, D.L.: Integrity constraints in OWL. In: Proceedings of the 24th AAAI Conference on Artificial Intelligence (AAAI-10), Atlanta, Georgia, USA, 11–15 July 2010
10. SPARQL 1.1 Query Language W3C Recommendation, 21 March 2013. https://www.w3.org/TR/sparql11-query/. Accessed 6 May 2017
11. Sirin, E., Parsia, B., Cuenca Grau, B., Kalyanpur, A., Katz, Y.: Pellet: a practical OWL-DL reasoner. Web Semant. Sci. Serv. Agents World Wide Web 5(2), 51–53 (2007)
12. Kagal, L., Finin, T., Joshi, A.: A policy language for a pervasive computing environment. In: Proceedings IEEE 4th International Workshop on Policies for Distributed Systems and Networks (POLICY 2003), pp. 63–74. IEEE Computer Society, Washington, D.C. (2003)
13. Nejdl, W., Olmedilla, D., Winslett, M., Zhang, C.C.: Ontology-based policy specification and management. In: Gómez-Pérez, A., Euzenat, J. (eds.) ESWC 2005, vol. 3532, pp. 290–302. Springer, Heidelberg (2005)
14. Uszok, A., Bradshaw, J., Jeffers, R., Johnson, M., Tate, A., Dalton, J., Aitken, S.: KAoS policy management for semantic web services. IEEE Intel. Syst. 19(4), 32–41 (2004)
15. OWL 2 Web Ontology Language Primer, 2nd edn. https://www.w3.org/TR/owl2-primer/. Accessed 6 May 2017

Secure and Scalable Remote Access Tunnels for the IIoT: An Assessment of openVPN and IPsec Performance

Frederic Pohl[✉] and Hans Dieter Schotten

Intelligent Networks Research Group, German Research Center for Artificial
Intelligence,Trippstadter Str. 122, 67663 Kaiserslautern, Germany
`frederic.pohl@dfki.de`

Abstract. Nowadays, industrial production already benefits from an
increased level of interconnection involving various heterogeneous production assets. Future development in the area is likely to lead to a
scenario often referred to as the Industrial Internet of Things (IIoT), a
promising factor in achieving unseen productivity goals. One of the key
IIoT use cases is remote access, which can drastically reduce the requirement for on-site presence of technicians and thus eliminate a large cost
factor. In this paper, we present a detailed examination of two widespread Virtual Private Network (VPN) remote access frameworks and
analyse their suitability for IIoT remote access facilities. We introduce
a cloud architecture that seamlessly integrates with existing highly segmented and firewalled industrial networks, yet providing secure connec-
tivity through the use of openVPN and IPsec technology. With scalability
being a key factor for a cloud architecture, we give an analysis of our
favoured protocols in order to derive potential performance bottlenecks.
We finally verify our assumptions by providing empirical performance
measurements.

Keywords: Industrial Internet of Things · Network security · Remote
access · Virtual Private Networks · IPsec · openVPN

1 Introduction and Motivation

Complex industrial production processes, as of today, are highly computerized
and involve a large number of interconnected devices. Yet, interconnection of
production environments as a driver for highly optimized production processes
is predicted to continue in the future, thus allowing for novel business models
often summarized by the visionary term of a "fourth industrial revolution" [11].

Within this vision of heavily interconnected "smart factories" [19], a key element is remote access to the interconnected components involved in production
processes. A robust remote access framework not only allows to reduce costs by
reducing on-site maintenance and incident durations but also is an enabler for

© IFIP International Federation for Information Processing 2017
Published by Springer International Publishing AG 2017. All Rights Reserved
F. De Paoli et al. (Eds.): ESOCC 2017, LNCS 10465, pp. 83–90, 2017.
DOI: 10.1007/978-3-319-67262-5_7

various machine-to-machine interaction scenarios. Malicious use of remote access frameworks, however, must be prevented by enforcing secure authentication and encryption facilities, which should be flanked by an anomaly detection framework. IPsec [13] and openVPN [1] are well-established solutions to achieve the first goal on the network layer; the second goal, despite being out of the scope of this work, can be achieved on the same cloud infrastructure by inspecting traffic that is forwarded by a centralized VPN endpoint between the involved entities.

This paper evaluates the suitability of the aforementioned VPN technologies for such a massive IIoT remote administration architecture and is organized as follows: Sect. 2 gives an overview of the related work. Section 3 describes our evaluation platform and compares involved IPsec and openVPN protocol properties. In Sect. 4 we present an empirical performance evaluation of the core cloud component for both protocols. Section 5 discusses the results we obtained and concludes this work.

2   State-of-the-Art and Related Work

The wide availability of Internet Protocol (IP) based packet switched networks, in conjunction with IP-based VPN protocols allowing to tunnel traffic to and from different private domains[1], allows for flexible remote access setups. Nowadays, there exists a variety of VPN protocols to tunnel network or data link layer traffic, yet many of them provide little to no security [14]. With an increasing awareness of security requirements in the internet domain, the most widely used VPN technologies therefore either comply with the IPsec standard or use a Transport Layer Security (TLS) [9] framework, as openVPN does.

In the context of IIoT scenarios involving thousands of connected devices, the performance of VPN technology is very important. A comparison of maximally achievable bandwidths and response times using IPsec and openVPN was performed by Kotuliak, Rybár, and Truchly [15] with IPsec outperforming openVPN. Migault et al. analysed processor overheads of different IPsec and cipher suite operation modes and observed significant performance improvement upon activation of hardware acceleration for encryption [16].

Most related work however focuses on evaluating performance in bidirectional VPN setups and thus only partly applies for the remote access platform we will present in Sect. 3. Our contribution consists in a performance evaluation of a remote access platform taking the role of a trusted intermediary in secure tunnelling scenarios for the IIoT.

3   Platform Architecture

Figure 1 depicts our evaluation architecture for secure, session-based end-to-end tunnelling between entities located in disjoint private network zones A, B, each isolated by at least one firewall and/or Network Address Translation (NAT) [20]

---

[1] Employing private IPv4 address ranges according to [18].

layer. An entity in this context represents any IP addressable device. The architecture's core component is a cloud platform trusted by the operators of both private networks, which consists of:

- a session database that contains all scheduled tunnelling events,
- a VPN endpoint that provides encryption and authentication facilities,
- a routing engine that forwards incoming packets to the respective recipient.

The cloud platform is located in zone C and must be reachable from the private zones. Tunnels are established by the entities in the private subnets, traffic within the remote access tunnel is therefore always directed to and originated from the platform's VPN endpoint, minimizing firewall configuration effort for operators of the respective private zones.

The platform is not limited to traffic forwarding tasks. An important architectural property lies within traffic being available in decrypted plain-text inside the platform, which we deem beneficially in the context of data aggregation and anomaly detection scenarios as described in [10]. Other processing scenarios such as accounting and monitoring are conceivable. Note that the architecture does not break with application layer security entities may employ to prevent deep packet inspection within the platform.

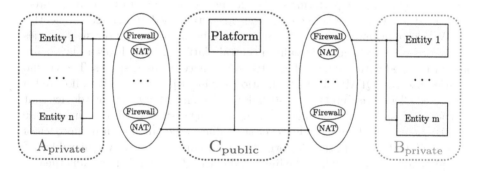

Fig. 1. Platform and test-bed architecture

In the context of these remote access scenarios, we deem high relevance to the performance of the platform's VPN endpoint in high traffic load conditions and a large number of connection attempts. From a cryptographic point-of-view, there exist various optimizations [7] which allow for fast cryptographic processing of VPN traffic. Nonetheless, different implementation approaches of IPsec and openVPN introduce overheads: openVPN encrypts and decrypts VPN traffic in user space and uses TUN/TAP interfaces to interact with system space routines responsible for actual traffic dispatching via physical network interfaces; session keys are exchanged using a TLS handshake [17]. IPsec traffic, in contrast, is processed by system space routines based on traffic selection and session key container structures called Security Associations (SA). SAs can be setup in the system space using the Internet Key Exchange (IKE) [12] protocol that allows for session key exchange with a reduced number of messages in comparison with the TLS handshake.

Given these considerations and due to the fact that switching from user to system space and vice versa introduces a context switching overhead, we expect IPsec to perform more efficiently under heavy traffic load conditions as it should not be subject to context switching overhead. Yet, both IPsec/IKE and openVPN should provide similar performance when confronted with a large number of key exchange requests.

4   Experimental Performance Evaluation

In order to verify our assumptions, we provide two separate evaluations of the performance of the central platform depicted by Fig. 1. The first measurement targets at the maximum achievable platform throughput that can be realized with openVPN and IPsec and compares the resulting CPU utilization. The second measurement evaluates the platform's CPU utilization for both VPN endpoints upon being confronted with a large number of key exchanges. While maximum throughput provides a good performance measure in a highly active network, key exchange performance is relevant in the context of massively inter-connected IoT devices where connections are established and closed frequently.

We use an evaluation test-bed consisting of both virtual and physical entities in the private zones and a virtualized central platform. NAT/Firewall layers are also virtualized with the help of isolated kernel network namespaces. The virtual entities use the QEMU [3] virtualization engine with each entity allocated a dedicated CPU core (Intel Core i7-6700K) and a Virtual/IO-Network device that provides link speeds in the range of the underlying system's PCI Bus, in our case 25 GBit/s. It should be noted however that, due to the architectural approach of routing all traffic within the platform, the maximum theoretically achievable end to end bandwidth is only half the link bandwidth, thus 12,5 GBit/s. Nonetheless, this setup allows us to efficiently stress the central platform without needing to deploy hundreds of IIoT devices.

openVPN as well as the strongSwan [4] IPsec suite were evaluated using the AES [5] symmetric cipher in Cipher Block Chaining (CBC) mode with 128-Bit key size in conjunction with HMAC-SHA256 [6] as PRF and for integrity checking. The AES algorithm was selected with respect to AES NI hardware acceleration available in the testbed. Nonetheless, with a measured maximum AES en-/decryption rate of 1.5 GB/s, we ensured that the CPU, not the link, formed the platform's bottleneck. All CPU and network metrics were recorded on the central platform and evaluated using the Performance Co-Pilot open source software suite [2].

4.1   Maximum Throughput

Figure 2 shows the maximum platform throughput achieved for openVPN and IPsec and highlights that IPsec clearly outperforms openVPN in this respect. The main reason can be recognized from Fig. 3a, which shows the CPU partly running in `user`, `kernel` and `irq`. `irq` mode handles interrupt routines required when switching from `user` to `kernel` mode and vice-versa, but in Linux systems also performs IPsec packet processing. This is visualized in Fig. 3b, which highlights that IPsec processing does not trigger expensive context switches and confirms our previous implications.

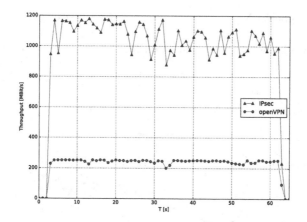

Fig. 2. Maximum platform throughput achieved by IPsec and openVPN

4.2   Key Exchange

In order to compare the platform's key negotiation performance for openVPN and strongSwan, we repeatedly initiated tunnel initiation floods originating from a total of four entities towards the openVPN platform endpoint. After successful key exchange, tunnels were closed immediately. We determined a maximum frequency $f_{max} = 0.04\,s$ where all key exchanges were still successful. Figure 4a shows a 60 s key exchange flood towards the platform's openVPN endpoint. Processing mostly occurs in user space, which is what we expected. However, one easily observes the remarkable portion of overall `idle` CPU time frames, which we can only suspect to be caused by openVPN implementing an internal key exchange rate limiter not known to us.

To provide better comparability, we flooded strongSwan using the same parameters. Figure 4b shows that strongSwan deals more efficiently with the key exchange, despite often switching between `user` and `kernel` mode which most likely results from installing negotiated IKE and IPsec SAs in the respective kernel structures.

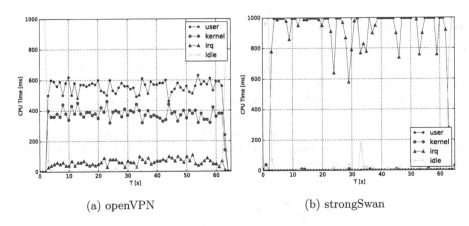

(a) openVPN   (b) strongSwan

Fig. 3. Platform CPU utilization during throughput measurement

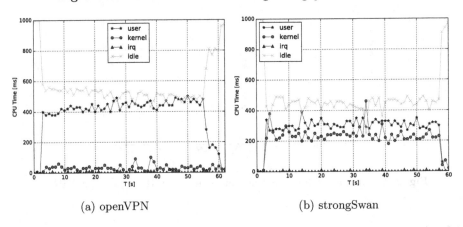

(a) openVPN   (b) strongSwan

Fig. 4. Platform CPU utilization during key exchange flood at f_{max} from four entities

5   Conclusion and Outlook

In this paper, we presented a scalable architecture that is able to flexibly inter-
connect heterogeneous IIoT entities located within segmented and highly firewalled environments. We therefore focused on the widespread and well-known
openVPN and IPsec tunnel protocols which not only provide good security mechanisms but also are able to carry legacy protocols, which is extremely important
in industrial contexts. Our work gives abstract estimates on their packet processing and key exchange performance, which are widely confirmed by our empirical
measurements. Both theoretical and empirical results strongly suggest that in
case of a critical performance, either imposed by throughput or by key exchange
rate requirements, IPsec is favourable over openVPN. A promising approach of
an IKEv2 mediation server that mediates direct IPsec host-to-host connections

has been proposed by [8] and would even increase IPsec performance in similar architectures.

These performance parameters however, do not denote all aspects of both protocols. Although openVPN suffers from weak performance, its very simple configuration by far outperforms IPsec complexity and possible resulting security issues on the other hand. The simple portability of openVPN additionally makes it more attractive in certain situations.

While in the future, remote assistance protocols might arise that integrate more specifically with the IoT and IIoT specifically, we have shown that state of the art VPN solutions can provide a scalable bridging technology that enables end-to-end tunnelling for legacy as well as novel devices.

Acknowledgement. This work has been supported by the Federal Ministry of Education and Research of the Federal Republic of Germany (Förderkennzeichen KIS4ITS0001, IUNO). The authors alone are responsible for the content of the paper.

References

1. openVPN. https://openvpn.net/
2. Performance co-pilot. http://pcp.io
3. QEMU, the fast! processor emulator. http://www.qemu.org
4. strongSwan, opensource IPsec-based VPN solution. https://strongswan.org/
5. FIPS PUB 197, Advanced Encryption Standard (AES) , U.S. Department of Commerce/National Institute of Standards and Technology (2001)
6. FIPS PUB 180–2, secure hash standard, U.S. Department of Commerce/National Institute of Standards and Technology (2002)
7. Bogdanov, A., Lauridsen, M.M., Tischhauser, E.: AES-based authenticated encryption modes in parallel high-performance software. IACR Crypt. ePrint Arch. **2014**, 186 (2014)
8. Brunner, T.: IKEv2 mediation extension. Internet-Draft draft-brunner-ikev2-mediation-00, IETF Secretariat , April 2008. http://www.ietf.org/internet-drafts/draft-brunner-ikev2-mediation-00.txt
9. Dierks, T., Rescorla, E.: The Transport Layer Security (TLS) protocol version 1.2. RFC 5246, RFC Editor, August 2008. http://www.rfc-editor.org/rfc/rfc5246.txt
10. Duque Antón, S., Fraunholz, D., Zemitis, J., Pohl, F., Schotten, H.D.: Highly scalable and flexible model for effective aggregation of context-based data in generic IIoT scenarios. In: Kopp, O., Lenhard, J., Pautasso, C. (eds.) 9th Central European Workshop on Services and Their Composition, Central European Workshop on Services and Their Composition (ZEUS-2017), CEUR Workshop Proceedings, 13–14 February, Lugano, Switzerland, pp. 51–58 (2017). 4
11. Kagermann, H., Wahlster, W., Helbig, J.: Recommendations for implementing the strategic initiative INDUSTRIE 4.0: securing the future of German manufacturing industry. Forschungsunion (2013)
12. Kaufman, C., Hoffman, P., Nir, Y., Eronen, P., Kivinen, T.: Internet key exchange protocol version 2 (IKEv2). RFC 7296, RFC Editor, October 2014. https://www.rfc-editor.org/rfc/rfc7296.txt
13. Kent, S., Seo, K.: Security architecture for the internet protocol. RFC 4301, RFC Editor, December 2005. https://www.rfc-editor.org/rfc/rfc4301.txt

14. Khanvilkar, S., Khokhar, A.: Virtual private networks: an overview with performance evaluation. IEEE Commun. Mag. **42**(10), 146–154 (2004)
15. Kotuliak, I., Rybár, P., Truchly, P.: Performance comparison of IPsec and TLS based VPN technologies. In: 2011 9th International Conference on Emerging eLearning Technologies and Applications (ICETA), pp. 217–221. IEEE (2011)
16. Migault, D., Palomares, D., Guggemos, T., Wally, A., Laurent, M., Wary, J.P.: Recommendations for IPsec configuration on homenet and M2M devices. In: Proceedings of the 11th ACM Symposium on QoS and Security for Wireless and Mobile Networks, Q2SWinet 2015, pp. 9–17, NY, USA (2015). http://doi.acm.org/10.1145/2815317.2815323
17. Novickis, T.: Protocol state fuzzing of an openVPN (2016)
18. Rekhter, Y., Moskowitz, B., Karrenberg, D., de Groot, G.J., Lear, E.: Address allocation for private internets. RFC 1918, RFC Editor, January 1996. https://www.rfc-editor.org/rfc/rfc1918.txt
19. Sadeghi, A.R., Wachsmann, C., Waidner, M.: Security and privacy challenges in industrial internet of things. In: 2015 52nd ACM/EDAC/IEEE Design Automation Conference (DAC), pp. 1–6. IEEE (2015)
20. Srisuresh, P., Egevang, K.: Traditional IP Network Address Translator (Traditional NAT). RFC 3022, RFC Editor, January 2001. https://www.rfc-editor.org/rfc/rfc3022.txt

Cloud Resources

Two Are Better Than One: An Algorithm Portfolio Approach to Cloud Resource Management

Zoltán Ádám Mann[✉]

paluno – The Ruhr Institute for Software Technology,
University of Duisburg-Essen, Essen, Germany
zoltan.mann@gmail.com

Abstract. Several different algorithms have been proposed in recent years for the dynamic optimization of resource allocation in virtualized data centers. The proposed methods range from fast and simple heuristics to exact algorithms that yield optimal results but take much longer. This paper suggests an algorithm portfolio approach in which multiple algorithms coexist. Based on continual monitoring and analysis of the state of the data center, the optimization algorithm that is most suitable is chosen on the fly. This way, the balance between optimization quality and reaction time can be tuned adaptively. Empirical results show that this approach leads to improved overall results.

1 Introduction

The last years have witnessed a tremendous uptake of cloud computing. The compelling advantages of the cloud, like the instantaneous access to services without the need for upfront investments and the elastic scaling backed by a seemingly unlimited pool of resources continue to drive ever more customers to the cloud.

For a provider of Infrastructure-as-a-Service (IaaS), several important challenges must be addressed to provide the service economically and in good quality [10]. First, the operation of the physical infrastructure is associated with high costs. Especially the costs for electricity play an important role for operating servers and cooling equipment [8]. For this reason, virtualization is widely used to achieve high utilization of physical servers and switch off unused ones. In particular, live migration of virtual machines (VMs) between physical machines (PMs) makes it possible to react to changes in the workload and continually consolidate VMs to just the required number of PMs [35].

Second, customers require a high level of service quality. In the case of IaaS, the most important quality objective is that the amount of resources requested for a VM should be available whenever the application in the VM requires it. This objective of the customers is in conflict with the economic objective of

F. De Paoli et al. (Eds.): ESOCC 2017, LNCS 10465, pp. 93–108, 2017.
DOI: 10.1007/978-3-319-67262-5_8

the providers. The latter would dictate aggressive consolidation of VMs, but if the resources of a PM are over-subscribed by multiple VMs and the load of the VMs starts to rise, this can quickly lead to an overload of the physical resources, resulting in a situation where VMs do not obtain the requested amount of resources. This may lead to degraded performance for client applications, thus to customer dissatisfaction which may manifest itself in penalties (if the service level agreement mandates this) or customer churn.[1]

As can be seen, it is vital for the provider to find the right balance between the conflicting objectives of minimizing the number of used PMs and minimizing the situations where a PM is overloaded. This leads to an interesting optimization problem called the *VM consolidation problem* [24]. Most of the realistic formulations of the VM consolidation problem are NP-hard to solve optimally or even to approximate with low approximation factors [23]. Still, because of its practical relevance, many algorithms have been proposed to solve this problem.

Many of the suggested algorithms are greedy heuristics that deliver a solution very quickly. However, there is no guarantee on how close the found solution will be to the optimum and in unfortunate cases, it can be very far from it. On the other extreme, some researchers have also proposed exact algorithms that are guaranteed to find the optimum, although at the cost of exponential execution times. To be practical, such algorithms must be furnished with a timeout so that overly long runs are prohibited (in which case the algorithm returns the best solution it has found). This way, the found solution is not guaranteed to be optimal; however, experience shows that this way significantly better results can be achieved than with the simple greedy heuristics, although with also significantly higher execution time.

It is not clear which of these approaches is the most appropriate. For example, in a situation where the workload is quickly rising (e.g., as a result of the flash crowd phenomenon [29]), it is paramount to react quickly. In this case, a greedy algorithm that delivers a suboptimal result within a second is clearly preferred over a more sophisticated algorithm that would give a better result after a minute because by that time PMs may already be overloaded. On the other hand, in a peaceful period of low load, it would pay off to wait for the better allocation returned by the longer-running algorithm.

Based on these considerations, we propose here an *algorithm portfolio* approach, in which the provider has a set of algorithms at its disposal and chooses from them dynamically, based on the current situation of the cloud. This way, the strengths of different algorithms can be combined.

In this paper, we describe a general approach for using an algorithm portfolio for VM allocation, as well as a specific preliminary implementation using two algorithms. Empirical results show that already our preliminary implementation leads to better results than those of the individual algorithms.

---

[1] Beyond these two basic objectives, there can be also several other factors that the provider must take care of, such as security and privacy requirements, optimization of data transfer among the VMs, thermal issues etc.

2   Previous Work

The VM consolidation problem has received a lot of attention in recent years. Several different versions of the problem have been studied and many different algorithms have been proposed to solve it [22,26]. The proposed algorithms realize different trade-offs between solution quality and algorithm execution time.

The fastest algorithms are greedy heuristics: their running time is at most quadratic in the size of the problem instance, leading to very low execution times, but also to solutions, the quality of which may not be so good. Typical examples include the packing heuristics adopted from the related bin-packing problem, such as First-Fit, Best-Fit, First-Fit-Decreasing etc. [4,5,13,17,20,30,36,37] and also some proprietary methods [4,32,33,38,39].

Exact methods (i.e., algorithms that are guaranteed to yield optimal results) are the other extreme. The proposed exact algorithms rely almost always on some form of mathematic programming (e.g., integer linear programming) and appropriate solvers [13,14,25,31,41]. Unfortunately, these approaches do not scale to practical problem sizes, so their running has to be limited.

There are also some further algorithms. These include meta-heuristics, the execution time and quality of which can be tuned with multiple parameters, e.g., simulated annealing [16,27], genetic algorithms [11], particle swarm optimization [18], ant colony optimization [9], and biogeography-based optimization [19,42]. Also, some complex proprietary heuristics fall into this category [2,17,28].

The algorithm portfolio approach advocated in this paper was originally suggested by Huberman et al. [15] and then popularized in the artificial intelligence community by Gomes and Selman [12] with the aim of attacking hard combinatorial problems. The fundamental idea is to select from a pool of available algorithms the most appropriate one for each specific problem instance, based on quickly computable features of the problem instance and a model of expected behavior of the algorithms on problem instances with the given features. The most well-known application of this approach has been the SATzilla solver for the Boolean satisfiability (SAT) problem [40], which has consistently achieved top results in the SAT competitions. The approach has also been used in the context of automated synthesis and deployment of cloud applications [1,7].

3   General Problem Description

As shown in Fig. 1, the inputs to the VM consolidation problem consist of (i) information about the PMs, (ii) information about the VMs, (iii) the current mapping of VMs on PMs, and (iv) further constraints.

Each PM is characterized by its capacity, current state, and its power consumption characteristic. The capacity can be one-dimensional if only a single resource type (typically the CPU) is considered, or multi-dimensional if multiple resources types (e.g., CPU, RAM, disk) are taken into account. The state of the PM can be either "on" or "off". The power consumption characteristic of the PM is a function that defines how much power the PM consumes depending on the load of the PM.

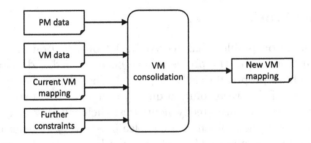

Fig. 1. Inputs and outputs of VM consolidation

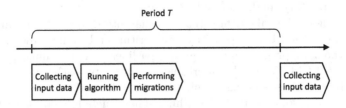

Fig. 2. Time-line of VM consolidation

A VM is characterized by its resource requirements. If d resource types are considered for the capacity of PMs, then also the resource requirements of the VMs are d-dimensional.

Some of the VMs may already exist and be placed on a PM. There can also be newly requested VMs whose placement is not decided yet. Hence, the current mapping of VMs on PMs defines for a subset of the VMs on which PM they currently reside. Further, it is also possible that the termination of some VMs has been requested; such VMs also appear in the current mapping of VMs on PMs, but can be removed.

There can also be further constraints that VM consolidation has to respect. For example, anti-colocation constraints prescribe that certain pairs of VMs must not be placed on the same PM for reasons of security or fault tolerance.

The aim of VM consolidation is to determine a new mapping of VMs on PMs. This mapping must define for each VM – including both existing and newly requested VMs – the PM that should host it. For the newly requested VMs, the new mapping defines on which PM they should be deployed. For existing VMs, if the new mapping defines a different host from the current one, then a migration must be carried out; otherwise, no action is required.

VM consolidation has two main objectives: (i) minimizing total energy consumption and (ii) minimizing PM overloads. These two objectives are conflicting: minimizing energy consumption can be achieved by aggressively consolidating the VMs to as few highly loaded PMs as possible, but this would increase the probability of PM overloads. Therefore, the aim is to find a good balance between these two objectives.

Timing also plays an important role in VM consolidation. The workload keeps changing, and so the mapping of VMs on PMs should be re-optimized regularly to react to the changes. Figure 2 depicts a typical time-line. According to this, VM consolidation is carried out periodically, with a period of T. In each period, first the input data – in particular, the current load of the VMs – are collected, which are then fed into the consolidation algorithm. Finally, the migrations that the algorithm decided are executed.

Collection of input data can be done in a decentralized manner and hence in parallel, so that the time required for that is not so high. In contrast, the time for running the algorithm can be substantial depending on the specific algorithm used. Also the migrations can take long depending on several factors like memory size of the migrated VMs or the available network bandwidth [34].

The time that elapses between collecting the input data and reaching the new state is critical for two reasons. First, the more time passes, the less effective is the reaction of the system: in case of a PM overload, it takes longer to remedy the problem; if there are consolidation opportunities, it takes longer to exploit them, thereby wasting energy. Second, the workload also changes during this time, so that the state actually reached will be different from the one that the algorithm determined based on the old load levels, and the longer it takes to reach the new state, the higher the difference can be.

For these reasons, the usefulness of a VM consolidation algorithm not only depends on how well it can consolidate the VMs and how well it can eliminate PM overloads, but also how fast it is. The algorithms that have been proposed so far in the literature differ strongly along these dimensions: some are slow but deliver very good results, whereas others are much faster but deliver weaker results. The question that we are trying to address is how the complementary strengths of existing algorithms can be combined.

4 Proposed Approach

An overview of our proposed approach is sketched in Fig. 3. The main idea is to use multiple VM consolidation algorithms that offer different trade-offs between speed and quality. In each period, it is decided dynamically which of the available algorithms should be used in the current optimization period. This decision is based on a quick analysis of the current system state, consulting a knowledge base containing information about the characteristics of the available algorithms. The analysis has to be quick because it is on the critical path of the decision-making process. Hence it should consist of simple rules that are based on aggregate system metrics. For example, such a rule could state that the fastest algorithm should be chosen if there are several overloaded PMs or if violations of some security-related constraints have been detected.

Some algorithms have important parameters with which their behavior can be configured. Some parameters may relate to quantities of the problem domain; for instance, some algorithms support explicit thresholds on the number of

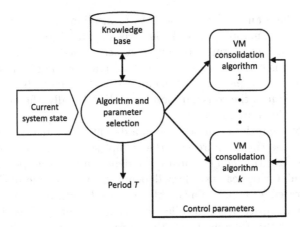

Fig. 3. Overview of the proposed approach

migrations [3] or the headroom to leave on PMs to prevent overloads [5]. Other algorithms have internal, algorithm-specific parameters that influence their efficiency and effectiveness; for example, evolutionary algorithms can be tuned with parameters like population size, mutation rate etc. Similarly to the selection of the most appropriate algorithm for the given system state, also its most appropriate parameter configuration can be set on the fly, provided that the necessary rules are known. For example, in the case of heavy network traffic, the number of allowed migrations can be limited.

Beside selecting the algorithm and its parameters, a further customization possibility relates to the re-optimization period T, i.e., the time until the re-optimization cycle starts again. All previous works that we are aware of assumed T to be constant; however, this need not always be the case. If we choose a quick algorithm and limit it to just a few migrations so as to react quickly to an emergency situation, then it makes sense to lower T so that the next re-optimization happens earlier. This way, it can be checked in a timely manner whether the emergency has been resolved: if yes, other optimizations can be performed that were previously not done because of the higher-priority mitigation steps; if no, further measures can be taken to mitigate the issue.

5   Specific Implementation

So far, we have described both the addressed problem and our proposed approach in a generic way. The reason is that the VM consolidation problem exists in many different flavors [22], but the presented approach can be applied to any variant in conceptually the same way. However, the specific algorithms that make up the portfolio, their parameters, as well as the specifics of the data center and the served workload may influence the details of how the proposed method should be applied. To validate our approach, we implemented it in a specific setting which we describe in the following.

5.1 Problem Model

We focus on CPU usage as the most important resource for consolidation. The set of available PMs is denoted by P. Each PM $p \in P$ is associated with a CPU capacity c_p and power consumption w_p. The set of active or requested VMs is denoted by V. Each VM $v \in V$ is associated with a – current or predicted – CPU size s_v. The current mapping of VMs to PMs is given for a subset of the VMs $V_0 \subseteq V$ by $m_0 : V_0 \rightarrow P$. The aim is to determine a new mapping $m : V \rightarrow P$ of each VM to a PM that fulfills the capacity constraints, also leaving some headroom on each PM:

$$\forall p \in P : \sum_{v \in m^{-1}(p)} s_v \leq \lambda \cdot c_p. \tag{1}$$

Here, $m^{-1}(p)$ is the set of VMs mapped by m to PM p and $0 < \lambda \leq 1$ is a given constant, defining the headroom.

A further constraint is that the number of migrations should not be too high. The number of migrations can be computed as $|\{v \in V_0 : m(v) \neq m_0(v)\}|$.

The optimization objective is to minimize the total power consumption, which is given by the sum of the power consumption of the PMs that are active: $\sum\{w_p : p \in P_a\}$, where $P_a \subseteq P$ is the set of active PMs.

5.2 Used Algorithms

We use a portfolio of two typical but very different algorithms. The first algorithm is the heuristic of Beloglazov et al. [5]. This is based on a packing heuristic called Modified Best Fit Decreasing (MBFD), in which the VMs to be placed are first sorted in non-increasing order of their CPU size, and then each VM is placed in the PM that can host it with the smallest increase in power consumption.

Newly requested VMs are placed directly using the MBFD heuristic. For re-optimizing the placement of existing VMs, the algorithm of Beloglazov et al. first determines the PMs whose utilization is above λ. From these PMs, some VMs are removed until their utilization gets below λ. The VMs removed this way are migrated to other PMs determined using again the MBFD heuristic. Finally, the algorithm tries for each PM whether it can be emptied by migrating all the VMs it hosts to some other PM – if this is possible, these migrations are carried out and the PM is shut down; otherwise, the migrations are not carried out.

The second algorithm consists of converting the VM consolidation problem to an integer linear program (ILP) and using an off-the-shelf ILP solver to solve it. The conversion mostly follows the approach of [3], and is described next.

Indexing VMs as v_i ($i = 1, \ldots, |V|$) and PMs as p_j ($j = 1, \ldots, |P|$), the following binary variables are introduced:

$$Alloc_{i,j} = \begin{cases} 1 & \text{if } v_i \text{ should be allocated on } p_j \\ 0 & \text{otherwise} \end{cases}$$

$$Active_j = \begin{cases} 1 & \text{if } p_j \text{ should be active} \\ 0 & \text{otherwise} \end{cases}$$

$$Migr_i = \begin{cases} 1 & \text{if } v_i \text{ should be migrated} \\ 0 & \text{otherwise} \end{cases}$$

Using these variables, the integer program can be formulated as follows ($i = 1, \ldots, |V|$ and $j = 1, \ldots, |P|$):

$$\min \quad \alpha \cdot \sum_{j=1}^{m} w_{p_j} \cdot Active_j + \mu \cdot \sum_{i=1}^{n} Migr_i \tag{2}$$

$$\text{s. t.} \quad \sum_{j=1}^{m} Alloc_{i,j} = 1 \qquad \qquad \forall i \tag{3}$$

$$Alloc_{i,j} \leq Active_j \qquad \qquad \forall i, j \tag{4}$$

$$\sum_{i=1}^{n} s_{v_i} \cdot Alloc_{i,j} \leq \lambda \cdot c_{p_j} \qquad \qquad \forall j \tag{5}$$

$$Migr_i = 1 - Alloc_{i,m_0(v_i)} \qquad \qquad \forall v_i \in V_0 \tag{6}$$

$$\sum_{i=1}^{n} Migr_i \leq K \tag{7}$$

$$Alloc_{i,j}, Active_j, Migr_i \in \{0,1\} \qquad \qquad \forall i, j \tag{8}$$

The objective function (2) is the weighted sum of the total power consumption and the number of migrations ($\alpha, \mu \geq 0$ are given weights). Equation (3) ensures that each VM is allocated to exactly one PM, whereas constraint (4) ensures that for a PM p_j to which at least one VM is allocated, $Active_j = 1$. Together with the objective function, this ensures that $Active_j = 1$ holds for *exactly* those PMs that accommodate at least one VM. Constraint (5) is the capacity constraint. Equation (6) determines the values of the $Migr_i$ variables and Eq. (7) constrains the number of migrations ($K > 0$ is a given constant).

5.3   Algorithm and Parameter Selection Logic

Our selection logic is based on a simple but powerful indicator of the current system state: the number of PMs currently not satisfying Eq. (1). If this number, denoted as L, is higher than a predefined threshold L_0, then we assume that a quick reaction is necessary; otherwise, the reaction can be more relaxed.

The rationale behind using this metric is the following. We can assume that in the previous re-optimization cycle, VMs were re-distributed among PMs in such a way that the utilization of each PM is below λ, and for most PMs it is near λ. If the workload is in an upturn, then the PMs whose load was just under the limit will exceed the limit; and indeed a quick reaction is needed to avoid negative consequences of further load increase. On the other hand, if the workload is stagnating or decreasing, then the load of the PMs still satisfies Eq. (1). In this case, there is more time to determine the new placement of the VMs. Hence the number of PMs not satisfying Eq. (1) is indeed a good indicator of how quickly a reaction is needed.

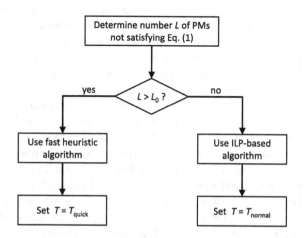

Fig. 4. Specific algorithm and parameter selection strategy

We assume that the heuristic of Beloglazov et al. is significantly faster than the ILP-based algorithm, but typically the ILP-based algorithm delivers better results. For this reason, we apply the fast heuristic if a quick reaction is necessary (i.e., $L > L_0$) and the ILP-based algorithm otherwise (see also Fig. 4).

Also the time T until the next re-optimization cycle is set adaptively, based on a similar decision logic. If the ILP-based algorithm is carried out, then T is set to its normal value. However, if we established that a quick reaction is necessary and hence run the heuristic algorithm, then we set T to a lower value. The reason is that we should keep the ability to respond quickly if the workload continues to rise. Cloud workloads are known to be amenable to the flash crowd phenomenon, which can quickly lead to severe violation of service level objectives. This is why we have to be careful if the load starts to rise. On the other hand, if the load is not rising, performing VM consolidation too often would be counterproductive because of the overhead associated with migrations.

6   Empirical Results

Simulations were used to assess the effects of our adaptive VM consolidation approach, using the CloudSim simulator [6], version 4.0. CloudSim already contains the VM consolidation algorithm of Beloglazov et al. We implemented the ILP-based algorithm using the Gurobi Optimizer, version 7.0.2. In addition, we implemented the algorithm and parameter selection logic described in Sect. 5.3. In all cases, λ was set to 0.8.

We simulate a cluster of 100 PMs serving 500 VMs. The PMs belong to three types (with one third of the PMs belonging to each type), having CPU capacities of 2000, 4000, and 8000 MIPS. The VMs' requested CPU size ranges from 200 to 1500 MIPS, and their actual CPU size is always defined as percentage of their requested size, as explained below. Re-optimization is normally carried out every 5 min (i.e., $T_{normal} = 300s$) like in many previous works (e.g., [21]). When T should be reduced to respond quickly, it is set to $T_{quick} = T_{normal}/2 = 150s$. The ILP-based algorithm is given a time budget of 60 s; the execution time of the heuristic algorithm is negligible (it was below 1 s in all of our experiments). Migrations take on average about 32 s. The power consumption of a running PM is 400 W. The experiments were performed on a Lenovo ThinkPad X1 laptop with Intel Core i5-4210U CPU @ 1.70 GHz and 8 GB RAM.

We tested several different workload patterns to assess how our approach works in different settings. Each pattern takes 1 h. In each case, the proposed approach is compared with the two pure strategies of using always the ILP-based algorithm or always the heuristic algorithm. The criteria for comparison are the number of active PMs, the total energy consumption, and the number of times a PM was overloaded, where the latter is assessed every 60 s.

Table 1. Aggregated results of the experiments

Workload	Energy [kWh]			Overloads		
	Heuristic	ILP	Portfolio	Heuristic	ILP	Portfolio
Constant	11.63	9.04	9.04	0	0	0
Decrease	16.60	15.21	14.93	0	0	0
Increase	18.90	19.11	20.12	146	60	39
Peak	18.99	16.09	18.51	104	60	2
Valley	16.15	14.81	15.93	133	135	40
Sinus small	12.39	10.35	9.88	0	0	0
Sinus big	18.77	17.40	17.15	75	69	13
Total	113.43	102.01	105.56	458	324	94

The results of the experiments are summarized in Table 1. In the first experiment, the workload was constant 50% of the requested capacity. As expected, all algorithms were able to perform consolidation without incurring PM overloads.

The ILP-based algorithm resulted in about 22% reduction in power consumption compared to the heuristic algorithm. Since there was no rise in the workload, the portfolio-based approach always chose the ILP-based algorithm, hence it led to the same result.

The situation is similar in the second experiment, in which the load decreases from 90% to 10% of the requested capacity. Again, there was no PM overload. The three algorithms led to similar energy consumption, with the portfolio-based approach leading to about 10% reduction in energy consumption over the heuristic and about 2% over the ILP-based algorithm[2].

In the third experiment, the opposite happens: the load is increased from 10% to 90%. As can be seen, the order of the algorithms also becomes opposite: now the portfolio-based approach leads to 5–6% higher energy consumption than the others. However, there are considerable differences in terms of PM overloads: the ILP-based algorithm leads to 54% more PM overloads, the heuristic to 274% more PM overloads than the portfolio-based approach. The details are shown

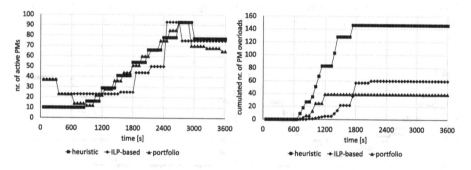

Fig. 5. Effects of the load increasing from 10% to 90%

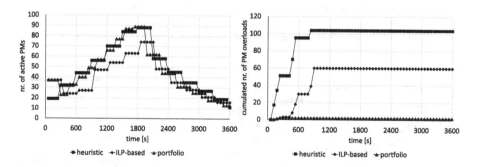

Fig. 6. Effects of the load first increasing from 10% to 90%, then decreasing back to 10%

---

[2] In almost all re-optimization cycles, the portfolio-based approach chooses the ILP-based algorithm, hence they behave almost the same. The only exception is the first cycle: since the workload starts at 90%, the initial placement of the VMs leads to several PMs with utilization above λ, so that the fast heuristic is chosen.

in Fig. 5. As can be seen, the portfolio-based approach can react faster to the change than the other algorithms.

The fourth experiment, called "peak," is a combination of the preceding two: in the first half of the time window, the load increases from 10% to 90%, then in the second half it decreases back to 10%. As can be seen, the energy consumption achieved by the three evaluated approaches is again very similar to each other; however, in terms of the number of PM overloads, the portfolio-based approach is again clearly superior. The details are shown in Fig. 6. Not surprisingly, the difference between the three approaches arises in the first half of the time window, where the portfolio-based approach provides faster and better reaction to the change than the others.

The fifth experiment, called "valley," is the opposite of the previous one: in the first half of the time window, the load decreases from 90% to 10%, then in the second half it increases back to 90%. The results, shown in detail in Fig. 7, are similar to the previous ones.

In the next two experiments, the load follows a sinus curve around 50%. In the experiment termed "sinus small," the amplitude of the sinus curve is 5%, whereas in the "sinus big" experiment it is 20%. In both cases, the portfolio-based

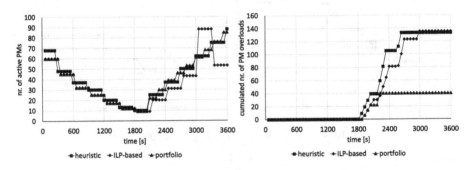

Fig. 7. Effects of the load first decreasing from 90% to 10%, then increasing back to 90%

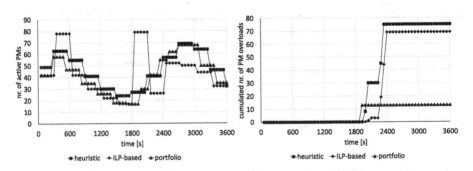

Fig. 8. Effects of the load following a sinus curve around 50% with amplitude 20%

approach outperforms the other two. The details for the "sinus big" experiment are shown in Fig. 8.

The aggregated figures (last line of Table 1) reveal that the portfolio-based approach improves energy consumption by 7% compared to the heuristic, but this result is still 3% worse than that of the ILP-based algorithm. Concerning the number of overloads, the portfolio-based approach emerges as clear winner.

7   Conclusions and Future Work

In this paper, we investigated how different algorithms for the VM consolidation problem can be combined into an algorithm portfolio from which an automated decision-making mechanism can choose dynamically at run-time based on the current system state. This way, the complementary advantages of different algorithms can be leveraged. In particular, we have shown how a fast but simple heuristic can be combined with a more sophisticated but slow ILP-based algorithm. Beside the choice of algorithm, also algorithm parameters as well as the re-optimization interval can be chosen by the same mechanism.

The simulation results demonstrate that the suggested approach is promising because in most cases it leads to a better trade-off between energy consumption and PM overloads than the two underlying algorithms.

Obviously, our current implementation is rather simple and could be improved in several ways. For example, the used knowledge about the two underlying algorithms is simplistic: the ILP-based algorithm is assumed to always lead to better quality than the heuristic. In reality, this is not always the case, so that a more sophisticated model of the algorithms' performance could result in better decisions. The model of algorithm performance could also be learned during run-time through appropriate machine learning techniques.

Also the decision-making is based on a simple metric. More intelligence could be added, for instance in the form of time series analysis, to make better decisions. Further possibilities include the addition of more algorithms to the portfolio or running multiple algorithms from the portfolio in parallel if sufficient parallel resources are available.

Acknowledgments. This work was partially supported by the Hungarian Scientific Research Fund (Grant Nr. OTKA 108947) and by the European Union's Horizon 2020 research and innovation programme under grant 731678 (RestAssured).

References

1. Ábrahám, E., Corzilius, F., Johnsen, E.B., Kremer, G., Mauro, J.: Zephyrus2: on the fly deployment optimization using SMT and CP technologies. In: Proceedings of the 2nd International Symposium on Dependable Software Engineering, pp. 229–245 (2016)
2. Ahvar, E., Ahvar, S., Mann, Z.A., Crespi, N., Garcia-Alfaro, J., Glitho, R.: CACEV: a cost and carbon emission-efficient virtual machine placement method for green distributed clouds. In: Proceedings of the 13th IEEE International Conference on Services Computing, pp. 275–282 (2016)

3. Bartók, D., Mann, Z.A.: A branch-and-bound approach to virtual machine placement. In: Proceedings of the 3rd HPI Cloud Symposium "Operating the Cloud", pp. 49–63 (2015)
4. Beloglazov, A., Abawajy, J., Buyya, R.: Energy-aware resource allocation heuristics for efficient management of data centers for cloud computing. Future Gener. Comput. Syst. **28**, 755–768 (2012)
5. Beloglazov, A., Buyya, R.: Optimal online deterministic algorithms and adaptive heuristics for energy and performance efficient dynamic consolidation of virtual machines in cloud data centers. Concurrency Comput. Pract. Exp. **24**(13), 1397–1420 (2012)
6. Calheiros, R.N., Ranjan, R., Beloglazov, A., De Rose, C.A.F., Buyya, R.: CloudSim: a toolkit for modeling and simulation of cloud computing environments and evaluation of resource provisioning algorithms. Softw. Pract. Exp. **41**(1), 23–50 (2011)
7. Cosmo, R.D., Lienhardt, M., Treinen, R., Zacchiroli, S., Zwolakowski, J., Eiche, A., Agahi, A.: Automated synthesis and deployment of cloud applications. In: ACM/IEEE International Conference on Automated Software Engineering, pp. 211–222 (2014)
8. Digital Power Group: The cloud begins with coal - Big data, big networks, big infrastructure, and big power (2013)
9. Gao, Y., Guan, H., Qi, Z., Hou, Y., Liu, L.: A multi-objective ant colony system algorithm for virtual machine placement in cloud computing. J. Comput. Syst. Sci. **79**, 1230–1242 (2013)
10. Garca-Valls, M., Cucinotta, T., Lu, C.: Challenges in real-time virtualization and predictable cloud computing. J. Syst. Architect. **60**(9), 726–740 (2014)
11. Gmach, D., Rolia, J., Cherkasova, L., Belrose, G., Turicchi, T., Kemper, A.: An integrated approach to resource pool management: policies, efficiency and quality metrics. In: IEEE International Conference on Dependable Systems and Networks, pp. 326–335 (2008)
12. Gomes, C.P., Selman, B.: Algorithm portfolios. Artif. Intell. **126**(1–2), 43–62 (2001)
13. Guazzone, M., Anglano, C., Canonico, M.: Exploiting VM migration for the automated power and performance management of green cloud computing systems. In: Huusko, J., de Meer, H., Klingert, S., Somov, A. (eds.) 1st International Workshop on Energy Efficient Data Centers, vol. 7396, pp. 81–92. Springer, Heidelberg (2012)
14. Guenter, B., Jain, N., Williams, C.: Managing cost, performance, and reliability tradeoffs for energy-aware server provisioning. In: Proceedings of IEEE INFOCOM, pp. 1332–1340. IEEE (2011)
15. Huberman, B.A., Lukose, R.M., Hogg, T.: An economics approach to hard computational problems. Science **275**(5296), 51–54 (1997)
16. Hyser, C., McKee, B., Gardner, R., Watson, B.J.: Autonomic virtual machine placement in the data center. Technical report HP Laboratories (2008)
17. Jung, G., Hiltunen, M.A., Joshi, K.R., Schlichting, R.D., Pu, C.: Mistral: dynamically managing power, performance, and adaptation cost in cloud infrastructures. In: IEEE 30th International Conference on Distributed Computing Systems, pp. 62–73 (2010)
18. Li, H., Zhu, G., Cui, C., Tang, H., Dou, Y., He, C.: Energy-efficient migration and consolidation algorithm of virtual machines in data centers for cloud computing. Computing **98**(3), 303–317 (2016)
19. Li, R., Zheng, Q., Li, X., Wu, J.: A novel multi-objective optimization scheme for rebalancing virtual machine placement. In: IEEE 9th International Conference on Cloud Computing, pp. 710–717 (2016)

20. Li, W., Tordsson, J., Elmroth, E.: Virtual machine placement for predictable and time-constrained peak loads. In: Vanmechelen, K., Altmann, J., Rana, O.F. (eds.) GECON 2011. LNCS, vol. 7150, pp. 120–134. Springer, Heidelberg (2012). doi:10.1007/978-3-642-28675-9_9

21. Li, Z., Yan, C., Yu, X., Yu, N.: Bayesian network-based virtual machines consolidation method. Future Gener. Comput. Syst. **69**, 75–87 (2017)

22. Mann, Z.A.: Allocation of virtual machines in cloud data centers - a survey of problem models and optimization algorithms. ACM Comput. Surv. **48**(1) (2015). Article nr. 11

23. Mann, Z.A.: Approximability of virtual machine allocation: much harder than bin packing. In: Proceedings of the 9th Hungarian-Japanese Symposium on Discrete Mathematics and Its Applications, pp. 21–30 (2015)

24. Mann, Z.A.: Modeling the virtual machine allocation problem. In: Proceedings of the International Conference on Mathematical Methods, Mathematical Models and Simulation in Science and Engineering, pp. 102–106 (2015)

25. Mann, Z.A.: Multicore-aware virtual machine placement in cloud data centers. IEEE Trans. Comput. **65**(11), 3357–3369 (2016)

26. Mann, Z.Á, Szabó, M.: Which is the best algorithm for virtual machine placement optimization? Concurrency Comput. Pract. Exp. **29**(10), e4083 (2017)

27. Marotta, A., Avallone, S.: A simulated annealing based approach for power efficient virtual machines consolidation. In: Proceedings of the 8th IEEE International Conference on Cloud Computing, pp. 445–452 (2015)

28. Mishra, M., Sahoo, A.: On theory of VM placement: anomalies in existing methodologies and their mitigation using a novel vector based approach. In: IEEE International Conference on Cloud Computing, pp. 275–282 (2011)

29. Qu, C., Calheiros, R.N., Buyya, R.: Mitigating impact of short-term overload on multi-cloud web applications through geographical load balancing. Concurrency Comput. Pract. Exp. **29**(12), e4126 (2017)

30. Rampersaud, S., Grosu, D.: Sharing-aware online algorithms for virtual machine packing in cloud environments. In: Proceedings of the 8th IEEE International Conference on Cloud Computing, pp. 718–725 (2015)

31. Ribas, B.C., Suguimoto, R.M., Montano, R., Silva, F., de Bona, L., Castilho, M.A.: On modelling virtual machine consolidation to pseudo-Boolean constraints. In: 13th Ibero-American Conference on AI, pp. 361–370 (2012)

32. Salehi, M.A., Krishna, P.R., Deepak, K.S., Buyya, R.: Preemption-aware energy management in virtualized data centers. In: 5th International Conference on Cloud Computing, pp. 844–851. IEEE (2012)

33. Shi, L., Furlong, J., Wang, R.: Empirical evaluation of vector bin packing algorithms for energy efficient data centers. In: IEEE Symposium on Computers and Communications, pp. 9–15 (2013)

34. Strunk, A.: Costs of virtual machine live migration: a survey. In: 8th IEEE World Congress on Services, pp. 323–329 (2012)

35. Svärd, P., Li, W., Wadbro, E., Tordsson, J., Elmroth, E.: Continuous datacenter consolidation. In: IEEE 7th International Conference on Cloud Computing Technology and Science (CloudCom), pp. 387–396 (2015)

36. Tomás, L., Tordsson, J.: An autonomic approach to risk-aware data center overbooking. IEEE Trans. Cloud Comput. **2**(3), 292–305 (2014)

37. Verma, A., Dasgupta, G., Nayak, T.K., De, P., Kothari, R.: Server workload analysis for power minimization using consolidation. In: Proceedings of the 2009 USENIX Annual Technical Conference, pp. 355–368 (2009)

38. Wood, T., Shenoy, P., Venkataramani, A., Yousif, M.: Sandpiper: black-box and gray-box resource management for virtual machines. Comput. Netw. **53**(17), 2923–2938 (2009)
39. Xiao, Z., Song, W., Chen, Q.: Dynamic resource allocation using virtual machines for cloud computing environment. IEEE Trans. Parallel Distrib. Syst. **24**(6), 1107–1117 (2013)
40. Xu, L., Hutter, F., Hoos, H.H., Leyton-Brown, K.: SATzilla: portfolio-based algorithm selection for SAT. J. Artif. Intell. Res. **32**, 565–606 (2008)
41. Zhang, Z., Hsu, C.C., Chang, M.: CoolCloud: a practical dynamic virtual machine placement framework for energy aware data centers. In: Proceedings of the 8th IEEE International Conference on Cloud Computing, pp. 758–765 (2015)
42. Zheng, Q., Li, R., Li, X., Wu, J.: A multi-objective biogeography-based optimization for virtual machine placement. In: Proceedings of the 15th IEEE/ACM International Symposium on Cluster, Cloud and Grid Computing, pp. 687–696 (2015)

A Fuzzy Load Balancer for Adaptive Fault Tolerance Management in Cloud Platforms

Hamid Arabnejad[1], Claus Pahl[2]([⊠]), Giovani Estrada[3], Areeg Samir[2], and Frank Fowley[1]

[1] IC4, Dublin City University, Dublin, Ireland
[2] Free University of Bozen-Bolzano, Bolzano, Italy
claus.pahl@unibz.it
[3] Intel, Leixlip, Ireland

Abstract. To achieve high levels of reliability, availability and performance in cloud environments, a fault tolerance approach to handle failures effectively is needed. In most existing research, the primary focus has been on explicit specification-driven solutions which requires too much effort for application developers, and leads to inflexibility. We propose a fuzzy job distributor (load balancer) for fault tolerance management to reduce levels of management complexity for the user. The proposed approach aims to *reduce* the possibility of *fault occurrences* in the system by a fair distribution of user job requests among available resources. In our self-adaptive approach, the system manages anomalous situations that might lead to failure by distributing the incoming job request based on the reliability of processing nodes, i.e., virtual machines (VMs). The reliability of VMs is a variable parameter and changes during its lifetime. Our approach is implemented and comparatively analysed using OpenStack. The experimental results show a significant reduction in the occurrence of faults in comparison with other load balancing algorithms.

Keywords: Load balancing · Job distributor · Fault tolerance · Fuzzy logic · Cloud computing · Anomaly detection · OpenStack

1 Introduction

Cloud computing offers a large-scale distributed computing environment through a pool of abstracted, virtualized, dynamically-scalable and configurable computing resources. Unfortunately, due to unreliability in hardware or software, failure as the major obstacle to high service availability in cloud computing, is unavoidable. A fault tolerance feature provided by cloud vendors aims to overcome the impact of system failures and continue their functionality correctly even after the occurrence of failures, is needed. Currently, several fault tolerance models [1,6,8] are proposed generally involving the application developer to configure and operate cloud software based on cloud-specific features in order to run reliably. The major drawback and limitation of this type of approach is that requires

© IFIP International Federation for Information Processing 2017
Published by Springer International Publishing AG 2017. All Rights Reserved
F. De Paoli et al. (Eds.): ESOCC 2017, LNCS 10465, pp. 109–124, 2017.
DOI: 10.1007/978-3-319-67262-5_9

knowledge and experience from the developer in order to configure and integrate applications in an available fault-tolerance framework. This difficulty arises due to (i) high complexity of the cloud platform, (ii) low available information about the underlying cloud infrastructure to its users. This results in intransparency and inflexibility of the Cloud architecture, and requiring too much effort by the application developer. Therefore, there is a demand for a reliable and automatic fault-tolerance management system without requirement for configuration and integration of applications by user. An efficient job distributor (load balancer) helps to remove critical conditions such as overload that causes a system failure and aims to improve system performance to make systems more reliable and fault-tolerant. Furthermore, as a part of a service layer, it brings more transparency in cloud infrastructures from a user's perspective. Recently, intelligent approaches have received attention for cloud job distribution and load balancing. Fuzzy theory [24], as a well-known artificial intelligence approach, has various characteristics that make it a suitable for control problems [12]. For us, it allows multiple possibly conflicting options – whether arising from an automated (machine) learning approach as multiple options or provided by different experts [3] – to be joined into a single decision that can be effectively enforced.

This paper proposes a fuzzy job distributor technique that ensures fault tolerance by properly distributing user job requests load among current available resources using anomaly and fault detection. By monitoring the current state of system and fairness in job distribution, we calculate the priority value for each resource and try to avoid overloading problems that are the cause of system failure. Upon detection of anomalies, the algorithm directs the system to apply a fault rejuvenation mechanism to an anomalously behaving virtual machine.

2   Fault Tolerance: Related Work and Positioning

Fault tolerance (FT) is the ability of a system to perform its function correctly even in the presence of internal faults. The purpose of fault tolerance is to increase the dependability of a system. Fault recovery mechanisms enable systems to correct the damaged state and restore to a known safe state after the system detects and verifies faults and anomalies leading to faults. Fault tolerance techniques can be classified into three main categories [6]: (i) redundancy techniques, (ii) load balancing strategies, and (iii) fault tolerance policies.

Redundancy is providing replication of system components such as hardware and software to provide more reliability in systems. Hardware redundancy techniques exploit additional hardware components. All redundant hardware executes the same task in parallel, and fault detection and masking can be achieved by majority voting techniques [18].

Load balancing fault tolerance strategies are based on improving fault tolerance based on load balancing performed using software models. In this case, a load dispatcher component distributes all incoming job requests among available resources. For example, Amazon EC2 uses elastic load balancing (ELB) to control how incoming requests are handled. Basically, in this context, it tries to *reduce* the likelihood of fault occurrences in the system by adequately distributing user job requests among available resources.

Fault tolerance policies can divided into *proactive* and *reactive* policies. The principle of proactive fault tolerance is to avoid recovery from errors and failure through preventative measures and proactively replace the suspected anomalous components by other working components. In contrast, reactive fault tolerance policies performs recovery from experienced failures.

Reactive Fault Tolerance is implemented in different ways. Firstly, *Checkpointing* records the system state periodically, allowing to restart the failed task from a recent checkpoint rather than from the beginning. Zhang et al. [26] propose a checkpointing strategy at user-level. The main drawback of this method is cost, which is significant in the case of large numbers of VM images in terms of storage space and restore processes. [25] proposes an asynchronous FT approach based on checkpointing by preserving data on surviving nodes to potentially accelerate recovering lost data with no overhead for checkpointing.

Secondly, *Replication* runs several task replicas on different resources. In the active model, all replicas receive the requests in the same order. In the passive model, one replica as the primary node receives the requests and all other replicas interact with the primary replica. To address reliability demands in PaaS cloud, a framework that automatically coordinates fault-tolerant applications based on the Byzantine fault-tolerant (BFT) protocol is proposed in [16]. In [19] an FT approach is proposed based on a checkpoint/replay technique for real-time computing to reduce the service time on the cloud infrastructure. Another reactive approach is *Job migration*, which migrates the failed task to another resource. *Task resubmission* is also widely used: the failed task is recommitted either to the same or a different resource.

Proactive Fault Tolerance can be distinguished into two important types:

Software Rejuvenation: it immediately terminates an application and restarts it with a clean state at every rejuvenation interval [10]. *Pre-emptive Migration*: it counts on a feedback-loop control mechanism, i.e., constantly monitors and analyzes. It migrates the parts of an application that show anomalous behaviour and are likely to fail [7,20]. In [17], a proactive coordinated FT (PCFT) approach based on particle swarm optimization (PSO) to minimizing the overall transmission overhead, overall network resource consumption is proposed. In [5], a VM placement model based on adaptive selection of fault-tolerant strategy for cloud applications is proposed. A predictive control approach for fault management in computing systems is presented in [14]. In most current clouds, (i) checkpointing, the process of recording and capturing recovery system state periodically during failure-free execution, and (ii) replication, the process of replicating tasks, are the most common fault tolerance strategies. The drawback of replication strategies is that they are rather expensive, i.e., higher cost for a device which contains multiple replicas. The advantage of checkpointing is that it does not require a high amount of hardware redundancy. However, the major drawback of checkpointing strategies is the time overhead of performing checkpoints.

Positioning of presented approach. Usually, the time overhead due to usage of fault tolerance policies may result in a negative impact on resource performance. In this work, in order to reduce the time overhead and improve the resource utilization during the life cycle of system, we consider proactive fault tolerance strategies using load balancing as the central controller function [11,13] and propose a fuzzy load balancer for fault tolerance management.

The proposed framework considers multiple objectives: (i) resource CPU utilization, (ii) fairness of distribution of job requests, and (iii) the history of fault rates for each resource. Our solution combines proactive techniques such as software rejuvenation with pre-emptive migration.

3   Fault Tolerance Management System

The first step of designing a fault tolerance mechanism as a service in cloud infrastructure is defining how the system works.

3.1   Self-adaptive Anomaly and Fault Management Framework

Generally, the client jobs are deployed in VM instances. The fault tolerance properties of the system should be obtained through a core service that applies a coherent fault tolerance mechanism in a transparent manner. To this end, we define a fault tolerance controller as the fundamental module that monitors the current system state and enacts a fault tolerance mechanism. It allows us to control and handle hardware failure of user applications at the virtualization layer rather than for the application itself. The proposed fault tolerance approach is coded and run inside of it. Additionally, we use two more modules, namely *job distributor* and *anomaly/failure detector* components in our solution. The job distributor has the duty to distribute client job requests across a set of computing resources in resource pool based on current request load, priority and weight value for each resource. The anomaly and failure detector monitors resources to detect anomalies that might lead to failure and server crashes. A recovery mechanism can be applied after a failure is detected by this module. In this context, detection of node failures and application of the recovery mechanism are performed without requiring any changes to integrate a user application with fault tolerance approach.

Figure 1 shows the complete process of how the proposed fault tolerance system works. The fault tolerance controller gathers information from `ceilometer` and the current state of computing nodes in a resource pool. The `ceilometer` component provides telemetry services to collect metering data in OpenStack (which we use for implementation [2]). Then, the fault tolerance controller decides how to modify the priority and weight value of each node in the resource pool to reduce future anomalous behaviour. The job distributor distributes submitted jobs based on the weight value of each resource. During the life cycle of the system, the failure detector module detects anomaly and fault occurrences in the system and sends a recovery mechanism signal to the faulty node. Note that each module in Fig. 1 has its own set of functional attributes.

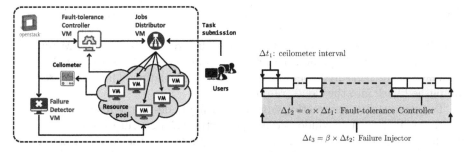

Fig. 1. Our fault tolerance framework   **Fig. 2.** Interval check

Our anomaly detection framework aims to proactively prevent or detect faults: (i) detect anomalous undesirable performance degradation (as a concrete anomaly) that might lead to failure, (ii) identify the symptoms and root causes of anomalous performance degradation to apply a proper corrective action, here using fuzzy job distribution, (iii) manage the relationships and dependencies between the symptoms, which are external manifestations of anomalous behaviour, and root causes, which are the reasons behind the performance degradation, and (iv) refine the future detection through applying a recovery mechanism on the identified faults and learning from the verified results to enhance the future fault detection and to continuously improve the deployment and the integration processes by using weight and priority adjustments. The following steps, aligned with the MAPE-K control loop framework [12], are carried out (see Fig. 1):

- *Monitoring*: Anomaly/Failure Detection. This step collects data from the controller using `ceilometer`, structures this data to provide a sequence presentation that can be used to detect the obfuscated behaviour in data.
- *Analysis*: Anomaly Identification and Diagnosis. To be able to identify and diagnose the fault root cause, we label the sequence representation in the anomaly detection step. The main points of that step are specifying the dependency and the relationships between faults, estimating the fault type (fault intensity level or the dispersal of anomaly within the managed resource) and distinguishing between fault (true anomaly diagnosing) and noise (false anomaly diagnosing). The distinction is specified based on assigning numerical values for each.
- *Planning and Execution*: Anomaly Recovery. After identifying and diagnosing faults, a recovery mechanism is applied to correct faults and remove their effects. The objective of fault removal is to isolate the affected component from the sequence presentation and delegate the incoming requests to another component or choosing an alternative solution to be used in the healing. This step is connected to the fault tolerance controller VM to re-assign a new weight for the affected component(s) to be able to store the verified path(s) according to their new weight.

Furthermore, Recovery Validation evaluates the effectiveness of the previous steps in detecting faults, in which different types of faults can be considered (such as CPU-related fault, memory-related fault, disk-related fault and VM-related fault). The latency, throughput and response time are measured to infer the performance of the measured components after faults isolation. The verified results are pushed back into the cloud (resource pool).

To gather status information from computing nodes in the resource pool, we use three different time windows during detection. Δt_1 specifies an interval after which the ceilometer component performs an update of the specified meter for the resource. Δt_2 is the sampling interval used by the fault tolerance controller machine, and the Δt_3 is used for sending periodic updates to the failure detector component. Generally, the time intervals Δt_2 and Δt_3 are proportional to the ceilometer interval parameter, i.e., Δt_1, in Fig. 2. For instance, if $\Delta t_1 = 10\,\mathrm{s}$, the value of Δt_2 and Δt_3 can be $10\,\mathrm{min}$ and $1\,\mathrm{h}$.

3.2 OpenStack

An important feature for users relates to the service uptime. To achieve high cloud availability and improve Service Level Objectives (SLOs) satisfaction, an efficient fault tolerance strategy needs to be employed. In contrast with a traditional manually configured approach, we propose an approach that used *active* and *runtime* monitoring for fault tolerance. It consists of several independent modules that work separately from each other in order to handle incoming job request load and perform fault tolerance in the target system.

In order to implement the fault tolerance controller and demonstrate its properties in an open IaaS solution, we have chosen the open-source OpenStack IaaS platform. It consists of components that control hardware pools of processing, storage, and networking resources throughout a data center. Users either manage it through a web-based dashboard, through command-line tools, or through a RESTful API. Figure 3 shows the OpenStack core services. (1) Neutron is a system for managing networks and IP addresses; (2) Nova is the computing engine for deploying and managing virtual machines; (3) Glance supports discovery, registration and delivery for disk and server images; (4) ceilometer provides telemetry services to collect metering data; (5) Keystone provides user/service/endpoint authentication and authorization and (6) Heat is a service for orchestrating the infrastructure needed for cloud applications to run.

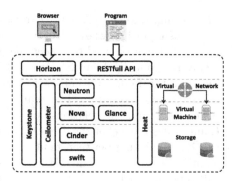

Fig. 3. An OpenStack block diagram

3.3   Job Distributor Strategies

Individual compute resources can easily suffer from heavy load or underload in the absence of a sufficient task dispatcher. The major cause for failure of the process at the VM layer is, however, overloading. The job distributor strategies can be classified into two major categories: (i) *Static* approaches divide the load evenly among all available resources. They do not consider the current state of the system, which may lead to heavy system load or underload conditions. (ii) *Dynamic* approaches monitor the current state of the system for managing the load and aim for a more efficient load distribution. The main aim of a job distributor is to improve system performance by efficient usage of resources. The most common job dispatcher/controller strategies are:

- *Round-Robin (RR):* In this strategy, as the name suggests, jobs are assigned to all servers in round-robin manner. *RR* does not consider factors such as the number of assigned job to the resource, CPU utilization, etc. Instead it treats all resources as equal and divides the traffic equally. It is the simplest strategy for implementation.
- *Weighted Round-Robin (WRR):* It is an extension *RR* strategy where resources receive jobs according to their given weight value. Each resource can be assigned a weight. Resources with higher weights receive new job requests first compared to those with less weight, and resources with higher weights get more jobs than those with less weights.
- *Dynamic Weighted Round-Robin (DWRR):* Since *RR* and *WRR* are static job distribution strategies and have to have knowledge of subsequent job requests, there are situations when already overloaded resources keep receiving more job requests although other idle resources are still available. By considering the real-time information and metrics of each resource such as current CPU utilization, *DWRR* applies dynamic weight assignment to avoid overloading and improves throughput of the whole system. The *DWRR* strategy reassigns a new weight value to the resources periodically.

3.4   Fuzzy Logic

Fuzzy logic [24] is an effective technique to describe complex systems with linguistic descriptions. A linguistic variable is a variable whose values are words in a natural language. For example, *"load"* is a linguistic variable, which can take the values as *"heavy"*, *"medium"*, *"light"* and so on. A Fuzzy Logic Systems (FLS) architecture consists of several components as shown in Fig. 4:

The *Fuzzification* module transforms the system inputs, which are crisp numbers, into fuzzy sets. The *Rules* (Knowledge Base) module stores IF-THEN rules provided by experts or learned from other sources. The *Inference* Engine simulates the human reasoning process by making fuzzy inference on the inputs and IF-THEN

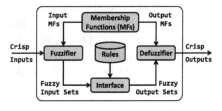

Fig. 4. Basic configuration of FLS

rules; the *Defuzzification* module transforms the fuzzy set obtained by the inference engine into a crisp value.

A membership function (MF) is a curve that defines how each point in the input space is mapped to a membership value (or degree of membership) between 0 and 1. MFs are used in the fuzzifier and defuzzifier modules of a FLS to map the non-fuzzy input values to fuzzy linguistic terms and vice versa.

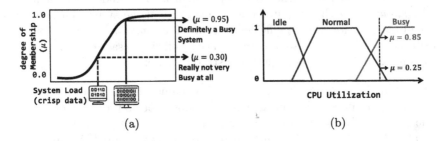

Fig. 5. Example of MFs

For example, Fig. 5(a) shows a smoothly varying curve that passes from a *not loaded* system to *heavily loaded* system. The curve is known as a membership function (μ). Both systems are busy to some degree, but one is significantly less busy than the other. An important characteristic of fuzzy logic is that a value can belong to multiple sets at the same time. There are different forms of membership functions. For example, according to Fig. 5(b), a CPU utilization value can be considered as *"normal"* and *"busy"* at the same time, with different degree of memberships. The most common types of membership functions are triangular, trapezoidal, and Gaussian shapes.

In a FLS, a rule base is constructed to control the output variable. Fuzzy rules are linguistic IF-THEN constructions that have the general form "IF A THEN B" where A and B are propositions contain linguistic variables. For instance, IF *load is high* and *target is medium* THEN *command is reduce*.

3.5   Fuzzy Fault Tolerance Management

Fuzzy control provides a solution to design a controller for a dynamic process based on available heuristic knowledge. Figure 1 earlier showed the general overview of our fault tolerance framework. Resulting from the Resource pool are the current weight and priority values for each available resource. Additionally, any changes of CPU utilization between two predefined intervals are collected from the ceilometer. The output of the fault tolerance controller is the modified weight value that determines whether the assigned job request for a resource should be increased or decreased in the next interval.

According to current state, the change of the weight value between two intervals is calculated by the fuzzy controller and send to the job distributor module as the adaptive weight value for the resource to be used for the next interval. Based on the change of CPU utilization and loaded job request to the resource in the previous interval, the fuzzy fault tolerance controller determines the new value for weight and priority of each available resource for the next interval.

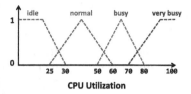

Fig. 6. Fuzzy membership functions for the input variable

As it described before, the fuzzifier and defuzzifier modules (Fig. 4) in the fuzzy controller internally work with linguistic variables and values. The input numeric values are measured and converted to the corresponding linguistic values by the fuzzification module, and the reverse operation is performed by the defuzzification module.

Based on the linguistic input value, the interface module selects the appropriate rule to be applied and produces the linguistic output value. Both fuzzifier and defuzzifier use an MF to convert numeric values to linguistic values and vice versa. The MF maps each numerical value to a membership value (certainty level) between 0 and 1 (0 completely uncertain, 1 completely certain). Figure 6 represents our membership function, where the x-axis represents CPU utilization values and the y-axis membership values. Based on possible levels of CPU utilization, which is the metric that represents how busy a processor core is, in this work, the linguistic variables representing the value of resource utilization level are divided into four levels: *idle*, *normal*, *busy* and *very busy*. To determine the boundary values of each linguistic variable, we collected the required data from several experts in cloud application management, and used the average of all the responses for each variable.

Our fuzzy fault tolerance controller uses the following anomaly identification rules that help in recognising possible failure and that result in job distribution and weight/priority adjustment as the response:

- A resources is defined as *overloaded* if its CPU utilization exceeds a given threshold for a predefined time frame. In this situation, the fuzzy controller determines the appropriate values of load weight and priority parameters for the target resource according to its current level of CPU usage. By adjusting the weight value, the job distributor will send less job requests to this resource until its CPU usage is in a safe mode.
- An *underload* situation occurs whenever the CPU usage of the resource becomes low value for a given time window, i.e., the resource has a low number of jobs to execute and mostly is in idle mode. In this case, the fuzzy controller modifies and increases the weight and priority value of idle resources to receive more job requests from job distributor, thus reducing likely failure elsewhere on other nodes.

Anomaly management happens in the following two ways. Firstly, overloading is an anomaly taken as an indication that failure is likely to happen, i.e., performance

Table 1. Description of compared strategies used in the controller evaluation

Technique	Strategy	Weight value
Equal weighted job distributor ($Equal$-W)	Resources receive job requests in a circular fashion without considering resource metric such as CPU utilization and fault tolerance, i.e., all resources have same weight value (W)[a]	$\forall\ r_i, r_j \in RP \mid W(r_j) = W(r_i)$
Least-CPU utilization weighted job distributor (cpu_{util}-W)	Resources are weighted based on their CPU utilization, and job requests are distributed in proportion to the weight value. Higher values will be assigned to the resource with lower CPU utilization[b]	$\forall\ r_j \in RP \mid W(r_j) = 100 - cpu_{util}(r_j, \Delta t_2)$
Fuzzy weighted job distributor ($Fuzzy$-W)	Resource weight value is obtained by the fuzzy fault tolerance controller based on the current CPU utilization and the history of weight value for the resource[c]	$\forall\ r_j \in RP \mid W(r_j) = Fuzzy(r_j, \Delta t_2)$

[a]Resource Pool contains of available resources.
[b]Average CPU utilization of resource r_j during previous time window Δt_2.
[c]Weight value of resource r_j based on CPU utilization during previous time window Δt_2.

degradation is a root cause for failures, and underload is an anomaly that signals an opportunity to reduce likely failure elsewhere by allocating load to the current node. Secondly, a further hypothesis of the anomaly framework is that incorrect weight and priority negatively impacts on fault occurrences. The incoming job load to each resource are determined based on its weight and priority values. Therefore, in order to have a fair distribution on user job requests and avoid of over/under load situations, our fuzzy controller has duty to modify these parameters based on loaded job request to the resource, the history of fault rates and the change of CPU utilization for target resource. In this way, a proactive pre-emptive migration FT strategy is applied.

4   Implementation

We implemented a prototype of the proposed fuzzy logic fault tolerance controller in OpenStack. The Fuzzy Fault Tolerance controller is a based on a fuzzy logic-based feedback control loop. It continuously monitors the resource utilization (using `ceilometer`) and triggers the controller at each interval check period.

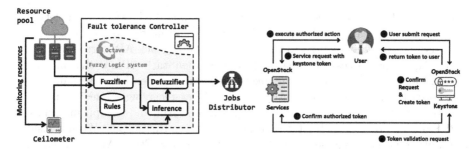

Fig. 7. Overview of the implemented fault tolerance controller

Fig. 8. cURL process of calling the OpenStack API

According to the utilization values for each available resources, the fuzzy controller module identifies appropriate load weight values in anomalous situations.

In our implementation, we assume one or more VM instances as members in the `Resource pool`. We use a minimal Linux distribution, namely the `cirros` image that was specifically designed for use as a test image on cloud platforms such as OpenStack. Each instance (VM) receives a job request and executes it. In our experiment, we consider all job requests submitted by different users as a CPU bounded type. In order to control and manage weight values of available resources by a fuzzy logic controller, we added an additional VM resource, which acts as a fault tolerance controller and decides and reassigns weight values periodically. For the fault tolerance controller, due the impossibility of installing any additional package in the `cirros` image, we considered a VM machine running Linux Ubuntu-based images. Figure 7 illustrates the implemented system in OpenStack. The created job distributor distributes user job requests across a set of resources, i.e., the `Resource pool`. The strategies used in the job distributor controller VM for evaluation (a comparison between our proposed fuzzy controller and two other traditional approaches) are summarized in Table 1.

Figure 7 shows the complete process of the proposed fuzzy fault tolerance approach. First, the fault tolerance controller gathers information from the job distributor, ceilometer and the current state of members (available resources) in the resource pool, then identifies appropriate load weight value for a resource according to the situation in order to adjust anomalous situations. For example, if a resource is overloaded, the controller determines that the incoming job load to the resource should be decreased, therefore it reassigns a new weight value for the resource to reduce the submitted job requests. The proposed fuzzy logic controller is coded and run inside of the fault tolerance controller machine.

For some parameters in the proposed algorithm, such as the current number of VM instances or workload, we need to call the OpenStack API. For example, the command `nova list` shows a list of running instances. The API is a RESTful interface, which allows us to send URL requests to the service manager to execute commands. Due to the unavailability of direct access to the OpenStack API inside of the fault tolerance controller machine, we used the popular command line utility cURL to interact with a couple of OpenStack APIs. cURL lets us transmit and receive HTTP requests and responses from the command line or a shell script, which enabled us to work with the OpenStack API directly.

In Fig. 8, the process of using cURL to call OpenStack APIs is shown. First, we send a request authentication token by passing credentials (username and password) from OpenStack Identity service. After receiving Auth-Token from Keystone, the user can combine the authentication token and Computing Service API Endpoint to send a HTTP request and receive the output. We use inside the fault tolerance controller machine to execute OpenStack APIs and collect required outputs. By combining these settings, we are able to run the fuzzy logic approach as the controller of fault tolerance management in OpenStack.

5   Experimental Comparison

The evaluation aims at showing the effectiveness of our fuzzy logic controller for fault tolerance management in comparison to other job distribution strategies.

5.1   Experimental Setup and Benchmark

In our experiment, the proposed fuzzy logic approach was implemented as full working systems and was tested in the OpenStack platform. The number of available resources considered in our experiment was set to 4 VMs. The term job workload refers to the user request arrival. Job workload is defined as the sequence of users submitting the job request that needs to be handled by the job distributor. To evaluate our proposed approach, we considered a multiple number of workloads. In each workload scenarios, there are a set of job requests submitted by individual users. Each job request submitted by a user is considered as a CPU bounded job. At each workload scenario, the duration of job execution was set by *Poisson Distribution*. Several workload scenarios were executed and the total duration of our experiment was 2 weeks.

In order to evaluate the proposed approach and generate/manage faults in the target system, we used a fault detector VM, shown in Fig. 1, as a single system fault model. By gathering information from the ceilometer about the current situation of each available VM, the fault detector is able to detect whether the resource goes into an anomalous state (over/underload) or not. Based on current CPU utilization of the resource in the defined time window, the fault detector module detects if a target resource is overloaded for a period, and sends a recovery signal to the target resource. To simplify the fault recovery process here, we consider hardware rejuvenation as the recovery fault tolerance strategy.

Additionally, we compared the proposed fuzzy fault tolerance approach with two other algorithms, namely *Equal-W* and cpu_{util}-*W*, as shown in Table 1. In the *Equal-W* approach, each available resource receives job requests in a circular fashion without considering resource metrics such as CPU utilization and fault tolerance, i.e., all resources have the same weight value (W). In contrast, the cpu_{util}-*W* approach, by monitoring resource CPU utilization, the weight values are assigned dynamically, and job requests are distributed in proportion to the weight value. There is other research on load balancing strategies [4,15,23], which aims to improve objectives such as resource response time, which are similar in terms of the monitoring set up, but not the configuration of the analyses and enactment strategies for fault tolerance.

5.2   Comparison Metrics

We measure the performance of the cloud environment during the whole period for each executed scenario. The metrics used for comparison are:

- *CPU utilization:* as a key metric considered in resource management across clouds, it is a function of time and is denoted by the amount of time a CPU is busy for handling work during a specific interval. It is reported as a percentage. CPU anomalies appear if its utilization goes beyond a high threshold (e.g., 80%) for a sustained period of time.
- *Failure rate:* is the representation of the total number of failures experienced during the experiment for each scenario. It widely used to represent the stability and reliability of a target system.

5.3   Results and Discussion

Figure 9 shows the distribution of the CPU utilization metric (cpu_util) obtained by comparing the algorithms during our experiment for each individual available resource. For all VMs, our approach (*Fuzzy-W*) obtained a better distribution range, with cpu_{util}-*W* consistently second best, followed by *Equal-W* as last. The wider range of CPU usage distribution shows that the job request load has a more fair distribution among all available resources. Fairness is defined based on the CPU usage of each resource and tries to avoid CPU overloading for a long period. In this context, fairness represents the quality of service provided by a cloud service and it tries to avoid SLA (Service Level agreement) violation due to host overloading. By using dynamic weight and priority values for load job request distribution, both *Fuzzy-W* and cpu_{util}-*W* algorithms try to overcome the overloading anomaly situation that causes system failures.

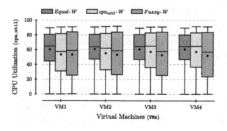

Fig. 9. CPU utilization (cpu_util)

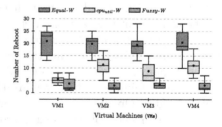

Fig. 10. Failure rates

In Figs. 11(a), (b), and (c), the bars represent the percentage frequency of CPU utilization among all available resources for the compared algorithms, i.e., *Equal-W*, cpu_{util}-*W* and *Fuzzy-W*, respectively.

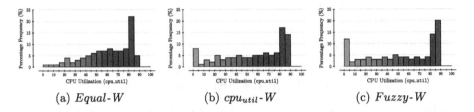

(a) *Equal-W*   (b) cpu_{util}-*W*   (c) *Fuzzy-W*

Fig. 11. Percentage frequency of CPU utilization

5.4   Comparison of Effectiveness

Figure 10 shows the distribution of reboot occurrences (resulting from failures) for individual resources during of our experiment under several workload scenarios. As it mentioned before, both *Fuzzy-W* and cpu_{util}-*W* approaches have better CPU usage distribution compared to *Equal-W* (Fig. 11). However, due to a higher distribution of CPU utilization in *Fuzzy-W*, at each time interval for the failure detector, we have lower average values for CPU utilization, and it shows a significant reduction of the number of reboot occurrences.

6   Conclusion

We have proposed a new fuzzy logic-based load balancer for fault tolerance in IaaS cloud platforms. The proposed approach employs a fuzzy logic strategy to assign a weight and priority value to each available resource as a proactive strategy in anomalous situations. By monitoring the current state of a system, it tries to adjust the weight value for each resource in order to achieve: (i) fairness job distribution, (ii) avoid anomalous situations such as overloading that causes a system failure, and (iii) improve throughput of the whole system. Overloading of a system may lead to poor performance which can increase failure rates and SLA violation. Underload is also dealt with to reduce anomalies elsewhere.

The assignment mechanism for choosing the appropriate weight value in the proposed approach is based on a fuzzy logic system (FLS) and collected metering data as its input. By considering the real-time information and collected metrics of each resource, it achieves a more efficient load distribution and reduces the occurrence of failures in the system. The proposed approach was coded and implemented in OpenStack, an open-source IaaS platform, to demonstrate the practical effectiveness of proposed approach, and evaluated based on important metrics, including distribution of CPU utilization and failure rate during of our experiment for each individual resource. The experimental results revealed that using a fuzzy approach the proposed approach outperformed the other strategies considering all the above mentioned metrics, especially in failure rate parameters, which is the main objective here.

We plan to apply the solution also to container-based virtualisation [9, 21] towards an edge-cloud management platform [22] in the future.

Acknowledgement. This work was partly supported by IC4 (the Irish Centre for Cloud Computing and Commerce), funded by EI and the IDA.

References

1. Amin, Z., Singh, H., Sethi, N.: Review on fault tolerance techniques in cloud computing. Int. J. Comput. Appl. **116**(18), 11–17 (2015)
2. Arabnejad, H., Jamshidi, P., Estrada, G., El Ioini, N., Pahl, C.: An auto-scaling cloud controller using fuzzy q-learning-implementation in openstack. In: European Conference on Service-Oriented and Cloud Computing (2016)
3. Arabnejad, H., Pahl, C., Jamshidi, P., Estrada, G.: A comparison of reinforcement learning techniques for fuzzy cloud auto-scaling. In: International Symposium on Cluster, Cloud and Grid Computing, CCGrid (2017)
4. Chaczko, Z., Mahadevan, V., Aslanzadeh, S., Mcdermid, C.: Availability and load balancing in cloud computing. In: International Conference on Computer and Software Modeling (2011)
5. Chen, X., Jiang, J.H.: A method of virtual machine placement for fault-tolerant cloud applications. Intel. Autom. Soft Comput. **22**(4), 587–597 (2016)
6. Cheraghlou, M.N., Khadem-Zadeh, A., Haghparast, M.: A survey of fault tolerance architecture in cloud computing. J. Netw. Comput. Appl. **61**, 81–92 (2016)
7. Engelmann, C., Vallee, G.R., Naughton, T., Scott, S.L.: Proactive fault tolerance using preemptive migration. In: International Conference on Parallel Distributed and Network-Based Proceedings (2009)
8. Ganesh, A., Sandhya, M., Shankar, S.: A study on fault tolerance methods in cloud computing. In: International Advance Computing Conference, pp. 844–849 (2014)
9. Heinrich, R., van Hoorn, A., Knoche, H., Li, F., Lwakatare, L.E., Pahl, C., Schulte, S., Wettinger, J.: Performance engineering for microservices: research challenges and directions. In: ACM International Conference on Performance Engineering Companion (2017)
10. Huang, Y., Kintala, C., Kolettis, N., Fulton, N.S.: Analysis, module and applications. In: International Symposium on Fault-Tolerant Computing, Software Rejuvenation (1995)
11. Jamshidi, P., Pahl, C., Mendonça, N.C.: Managing uncertainty in autonomic cloud elasticity controllers. IEEE Cloud Comput. **3**(3), 50–60 (2016)
12. Jamshidi, P., Sharifloo, A., Pahl, C., Arabnejad, H., Metzger, A., Estrada, G.: Fuzzy self-learning controllers for elasticity management in dynamic cloud architectures. In: ACM International Conference on Quality of Software Architectures (QoSA), pp. 70–79 (2016)
13. Jamshidi, P., Sharifloo, A.M., Pahl, C., Metzger, A., Estrada, G.: Self-learning cloud controllers: fuzzy q-learning for knowledge evolution. In: 2015 International Conference on Cloud and Autonomic Computing (ICCAC) (2015)
14. Jia, R., Abdelwahed, S., Erradi, A.: A predictive control approach for fault management of computing systems. Perform. Eval. Rev. **43**(3), 16–20 (2015)

15. Kansal, N.J., Chana, I.: Cloud load balancing techniques: a step towards green computing. Int. J. Comput. Sci. Issues **9**(1), 238–246 (2012)
16. Li, B., Kapitza, R.: BFT-Dep: automatic deployment of byzantine fault-tolerant services in PaaS cloud. In: Jelasity, M., Kalyvianaki, E. (eds.) DAIS 2016. LNCS, vol. 9687, pp. 109–114. Springer, Cham (2016). doi:10.1007/978-3-319-39577-7_9
17. Liu, J., Wang, S., Zhou, A., Kumar, S., Yang, F., Buyya, R.: Using proactive fault-tolerance approach to enhance cloud service reliability. IEEE TCC (2016). Pre-print online at http://ieeexplore.ieee.org/document/7469864/. Accessed 22 Aug 2017
18. Lyons, R.E., Vanderkulk, W.: The use of triple-modular redundancy to improve computer reliability. IBM J. Res. Dev. **6**(2), 200–209 (1962)
19. Mohammed, B., Kiran, M., Maiyama, K.M., Kamala, M.M., Awan, I.-U.: Failover strategy for fault tolerance in cloud computing environment. Pract. Exp. Softw. **47**(9), 1243–1274 (2017)
20. Nagarajan, A.B., Mueller, F., Engelmann, C., Scott, S.L.: Proactive fault tolerance for HPC with Xen virtualization. In: International Conference on Supercomputing (2007)
21. Pahl, C., Brogi, A., Soldani, J., Jamshidi, P.: Cloud container technologies: a state-of-the-art review. IEEE Trans. Cloud Comput. (2017). Pre-print online at http://ieeexplore.ieee.org/document/7922500/. Accessed 22 Aug 2017
22. Pahl, C., Helmer, S., Miori, L., Sanin, J., Lee, B.: A container-based edge cloud PaaS architecture based on raspberry pi clusters. In: IEEE International Conference on Future Internet of Things and Cloud Workshops (FiCloudW) (2016)
23. Randles, M., Lamb, D., Taleb-Bendiab, A.: A comparative study into distributed load balancing algorithms for cloud computing. In: AINA Workshops (2010)
24. Vas, P.: Artificial-intelligence-based electrical machines and drives: application of fuzzy, neural, fuzzy-neural, and genetic-algorithm-based techniques. OUP (1999)
25. Wang, Z., Gao, L., Gu, Y., Bao, Y., Yu, G.: A fault-tolerant framework for asynchronous iterative computations in cloud environments. In: ACM Symposium on Cloud Computing, pp. 71–83 (2016)
26. Zhang, Y., Wong, D., Zheng, W.: User-level checkpoint and recovery for LAM/MPI. Operating Syst. Rev. **39**(3), 72–81 (2005)

Data Preparation as a Service Based on Apache Spark

Nivethika Mahasivam[✉], Nikolay Nikolov, Dina Sukhobok,
and Dumitru Roman

SINTEF, Pb. 124 Blindern, 0314 Oslo, Norway
nivemaham@gmail.com, {nikolay.nikolov,dina.sukhobok,
dumitru.roman}@sintef.no

Abstract. Data preparation is the process of collecting, cleaning and consolidating raw datasets into cleaned data of certain quality. It is an important aspect in almost every data analysis process, and yet it remains tedious and time-consuming. The complexity of the process is further increased by the recent tendency to derive knowledge from very large datasets. Existing data preparation tools provide limited capabilities to effectively process such large volumes of data. On the other hand, frameworks and software libraries that do address the requirements of big data, require expert knowledge in various technical areas. In this paper, we propose a dynamic, service-based, scalable data preparation approach that aims to solve the challenges in data preparation on a large scale, while retaining the accessibility and flexibility provided by data preparation tools. Furthermore, we describe its implementation and integration with an existing framework for data preparation – Grafterizer. Our solution is based on Apache Spark, and exposes application programming interfaces (APIs) to integrate with external tools. Finally, we present experimental results that demonstrate the improvements to the scalability of Grafterizer.

Keywords: Distributed data parallel processing · Apache Spark · Big data preparation · Interactive data preparation

1 Introduction

The movement towards digitalization has spread in prominent domains such as health, industrial production, defense, and banking, to improve operations using data-driven decisions. Such domains deploy various tools including sensors, applications, logging and production databases to collect data in high velocity and large volumes, and extract relevant information in tabular or text formats [1]. This process produces raw data, often semi-structured or unstructured, that could contain missing, erroneous, incomplete, and duplicate values. The raw data needs to be cleaned and transformed into structured data to meet the expected quality for further usage. Data preparation is an important step to treat "dirty" datasets by collecting, combining and consolidating datasets that are suitable for further data analysis. Despite of the importance of data preparation, it remains a tedious and time-consuming process that requires significant

© IFIP International Federation for Information Processing 2017
Published by Springer International Publishing AG 2017. All Rights Reserved
F. De Paoli et al. (Eds.): ESOCC 2017, LNCS 10465, pp. 125–139, 2017.
DOI: 10.1007/978-3-319-67262-5_10

effort [2, 3]. Furthermore, data preparation in the context of big data introduces even more challenges, both functional and nonfunctional.

One of the main challenges related to large volume data preparation is that existing frameworks and tools require expert knowledge of specific programming languages, data models, and computational models. Examples include native language libraries such as Pandas in Python [4] or Data Frame in the R language[1], which are widely used for data wrangling and preparation. Further, distributed data parallelization (DDP) is the most widely realized computational model in big data processing [5]. The basic computational abstraction of DDP performs a computation in parallel, by distributing smaller data partitions among a set of machines or processes. It provides scalability, load balancing and fault tolerance. Frameworks that realise DDP, such as Apache Hadoop and Apache Spark, are used to implement scalable solutions in the big data domain, and significantly increase technical complexity of data workers' data preparation routines. Implementation of a solution based on the DDP model should consume a large dataset, split it into partitions, and process and accumulate the results without losing the semantics of the expected outcome.

A scalable data preparation tool or framework is essential to process large volumes of data, but existing solutions lack capabilities to effectively perform such operations. Due to their architecture, it is difficult to realize large-scale data processing techniques including distributed and concurrent processing. Such solutions include spreadsheet tools (e.g. Excel and Open Office) that are often used to prepare datasets, especially in companies that lack the expertise to make use of the frameworks and tools for big data preparation and processing [6]. Data preparation is often implemented as an iterative process where new data quality issues can appear while existing ones are being addressed. Consequent iterations are performed by reviewing the intermediate results produced from previous iterations. Existing data preparation tools support interactive preparation by providing immediate rendering of intermediate results and suggestions for improvements. OpenRefine[2], Pentaho Data Integration (Kettle)[3], and Trifacta Wrangler[4] are examples of interactive solutions that are used in industries to accelerate the data preparation process. Such solutions are primarily desktop-oriented applications that are not dedicated to handling large amounts of data.

In this paper, we propose a solution that addresses the scalability, usability and accessibility issues in data preparation through a mixed approach that combines interactivity of data preparation tools with the powerful features of frameworks that support data preparation for big data. Our solution is based on extensions to the web-based Grafterizer transformation framework [7] that is part of the DataGraft platform [8–10][5]. We propose improvements to Graftwerk – the existing data transformation back-end of Grafterizer, with the aim to augment its capability to effectively process larger datasets. Our solution is a scalable data preparation as a service back-end

---

[1] http://www.r-tutor.com/r-introduction/data-frame.

[2] http://openrefine.org/.

[3] http://community.pentaho.com/projects/data-integration/.

[4] https://www.trifacta.com/products/wrangler/.

[5] https://datagraft.io/.

that can dynamically build data preparation pipelines, and effectively support interactive cleaning and transformation of large volumes of data using DDP techniques.

The contributions of this paper are thereby two-fold:

1. First, we describe an approach for using DDP for scalable data preparation, based on the use of Apache Spark, which has been identified as a suitable framework that facilitates scalable data preparation.
2. Second, we propose a proof-of-concept realization of the approach for data preparation as a service in Grafterizer, along with validation and evaluation results that demonstrate the difference in performance between our proposed approach and the existing back-end.

The remainder of this paper is organized as follows. In Sect. 2, we provide a detailed description of our approach for DDP-based data preparation. In Sect. 3, we describe a proof-of-concept data preparation as a service back-end that realizes our proposed approach. Section 4 shows the performance of the implemented solution in experiments with large volumes of data. Section 5 discusses related works. Finally, Sect. 6 summarizes this paper, and outlines further development directions of the approach and implementation.

2 A Proposed Approach for DDP-Based Data Preparation

2.1 DDP for Data Preparation

Distributed Data Parallelization is a computational model, proven to effectively perform large scale data processing [5]. MapReduce is a popular implementation of the DDP model that has been adapted in many big data analytic tools [11]. Following the spike of MapReduce, other programming models were introduced, including in-memory computing [5] and iterative map-reduce [12]. In-memory computing is a general-purpose solution for large-scale computing problems. It is a special form of DDP, where a computation is performed on a read-only representation of data in memory. The memory representation is held on a distributed-shared-memory (DSM) that is composed of memory distributed across several machines. Since data preparation processes are iterative, an in-memory computing model is suitable for the implementation of such processes. This approach keeps intermediate results in-memory and avoids high disk input/output latency, unlike MapReduce frameworks. In the following paragraphs, we discuss some of the most important characteristics of designing a data preparation approach using DDP.

Handling Data Parallelism
Parallelism is an important aspect of DDP. We aim to achieve parallelism in two ways:

- *Data-flow parallelism:* In data-flow parallelism, data is chunked into several partitions and distributed to facilitate ingestion of multiple processors in parallel. This enables processing large datasets that cannot be processed using traditional computational models. To achieve data parallelism, a computational operation should be adapted to be executed in parallel and to use partitioned data. Subsequently, the output data from each partition needs to be aggregated according to the semantics of the operation to produce the final result. DDP operations such as *map, reduce, group, match* are all examples of existing DDP patterns [11].

- *Control-flow parallelism:* Control-flow parallelism is achieved by parallel execution of multiple operations that do not depend on other operations' results [13]. As mentioned earlier, data preparation is an iterative process where the data preparation operations are performed in a pipeline. Figure 1 exemplifies control-flow parallelism optimization on such a pipeline. Suppose that operations p1 and p2 in Fig. 1a operate independently on two parts of a dataset (i.e. they do not rely on their respective results). With control-flow parallelism, the total execution time of the control sequence *t1* of the given operation flow can be shortened to *t2* by executing them in parallel, as shown in Fig. 1b. Control-flow parallelism provides high throughput of execution time and optimises resource allocation.

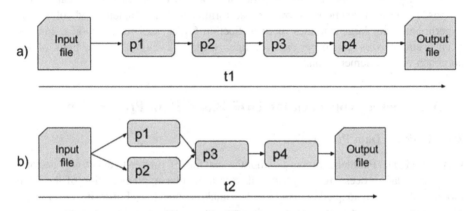

Fig. 1. Control-flow parallelization of a pipeline

Our proposed approach for DDP in data preparation is to use a combination of data-flow and control-flow parallelism using DDP. Data-flow parallelism is essential to enable large-scale data preparation that can scale horizontally. Control-flow parallelism can be used to improve the throughput by executing dynamically adapted pipelines that utilize optimal resources on data partitions.

Handling Data Ingestion

We want to allow cleaning and transformation of collected raw data that are available in various volumes and formats. A position article [14] shows that 80% of the published datasets are in tabular format. Hence, in our solution we aim to process datasets that are already collected and made available in common tabular formats such as CSV, TSV, Excel and other spreadsheet formats.

Data ingestion is a routine for receiving input data for data preparation processes. The most frequently used data ingestion techniques in big data context are stream processing, micro-batch processing and batch processing [15]. Batch processing techniques treat input data as a complete collection that needs to be considered for analysis [16]. Batch processing is generally used as "store-first, process second" model, where data is collected in advance and made available to be processed. In stream processing, the data is ingested as continuous, long running streams [17]. Data streams are produced based on event-by-event or the complex-event-model. Data streams are used for real-time analysis but are less appropriate when it comes to processing tabular formats of data. Micro-batch processing combines aspects of both batch processing and stream processing by treating data as a sequence of small batches. Streaming or micro-batching data can be a solution to overcome the problem of processing large data. However, since we aim to perform ETL operations on tabular data, these approaches assume data to be homogenous, and will not always result in the expected output, especially when performing collective operations or row-dependent operations. Hence, we focus on support for batch processing of input data since the approach is more suitable for processing the targeted input datasets.

2.2 Apache Spark as a Framework for DDP-Based Data Preparation

According to [18], the biggest challenge faced in data preparation solutions for big data is providing a processing model that can do complex reasoning of small volumes of data, simple processing of large volumes of data, and parallel processing of very large volumes of data. In [18], the authors argue that a feasible big data preparation tool should provide both expressiveness and scalability of functionalities. Thereby, we compared available highly expressive and scalable solutions. Native libraries such as Pandas in Python or Data Frame in the R language are widely used in data preparation implementations. However, deploying these frameworks as a scalable solution in a distributed environment is challenging since no native support for this type of deployment currently exists. On the other hand, big data frameworks provide native tools to deploy an application in a distributed environment out of the box. Among big data frameworks Apache Hadoop and Apache Spark are used to implement scalable, batch-processing solutions. Apache Spark has been selected for the implementation of our solution since experiments show that Spark has better performance than Hadoop for big data analytics [19].

Apache Spark is a general-purpose, in-memory data processing framework that realizes DDP. It runs on master-slave architecture, which can scale out with additional master and/or slave nodes. One of the advantages of Spark is its computational abstraction called *resilient distributed datasets (RDDs)* [20]. RDDs are immutable collections of objects that are partitioned across different Spark nodes in the network. It represents the data in-memory on a DSM to enable data flow parallelism and support batch-processing of large volumes of data.

Transformations in Spark are operations that do not depend on inputs from other partitions such as map, filter, rename. An RDD is transformed into another RDD when a transformation is executed. Spark implements the notion of lineage for RDDs to keep the information of how a newer RDD is derived from parent RDD. When a partition is lost, Spark rebuilds the partition from stored data to facilitate efficient fault-tolerance to the system and implement data-flow parallelism.

Furthermore, Spark benefits from lazy execution of transformations to create a directed acyclic-graph (DAG) of data and transformations instead of applying transformations immediately. Once the graph is followed by an action, Spark executes the formed DAG by distributing it as several tasks among nodes. An action in Spark is an operation that reduces the output from all partitions into a final value such as *reduce*. Lazy execution of transformations is used to further optimize the operations in accordance with the control-flow. As an example, if a user wants to apply two independent filters on two different parts of a dataset, and a global operation on the entire data, Spark would optimize by jointly (as opposed to sequentially) applying the independent filters without constructing the intermediate dataset after each filter. This optimization benefits the evaluation of several consecutive RDDs, and provides efficient implementation of iterative execution of the pipeline.

In addition, *DataFrame* is an extended model of RDD in the SparkSQL package, which organizes data into named columns, conceptually equivalent to a relational database structure [19]. It provides a domain-specific language for relational operations, including select, filter, join, groupBy, and enables users to perform SQL-like queries on *DataFrames*. By extending these APIs, we provide an expressive data preparation framework that accommodates most of the data cleaning operations in relatively less complex APIs. Finally, SparkSQL extends a novel optimizer called *Catalyst* [19], that implements query analysis, logical optimization and physical planning. Catalyst supports both rule-based and cost-based optimization of relational operations. Generating optimized queries based on the features in Catalyst allows us to indirectly realize relational query optimization and control-flow parallelization. Therefore, in our solution, a pipeline created using DataFrame in Spark will be optimized before it is executed using Catalyst.

3 Realization of DDP-Based Data Preparation Approach in Grafterizer

In this section, we introduce a proof-of-concept implementation of the approach to provide a scalable, dynamic data preparation service using Spark. The service is deployed as a data preparation back-end for Grafterizer that processes, cleans and transforms large volumes of tabular data. Currently, the implementation supports CSV, TSV, and flat-JSON files, and provides rich, procedural APIs for data preparation operations that can be easily used to build pipelines on Spark. Our solution allows for dynamic creation of pipelines, which is the ability to create and/or modify a data preparation pipeline during run-time. This enables the execution of the data preparation process interactively, so that users can perform incremental modifications of the data cleaning pipeline and observe the results.

3.1 Architecture

The high-level architecture of the service is illustrated in Fig. 2. Below, we describe each component and its functional and technical contributions in more detail.

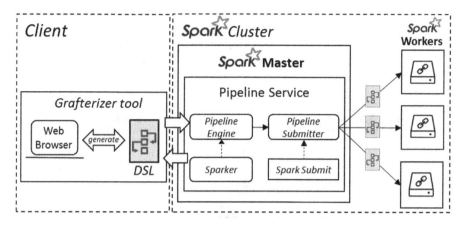

Fig. 2. High-level architecture of the service

Sparker

Sparker is a component that provides APIs to enable data preparation pipelines as Spark jobs. It implements data preparation operations [21] using DataFrame and RDD APIs, and provides pattern-oriented procedural APIs that can be used to build a pipeline. Sparker encapsulates the implementation complexity of data cleaning operations in Spark. It provides commonly used APIs in data preparation operations that are not already available in DataFrame. Especially reshape functions merging grouped data, concatenating multiple columns, splitting of a given column using a separator into multiple columns, custom group functions, filling missing values, custom query functions with simple filters, pagination of queried data and adding additional rows of values to a dataset are notable features. To adapt a pipeline to perform data preparation, we designed every API to receive DataFrame objects with additional parameters depending on the operation's semantics, and return the result as an altered DataFrame object according to the pipeline pattern. This allows us to create a chain of operations by using the output of any operation as an input to another operation. The main categories of Sparker's APIs are: (1) converting input files to DataFrame; (2) data cleaning/preparation operations; (3) converting DataFrame into suitable output format as shown in Fig. 3. A standard pipeline would start with the conversion of an input file, one or more data cleaning/preparation operations, and finally the generation of the final result as output.

Pipeline Service

The *Pipeline Service* provides dynamic creation of pipelines using Sparker APIs, and submits the current version of the pipeline to the Spark cluster. The *Pipeline Service* has two main components: The *Pipeline Generator* and the *Pipeline Submitter*. The *Pipeline Generator* initially receives requests with input data and corresponding pipeline instructions, and dynamically generates pipelines using the requested information. The pipeline is implemented in Clojure – a dynamic programming language that allows the creation, modification and execution of programming instructions during runtime.

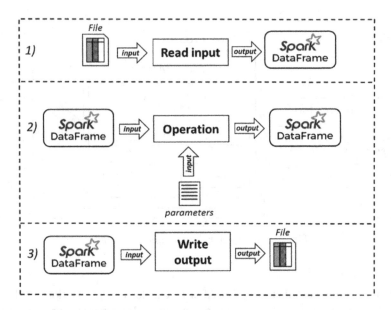

Fig. 3. Pipeline pattern implementation using DataFrames

Furthermore, pure functions in Clojure transform immutable data structures into some output format. We use the thread-first macro, which is denoted by "- > " in a pipeline. Taking an initial value as its first argument, the macro threads it through one or more expressions, thus constituting a pipeline. A sample pipeline using *Pipeline Service*'s APIs is depicted in Fig. 4.

```
1   (defn my-pipe
2       [data-file]
3
4       (->
5           (make-data-set data-file)
6           (make-first-row-as-column)
7           (make-data-set-with-columns 0 15)
8           (remove-duplicates `("Year" "Month" "DayofMonth" "DayofWeek"))
9       )
10  )
```

Fig. 4. A sample pipeline using Pipeline Service APIs realizes pipeline pattern

The Clojure function names are used as APIs in the Pipeline Service to enable creation and execution of Sparker pipeline instructions during run-time. Once a pipeline is created, the *Pipeline Generator* forwards the created pipeline to the *Pipeline Submitter*. The *Pipeline Submitter* submits given pipeline instructions as a Spark job using *spark-submit*. *spark-submit* is a script provided by Apache Spark that submits any given programming instruction created using Spark as a Spark job, which can then be executed on a Spark cluster. Once the job is executed *Pipeline Service* sends a response with the processed data.

These APIs are used to create a pipeline of data preparation operations in client applications. Figure 4 shows a sample pipeline that uses the Pipeline Service APIs and demonstrates how the pipeline pattern was implemented. Rows 1 and 2 define the pipeline function and the data input parameter to the pipeline through which we pass the dataset as argument. This is followed by the thread-first operator in line 4. Lines 5 through 8 are calls to the APIs exposed through the Pipeline Service. They consecutively create the data structure (DataFrame) out of the input data, take the first row as table headers, take the first 16 columns of data (discarding the rest), and, finally, filter out duplicate rows based on a vector of unique values of the cells in each row that correspond to the columns "Year", "Month", "DayofMonth" and "DayofWeek".

Grafterizer

Grafterizer has been integrated to generate pipelines using calls based on the DSL/APIs provided by the *Pipeline Service* during user interaction. Once a pipeline is created/altered an HTTP request is sent to the pipeline service with the metadata of input and the generated pipeline using the DSL/APIs. The pipeline is then executed by the Spark-based back-end and the resulting data/output is sent back as an HTTP response to Grafterizer and immediately previewed. The back-end service proposed in this paper has been integrated with the currently available user interface of Grafterizer, which is shown in Fig. 5 (the left part representing an example of data transformation pipeline and the table depicting the data on which the pipeline executes).

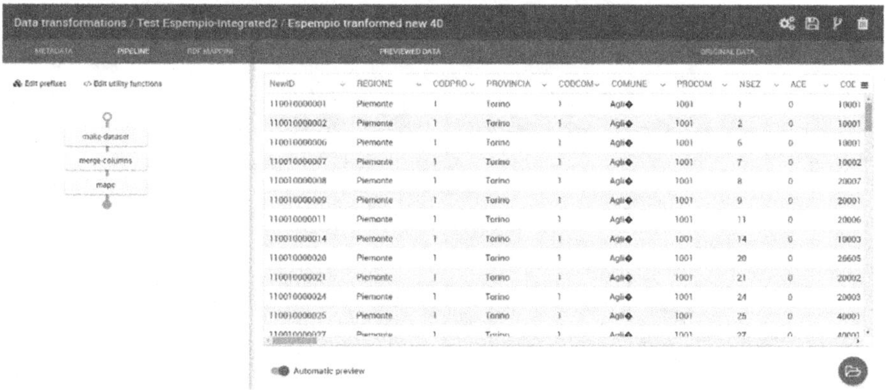

Fig. 5. Grafterizer's preview of cleaned data using current pipeline

4 Evaluation

We conducted a set of experiments to evaluate the performance of the proposed service. The experiments were conducted on a cluster consisting of a master node with Intel Core i7 3.3 GHz, 4 CPU Cores, 15 GB of RAM, 512 GB of SSD, running on Ubuntu 14.04 LTS and 4 worker nodes each having Intel Core i7 3.3 GHz, 12 CPU

Cores, 64 GB of RAM, 480 GB SSD and running on CentOS 7. A Spark executor is a process that serves a Spark application, and typically runs on a worker node. A Spark driver is a process that coordinates the execution of a Spark job on worker nodes. A Spark application can scale-out with more executors and scale-up with more concurrent tasks assigned to a process.

To analyze the scalability of the proposed solution, we tuned the Spark cluster with different numbers of executors to study its ability to scale out. By increasing the number of executors, we multiplied the memory allocated to process input, CPUs and concurrent tasks per executor. In this experiment, we used the Price Paid Data (PPD)[6] dataset which is approximately 3.5 GB. We created a sample data pipeline to load the input data, use the first-row as a header row for the schema and then use filters on selected columns followed by grouping of data. We executed the same pipeline on the given input dataset multiple times with varying number of executors, and recorded the execution times of the first request sent to the cluster once a cluster setup was initialized. In addition, we recorded the average of the three following requests sent to that cluster setup, because of the significant difference between the execution time of the first and any following requests. The difference is due to overhead of distributing dependent source files to worker nodes from drivers, which is done only when the first request is executed. The result of the experiment is illustrated in Fig. 6.

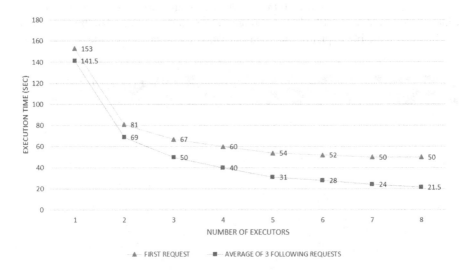

Fig. 6. Execution time of Pipeline Service with increasing number of executors

The experiment clearly shows that the execution time is gradually decreasing. This validates that the performance of the service increases for a given input when the cluster scales-out with more executors. Further, this proves that the proposed service can process large volumes of data and scale out with more executors. The service can

---

[6] https://www.gov.uk/government/statistical-data-sets/price-paid-data-downloads.

scale out with the size of input data, since it is based on in-memory computation, and adding more computing resources increases the capability of processing larger volumes of data.

Further, we benchmarked the performance of Grafterizer with the proposed service on a single host compared to original Grafterizer with traditional back-end to measure the improvement with respect to the current system. Due to the limitations in the ability to process large volumes of data by existing system, we created input datasets by sampling the UK Road Accidents Safety Data in different sizes. We created inputs that increase by approximately 10 MB from 10 MB to 100 MB. Experiments were performed on a computer with Intel Core i5 2.5 GHz processor with 4 CPU Cores, and 8 GB of RAM. Equivalent pipelines that can be executed by each system were created, and the execution time for each input of every system were recorded. The results of the experiment are depicted in Fig. 7.

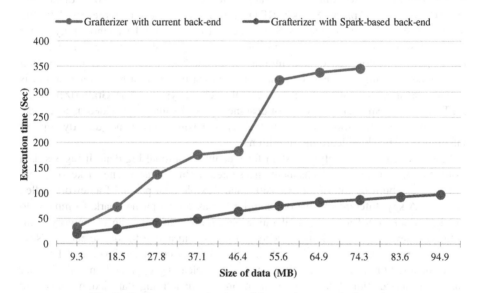

Fig. 7. Performance evaluation of the service on a single-node

The graph clearly shows that the proposed service is almost four times faster than the existing Grafterizer back-end on a single node deployment. Further, the existing Grafterizer back-end was not able to effectively process data bigger than 75 MB on the test hardware, whereas the proposed service could easily process larger input in a short time. This shows that the new service has significantly improved Grafterizer's performance and capacity to process large data even as a single-node deployment.

5 Related Work

The solution proposed in this paper is an alternative to the existing Grafterizer back-end: it enables Grafterizer to work with larger volumes of data by integrating a scalable-backend system that can effectively scale out on a distributed environment with the size of data, and efficiently execute data preparation pipelines. This solution eliminates the dependencies and complexities of implementing and executing a scalable data preparation pipeline in Grafterizer.

Furthermore, the work presented in this paper is related to scalable data processing systems, and data cleaning and transformation tools for big data. In the following we discuss the most relevant recent works in these areas, pointing out the main differences between existing solutions and our proposed approach.

SparkGalaxy [22] is a big data processing toolkit designed to perform complex experiments using data mining and analysis for large amounts of bio-medical data. SparkGalaxy uses Apache Spark's RDD and Graph features to represent data and workflows in a distributed fashion. SparkGalaxy follows a similar methodology to our proposed solution to solve scalability problems. SparkGalaxy focuses on enabling large-scale, workflow-based data mining of biomedical data whereas our solution focuses on enabling a general purpose scalable data preparation tool. Our solution is provided as a service and can be used by other client systems than Grafterizer, using HTTP requests. SparkGalaxy was not designed to be a solution provided as a service. On the other hand, compared to SparkGalaxy, our solution does not directly support integration of machine learning algorithms.

Cleanix [23] is a prototype system for cleaning relational big data. It ingests data from multiple sources and cleans them on a shared-nothing cluster. The backend system of Cleanix is built on top of an extensible and flexible data-parallel framework called Hyracks. A key difference is that our solution is based on Apache Spark. Compared to Spark, Hyracks does not support iterative algorithms and is not an in-memory computing framework [24], making Apache Spark more attractive for data cleaning. Nevertheless, we are not aware of any studies that directly compares Spark and Hyracks performance. Furthermore, Cleanix provides data cleaning operations mainly in four categories of operations (value detection, incomplete data filling, data deduplication and conflict resolution), while our solution supports expressive APIs to perform Cleanix's four types of operations, as well as other operations such as data reshaping and grouping. Furthermore, one could argue that our solution is more user-friendly compared to Cleanix since the data cleaning workflow is supported by graphical interactive previews, and data upload through an intuitive graphical drag-and-drop component.

OpenRefine[7] is an open-source tool for data cleaning/transformation and integration, and provides interactive user-interfaces with spreadsheet style interactions to easily support data cleaning, and previews similar to Grafterizer. OpenRefine was designed as a desktop application rather than a service. It is a memory-intensive tool that runs on a desktop system which limits the size of data that can be processed. There

---

[7] http://openrefine.org/.

are attempts to extend OpenRefine to support large data processing, e.g., BatchRefine[8] and OpenRefine-HD[9]. OpenRefine-HD extends OpenRefine to use Hadoop's MapReduce jobs on HDFS clusters. However, Apache Spark is considered faster for iterative data preparation process [23]. Such OpenRefine extensions require manual execution of transformation in a distributed environment whereas our solution eliminates such overhead by integrating it with Grafterizer in an automated workflow.

6 Summary and Outlook

In this paper, we proposed a data preparation as a service solution that addresses the scalability, usability and accessibility issues in data preparation. We proposed an approach for using DDP for scalable data preparation, based on the use of Apache Spark, and presented a proof-of-concept realization of the approach in Grafterizer, along with validation and evaluation results that demonstrate the difference in performance in data preparation between our proposed approach and the existing back-end of Grafterizer. Experiments show that the proposed implementation scales out with more executors, and performs better than the existing Grafterizer back-end on a single-node deployment. It is worth mentioning that the functional benefits of the proposed solution include user-friendliness, flexibility and ease of use for users with moderate technical skills. Overall, the service is effective and efficient for large-scale data preparation.

As part of future work, we are considering extending the proposed solution to support various data formats as input for data preparation, and operationalize it for the production environment of DataGraft.

Acknowledgements. The work in this paper is partly supported by the EC funded projects proDataMarket (Grant number: 644497), euBusinessGraph (Grant number: 732003), and EW-Shopp (Grant number: 732590). The authors would like to thank Bjørn Marius von Zernichow for his help in improving the readability of the camera-ready version of the paper.

References

1. Atzmueller, M., Oussena, S., Roth-Berghofe, T.: Data preparation for big data analytics: methods and experiences. In: Enterprise Big Data Engineering, Analytics, and Management, pp. 157–170. IGI Global (2016)
2. Kandel, S., Heer, J., Plaisant, C., Kennedy, J., Ham, F.V., Riche, N.H., Buono, P.: Research directions on data wrangling: visualizations and transformations. Inf. Vis. **10**(4), 271–288 (2011)
3. Krishnan, S., Franklin, M.J., Goldberg, K., Wu, E.: ActiveClean: an interactive data cleaning framework for modern machine learning. In: International Conference on Management of Data, San Francisco, California, USA. ACM (2016)

---

[8] https://github.com/fusepoolP3/p3-batchrefine.

[9] https://github.com/rmalla1/OpenRefine-HD.

4. McKinney, W.: Pandas: A Foundational Python Library for DataAnalysis and Statistics. NEM (Networked & Electronic Media) (2011)
5. Jackson, C.J., Vijayakumar, V., Quadir, A.M., Bharathi, C.: Survey on programming models and environments for cluster cloud, and grid computing that defends big data. In: Procedia Computer Science, 2nd International Symposium on Big Data and Cloud Computing (ISBCC 2015), pp. 517–523 (2015)
6. Kandel, S., Paepcke, A., Hellerstein, J., Heer, J.: Enterprise data analysis and visualization: an interview study. IEEE Trans. Vis. Comput. Graph. 18(12), 2917–2926 (2012)
7. Sukhobok, D., Nikolov, N., Pultier, A., Ye, X., Berre, A., Moynihan, R., Roberts, B., Elvesæter, B., Mahasivam, N., Roman, D.: Tabular data cleaning and linked data generation with Grafterizer. ESWC (Satell. Events) 2016, 134–139 (2016)
8. Roman, D., Nikolov, N., Putlier, A., Sukhobok, D., Elvesæter, B., Berre, A.J., Ye, X., Dimitrov, M., Simov, A., Zarev, M., Moynihan, R., Roberts, B., Berlocher, I., Kim, S., Lee, T., Smith, A., Heath, T.: DataGraft: one-stop-shop for open data management. Semantic Web J. (SWJ) – Interoperability, Usability, Applicability (2017, to appear). doi:10.3233/SW-170263. Published and printed by IOS Press, ISSN 1570-0844
9. Roman, D., Dimitrov, M., Nikolov, N., Putlier, A., Sukhobok, D., Elvesæter, B., Berre, A.J., Ye, X., Simov, A., Petkov, Y.: DataGraft: simplifying open data publishing. ESWC (Satell. Events) 2016, 101–106 (2016)
10. Roman, D., Dimitrov, M., Nikolov, N., Putlier, A., Elvesæter, B., Simov, A., Petkov, Y.: DataGraft: a platform for open data publishing. In: The Joint Proceedings of the 4th International Workshop on Linked Media and the 3rd Developers Hackshop, (LIME/SemDev @ESWC 2016)
11. Wang, J., Crawl, D., Altintas, I., Tzoumas, K., Markl, V.: Comparison of distributed data-parallelization patterns for big data analysis: a bioinformatics case study. In: Proceedings of the Fourth International Workshop on Data Intensive Computing in the Clouds (DataCloud) (2013)
12. Ekanayake, J., Li, H., Zhang, B., Gunarathne, T., Bae, S.-H., Qiu, J., Fox, G.: Twister: a runtime for iterative MapReduce. In: Proceedings of the 19th ACM International Symposium on High Performance Distributed Computing (2010)
13. Bala, M., Boussaid, O., Alimazighi, Z.: Big-ETL: extracting-transforming-loading approach for big data. In: Proceedings of International Conference on Parallel and Distributed Processing Techniques and Applications, Las Vegas, Neveda, USA (2015)
14. Krukowski, A., Kompatsiaris, Y., Papadopoulos, S., et al.: Big and Open Data Position Paper (2013). https://nem-initiative.org/wp-content/uploads/2013/11/NEM-PP-016.pdf
15. Akidau, T., Bradshaw, R., Chambers, C., Chernyak, S., Lax, R., Whittle, S.: The dataflow model: a practical approach to balancing correctness, latency, and cost in massive-scale, unbounded, out-of-order data processing. In: Proceedings of the 41st International Conference on Very Large Data Bases, pp. 1792–1803, VLDB Endowment, Kohala Coast, Hawaii (2015)
16. Sims, M., Kurose, J.F., Lesser, V.R.: Streaming versus batch processing of sensor data in a hazardous weather detection system. In: Proceedings of Second Annual IEEE Communications Society Conference on Sensor and Ad Hoc Communications and Networks (SECON 2005) (2005)
17. Shahrivari, S.: Beyond batch processing: towards real-time and streaming big data. Computers 3(4), 117–129 (2014)
18. Furche, T., Gottlob, G., Neumayr, B., Sallinger, E.: Data wrangling for big data: towards a lingua franca for data wrangling (2016)

19. Armbrust, M., Xin, R.S., Lian, C., Huai, Y., Liu, D., Bradley, J.K., Meng, X., Kaftan, T., Franklin, M.J., Ghodsi, A., Zaharia, M.: Spark SQL: relational data processing in spark. In: Proceedings of the 2015 ACM SIGMOD International Conference on Management of Data, pp. 1383–1394. ACM (2015)
20. Zaharia, M., Chowdhury, M., Das, T., Dave, A., Ma, J., McCauley, M., Franklin, M.J., Shenker, S., Stoica, I.: Resilient distributed datasets: a fault-tolerant abstraction for in-memory cluster computing. In: Proceedings of the 9th USENIX Conference on Networked Systems Design and Implementation, p. 2. USENIX Association (2012)
21. Sukhobok, D., Nikolov, N., Roman, D.: Tabular data anomaly patterns. In: 3rd International Conference on Big Data Innovations and Applications. Innovate-Data 2017 (2017, in press)
22. Riazi, S.: SparkGalaxy: workflow-based big data processing (2016)
23. Wang, H., Li, M., Bu, Y., Li, J., Gao, H., Zhang, J.: Cleanix: a parallel big data cleaning system. ACM SIGMOD Rec. **44**(4), 35–40 (2016)
24. Kaur, M., Dhaliwal, G.: Performance comparison of map reduce and Apache Spark. Int. J. Comput. Sci. Eng. **3**(11), 66–69 (2015)

Services

Human-in-the-Loop Simulation of Cloud Services

Nikolaos Bezirgiannis[1(✉)], Frank de Boer[2], and Stijn de Gouw[3]

[1] Leiden Institute for Advanced Computer Science, Leiden, The Netherlands
n.bezirgiannis@umail.leidenuniv.nl
[2] Centrum Wiskunde & Informatica (CWI), Amsterdam, The Netherlands
f.s.de.boer@cwi.nl
[3] Open University, Heerlen, The Netherlands
stijn.degouw@ou.nl

Abstract. In this paper we discuss an integrated tool suite for the simulation of software services which are offered on the Cloud. The tool suite uses the Abstract Behavioral Specification (ABS) language for modeling the software services and their Cloud deployment. For the real-time execution of the ABS models we use a Haskell backend which is based on a source-to-source translation of ABS into Haskell. The tool suite then allows Cloud engineers to interact in real-time with the execution of the model by deploying and managing service instances. The resulting human-in-the-loop simulation of Cloud services can be used both for training purposes and for the (semi-)automated support for the real-time monitoring and management of the actual service instances.

Keywords: Human-in-the-loop simulation · Cloud services · Monitors · Service Level Agreement

1 Introduction

The Abstract Behavioral Specification (ABS) language[1] is an executable modeling language which features powerful abstractions of virtualized resources [7] like CPU time, memory, and bandwidth. As such it is particularly tailored towards modeling and simulation of software services offered on the Cloud [1]. Further, a variety of tools[2] which include simulation with visualization support, deadlock analysis, cost analysis, deployment synthesis, and test case generation, supports the formal development and analysis of software models and their deployment as executable ABS.

The Erlang backend of ABS provides a symbolic interpretation of the abstractions modeling (CPU) time, that is, time is modeled by a symbolic clock which

---

Partly funded by the EU project FP7-610582 Envisage. This work was carried out on the Dutch national e-infrastructure with the support of SURF Foundation.
[1] http://docs.abs-models.org.
[2] http://abs-models.org/abs-tools.

© IFIP International Federation for Information Processing 2017
Published by Springer International Publishing AG 2017. All Rights Reserved
F. De Paoli et al. (Eds.): ESOCC 2017, LNCS 10465, pp. 143–158, 2017.
DOI: 10.1007/978-3-319-67262-5_11

is advanced by the execution of a certain kind of statements, so-called duration statements. In contrast, in this paper we introduce a new Haskell backend, in the sequel denoted by ABS_RT, which is based on a source-to-source translation of ABS into Haskell and which directly relates the ABS abstractions of time to the underlying hardware clock. It should be noted that the term "real-time ABS" has also been used, for example in [8], to refer to the ABS abstractions modeling (CPU) time themselves. In this paper however we use the term "real-time" to refer to the implementation of these abstractions with respect to some external clock, e.g., the hardware clock. This implementation allows for a different kind of simulation, so-called human-in-the-loop simulation, abbreviated in the sequel by HITL. In general this kind of simulations require human interaction and are used for training purposes. A typical example is that of flight simulations where trainees interact in real-time with a model of a plane in flight. Clearly, for such training to be effective the human interactions should be processed by the model in real-time as measured by the hardware clock.

In this paper we introduce the ABS_RT Haskell backend of ABS and present its use by Cloud engineers so that they can interact in real-time with the execution of the model of the services offered on the Cloud. This interaction consists of deploying and managing service instances and allows Cloud engineers to acquire knowledge of the real-time consequences of their decisions. We illustrate this use of HITL simulation of Cloud services by an industrial case study based on the Fredhopper Cloud Services.

Main contribution and related work. There exists a variety of cloud simulation tools including CloudSim [4], GreenCloud [9], and iCanCloud [10]; although all of these tools offer finer-grained analysis (e.g. network configuration and energy consumption in the Cloud) they rely on discrete-event computer simulation engines, which do not permit live HITL intervention on a running simulation. To the best of our knowledge HITL simulation of Cloud services has not been investigated before. As already stated above, HITL simulation allows Cloud engineers to acquire knowledge of the real-time consequences of their decisions directly in an interactive manner.

Our overall contribution is an integrated tool suite which supports HITL simulations of Cloud services. This suite integrates the SAGA tool [3] for the declarative specification of service metric functions, and SmartDeployer [6] for the formalization of deployment requirements and the automatic generation of provisioning scripts. At the core of this suite is a new Haskell backend ABS_RT of the ABS modeling language which supports a real-time interpretation of the timing constructs of ABS. We further illustrate the use of our tool-suite by an industrial case study based on the Fredhopper Cloud Services. The underlying ABS model of the Fredhopper Cloud Services builds on the one presented in [6] which focuses on automated generation of deployment actions. Here we extend that model to support HITL simulation and for the generation of more realistic deployment recommendations.

The general methodology underlying the use of ABS_RT in the HITL simulation of Cloud services involves the formalization of Service Level Agreements

(SLA's) as a property of a service metric function, as described in [5], with a new framework in ABS which captures various monitoring concepts – from QoS and SLAs to lower-level metrics, metric policies, and listenable and billable events. The monitoring framework allows the formal development and analysis of monitors as executable ABS.

Outline of the paper. In the next section we introduce the ABS_RT backend. In Sect. 3 we describe the ABS model of the Fredhopper Cloud Services. The use of ABS_RT in the HITL simulation of this model is described in Sect. 4. The experimental results are described in Sect. 5. Finally, in Sect. 6 we draw some conclusions.

2   The ABS Language

ABS is an executable resource-aware modeling language which at its core integrates an imperative layer based on concurrent objects and a functional layer based on algebraic data types. Concurrent objects are (strongly) typed by interfaces and communicate via asynchronous method calls. Such calls generate messages which are queued to be processed sequentially (by the object callee) up to method completion or deliberate yield of control (cooperative scheduling).

ABS further provides a high-level model of *deployment components* which encapsulate virtualized resources of a computer system like CPU time, memory, and bandwidth. These components are expressed by concurrent objects themselves and as such are an integral part of an ABS model. Objects dynamically deployed onto these components share their resources. Usually the ABS user does not create deployment component objects directly (by calling **new**), but instead through a higher object abstraction named *CloudProvider*, which serves both as a factory of deployment components as well as a communication endpoint to an infrastucture service (IaaS):

```
CloudProvider cp = new AmazonCloudProvider(params);
DeploymentComponent vm1 = cp.createInstance(map[Pair(
    Cores,4), Pair(Speed,35), Pair(Memory,16)]);
[DC: vm1] new WebServer(8080); // deployed object
```

High-level annotations of the ABS code are used to specify the corresponding cost model. A statement in ABS can be annotated by [Cost: intExp()] stmt; which means in practice that *stmt* will be only completed (and its side-effects instantaneously realised) after some time where *intExp* amount of resource *Speed* has been provided and consumed by the currently executing deployment component. This model of deployment as executable ABS allows for a formal analysis of the constraints induced by the shared resources in terms of a formal cost model and its relation to a formalization of Service Level Agreements (SLA's) as a property of a service metric function.

Whereas the *Cost* annotation induces the passage of time *locally* inside the deployment component, the timed-ABS extension of the language enables time to pass globally (over the whole model), always with respect to an external clock.

The statement `await duration(min,max)` means that the current process will be rescheduled for execution only after *min* and less than *max* time steps from now have passed on the clock; the statement `duration (min,max)` will accordingly block the object and all of its process for that time. If the ABS clock refers to symbolic (abstract) time—used for synchronizing distinct parts of the model—then the models' execution is essentially a computer simulation; however, a model running on the real (hardware) clock defines a user-interactive simulation.

Finally, since ABS was primarily designed as a modeling language, it lacks the common I/O functionality found in mainstream programming languages. To allow user interaction a new language extension was introduced to the language built around a REST API. The ABS user may annotate any object declaration with `[HTTPName: strExp()] I o = new ...` to make the object and its fields accessible from the outside as an HTTP endpoint. Any such object can have some of its method definitions annotated with `[HTTPCallable]` to allow them to be called from the outside; the arguments passed and the method's result will be serialized according to a standard JSON format.

The ABS_RT backend. The original Haskell backend of ABS was designed with speed in mind, as well as to offer distributed computing on the cloud [2]. The choice of Haskell was made since it provides language features that closely match those of ABS, and also certain runtime facilities that make the ABS straightforward to implement (e.g. first-class continuations).

At runtime, each ABS concurrent object (or ABS concurrent object group) is associated with one Haskell green thread. Each such thread listens to its own queue for new or re-activated processes and executes 1 at a time up to their next release point (`await` or `return`). The GHC runtime (Haskell's standard compiler) preempts over these green threads, which are automatically load-balanced to system threads to support Symmetric Multi-Processing (multi-core).

During an asynchronous method call, a caller creates a new process by applying the corresponding function to its arguments and ships its body (function closure) to the end of the callee's queue. This shipment is done for the parallel runtime through shared-memory, or for the distributed-runtime through Cloud Haskell (TCP/IP). To complement cooperative scheduling, awaiting on futures is implemented a-top of extra temporary green threads and utilizing an asynchronous I/O event library (e.g. epoll on Linux); await on boolean conditions are optimized to avoid unnecessary busy-wait polling through a more notification-like protocol.

Algebraic-datatypes, parametric polymorphism, interfaces, pure functions are all one-to-one mapped down to Haskell. Haskell's type system lacks subtyping polymorphism, and as such we implement this in the ABS_RT compiler itself through means of implicit coercive subtyping. The REST API extension of ABS utilizes WARP: a high-performance, high-throughtput server library written in Haskell.

Compared to some other backends (Erlang, Java), the Haskell backend does not treat active ABS processes as individual system threads, but instead as data (closures) that are stored in the queue of the concurrent object, which leads to a smaller memory footprint. This "data-oriented" implementation preserves local message ordering of method activations, although the ABS language specification cares to leave this unspecified.

We augment the original Haskell backend with support for the timed-ABS language extension, and name the resuling backend ABS_RT. The clock that ABS_RT uses is the available real-time hardware clock underneath. This means that compared to the backends with a symbolic clock (Erlang, Maude), the passage of time is not influenced by timed-ABS calls but instead by the real clock itself. The `duration` statement is implemented as a *sleep* call on the concurrent object's thread, whereas the `await duration` creates a new extra lightweight thread which will re-schedule its continuation back to the original object thread after the specified time. The `[Cost: x]` annotations are translated to a `executeCost()` method call on the deployment component object as seen in Fig. 1. The `instrPS` field refers to the number of instructions the particular deployment component is able to execute per second. The unit of time (default is seconds) is tunable as a runtime option.

```
Unit executeCost(Int cost) {
    Int remaining = cost;
    while (remaining > this.instrPS) {
      duration(1,1);
      suspend;
      remaining = remaining - this.instrPS;
    }
    Rat last = remaining / this.instrPS;
    duration(last,last);
}
```

Fig. 1. The implementation of cost annotation for the ABS_RT backend

It is worth noting that the GHC runtime scheduler dictates that any "sleeping" thread will be re-activated (preempted) no sooner than the specified time, but may be later than prescribed (not precise). This does affect the reproducibility, among the fact that there is no notion of simultaneous method calls (no specific ordering, thus non-deterministic hardware-dependent process-enqueuing of simultaneous callers) as it can be done with total ordering of symbolic time. Finally, we would like to mention that this real-time implementation as shown in Fig. 1 is generic for any ABS backend that uses the hardware clock and implements *duration/await duration* as a *sleep()* system call. Indeed, it would be straightforward to port it to the Erlang and Java backends as well.

3   FRH Case Study

Fredhopper[3] provides the Fredhopper Cloud Services to offer search and targeting facilities on a large product database to e-Commerce companies as services

---

[3] https://www.fredhopper.com/.

(SaaS) over the cloud computing infrastructure (IaaS). Fredhopper Cloud Services drives over 350 global retailers with more than 16 billion in online sales every year. A customer (service consumer) of Fredhopper is a web shop, and an end user is a visitor to the web shop.

The services offered by Fredhopper are exposed at endpoints. In practice, these services are implemented to be RESTful and accept connections over HTTP. Software services are deployed as *service instances*. The advantages of offering software as a service on the cloud over on-premise deployment include the following: to increase fault tolerance; to handle dynamic throughputs; to provide seamless service update; to increase service testability; and to improve the management of infrastructure. To fully utilize the cloud computing paradigm, software must be designed to be *horizontally* scalable[4]. Typically, software services are deployed as *service instances*. Each instance offers the same service and is exposed via the Load Balancing Service, which in turn offers a service endpoint (Fig. 2). Requests through the endpoint are then distributed over the instances.

The number of requests can vary greatly over time, and typically depends on several factors. For instance, the time of the day in the time zone where most of the end users are located, plays an important role. Typical lows in demand are observed daily between 2 am and 5 am. In the event of varying throughput, a different number of instances may be deployed and be exposed through the same endpoint. Moreover, at any time, if an instance stops accepting requests, a new instance may be deployed in place.

3.1   Architecture of the Fredhopper Cloud Services

Each service instance offers the same service and is exposed via Load Balancer endpoints that distribute requests over the service instances. Figure 2 shows a block diagram of the Fredhopper Cloud Services.

Load Balancing Service. The Load Balancing Service is responsible for distributing requests from service endpoints to their corresponding instances. Currently at Fredhopper, this service is implemented by HAProxy (www.haproxy.org), a TCP/HTTP load balancer.

Platform Service. The Platform Service provides an interface to the Cloud Engineers to manage customer information, deploy and manage service instances associated to the customers, and associate service instance to endpoints (load balancers). The Platform Service takes a service specification, which includes a *resource configuration* for the service, and creates and deploys the specified service. A service specification from a customer determines which type of service is being offered, the number of service instances to be deployed initially for that customer, and the kinds of *virtualized resources* on which the service instances should be deployed.

---

[4] en.wikipedia.org/wiki/Scalability#Horizontal_and_vertical_scaling.

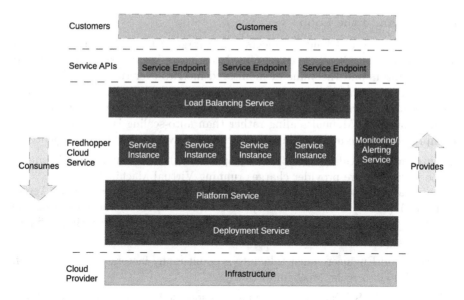

Fig. 2. The architecture of the Fredhopper Cloud Services

Deployment Service. The Deployment Service provides an API to the Platform Service to deploy service instances (using a dedicated Deployment Agent) onto specified virtualized resources provided by the *Infrastructure Service.* The API also offers operations to control the life-cycle of the deployed service instances. The Deployment Service allows the Fredhopper Cloud Services to be independent of the specific infrastructure that underlies the service instances.

Infrastructure Service. The Infrastructure Service offers an API to the Deployment Service to acquire and release virtualized resources. At the time of writing the Fredhopper Cloud Services utilizes virtualized resources from the Amazon Web Services (aws.amazon.com), where processing and memory resources are exposed through Elastic Compute Cloud instances (https://aws.amazon.com/ec2/instance-types/).

Monitoring and Alerting Service. The Monitoring and Alerting Service provides 24/7 monitoring services on the functional and non-functional properties of the services offered by the Fredhopper Cloud Services, the service instances deployed by the Platform Service, and the healthiness of the acquired virtualized resources.

If a monitored property is violated, an alert is raised to the Cloud Engineers via emails and SMS messages, and Cloud Engineers can react accordingly. For example, if the query throughput of a service instance is below a certain threshold, they increase the amount of resources allocated to that service. For broken functional properties, such as a run-time error during service up-time, Cloud Engineers notify Software Engineers for further analysis. Figure 6a shows a visualization of monitors in Grafana, the visualization framework used by ABS.

3.2 Human in the Loop

A dedicated team of Cloud Engineers is in charge of the day to day operation of the Fredhopper Cloud Services. Cloud Engineers keep track of alerts raised by the monitors and the value of monitored metrics over time. Based on their interpretation of this information, using their domain knowledge, Cloud Engineers decide if, when and how to scale up, down or restart services instances and Virtual Machines. Manual scaling rather than auto-scaling is used, as any bug or imprecision in an auto-scaling approach may have disastrous consequences:

1. Automatically scaling up too much jeopardizes the continuity of the business: the infrastructure provider charges running Virtual Machines.
2. Automatically scaling down too much may break the Service Level Agreement(s) (SLAs) between Fredhopper and customers. In the most extreme case, the web shop of a customer may become unavailable, resulting in financial and reputation damage.

The Cloud Engineers must take into account many factors when deciding if, when and how to scale. Most importantly:

– The target QoS values for service metrics specified in the SLA between Fredhopper and the customer.
– Logical and resource requirements on the deployment[5].
– General business KPIs.

Finding scaling actions resulting in a deployment satisfying all above desiderata, and applying them at the right time is a challenging task due to several reasons.

SLAs traditionally are informal natural language documents, not represented at the software level. Thus, metrics tracked by the monitoring system (i.e., memory consumption), are not directly related to SLAs between Fredhopper and its customers. The Cloud Engineer must manually infer a relation between a combination of the metrics from the monitoring system (typically lower-level), and the metrics in the SLA (typically higher-level, aggregated at the customer level).

Synthesizing a deployment satisfying all logical and resource requirements is a computationally complex task for Cloud Engineers. Even taking only the resource requirements into consideration, it is an instance of the NP-hard multi-dimensional multi-knapsack problem, where the items are service instances (whose weights are the resource requirements for the service, like the amount of memory needed, minimal speed of CPU, etc.), and the knapsacks are virtual machines. Logical requirements must also be taken into account. For example, which service instances should be co-located on the same VM, and which to deploy on a dedicated VM? For example, the Query service requires the presence of the Deployment service to function properly. Another logical requirement is to scale with multiple VMs simultaneously in different available zones (locations) in each region. This is mandated by most infrastructure providers to be eligible for compensation for faulty VMs.

In the next section we describe how HITL simulation of ABS models can be used to improve the above practice of Cloud engineers.

---

[5] A deployment associates service instances to Virtual Machines.

4   Human-in-the-loop Framework

Our tool suite for HITL simulations of Cloud services integrates several different tools.

- The SAGA tool [3] was tweaked for monitoring SLA metrics and the Grafana framework visualizes the metrics
- The SmartDeployer [6] for synthesizing deployment actions
- A logreplay tool for replaying real-world log files
- The new Haskell ABS_RT backend for real-time simulations (Sect. 2).

We discuss below how each of these tools was exploited to contribute to the support for realistic HITL simulations.

We defined a new layered declarative generic framework in ABS which captures various monitoring concepts – from QoS and SLAs to lower-level metrics, metric policies, and listenable and billable events. This framework exploits the SAGA tool for the declarative specification of service metric functions which are used to formalize SLA's. A service metric function is defined by a mapping of (time-stamped) event traces to values which indicate the different levels of the provided quality of service. These events represent client interactions with an endpoint of an exposed service API. Each monitor captures a single metric, and based on the value of that metric, suggest scaling actions to improve that metric. The `MonitoringService` periodically polls the registered monitors at a user-configured interval to retrieve its suggested scaling actions. An `await duration(1,1)` statement is used to advance the clock and determine which monitors to poll at the current time.

Our tool suite further integrates SmartDeployer [6] for the formalization of deployment requirements, and the automatical derivation of an executable (in ABS) provisioning script that synthesizes a deployment satisfying all specified requirements. By further integrating SmartDeployer actions into the executable, SLA-level monitors generated by SAGA, we have a formalized model that automatically suggests appropriate scaling actions at the right time: when the values of the SLA metrics give rise to it.

The simulation itself consists of replaying a log file generated by the actual system on the ABS model of the system. The logreplay tool is responsible for firing at appropriate times a REST API call (as explain in Sect. 2) to the running simulation for each request recorded in the log file. These requests will trigger ABS code that contains *Cost* annotations (Fig. 3), which has the effect of the real-time simulation as defined for the ABS_RT backend.

This model includes automatically generated monitors in ABS which integrate the declarative specification of service metric functions of SAGA and the provisioning scripts of SmartDeployer. In the simulation Cloud engineers then can interactively select the scaling actions recommended by the different monitors and thus acquire realtime knowledge of their consequences. In general, these selections requires specific domain knowledge which includes knowledge of past behavior. For simplicity, Cloud Engineers can interact with a running HITL simulation via an HTML/Javascript graphical user interface; a live screenshot is

```
Bool invoke(Int request){
  print("Executing request in service:"+serviceId);
  [Cost : cost(request)] reqCount = ( reqCount + 1 );
  return True;
}
```

Fig. 3. ABS method that process each incoming request from the log-file

shown in Fig. 5. This interface makes also use of the REST API (Fig. 4) extension as implemented in the ABS_RT backend, for fetching the metric history and recommendations.

```
{ // ... main block header omitted
[HTTPName:"monitoringService"] IMonitoringService ms
  =new MonitoringService();
[HTTPName:"monitor1"] IDegradationMonitor dm
  =new DegradationMonitor(deployer1);
ms!addMonitor(Rule(5000,dm)); // registers a new monitor
[HTTPName:"queryService"] IMonitoringQueryEndpoint ep
  =new MonitoringQueryEndpoint(loadBalancerEndPoints,dm);
println("Endpoints set up. Waiting for requests...");
}
```

Fig. 4. The main ABS block exposing the FRH services through the REST API.

This model-based approach of ABS and its toolset can also be used by the Cloud Engineers as a semi-automated support system: the Engineer still interacts with the Fredhopper Cloud Services to perform at the right time the desired scaling actions suggested by the framework. To achieve this the REST API can be used to forward queries in real-time from the production system to the ABS monitors, whereas the CloudProvider interface deploys actual IaaS virtual machines. Hence to allow the Cloud Engineer to engage in simulating real-world scenarios, or simply to interact with the system in a meaningful manner, we believe it is crucial that the simulation executes *in real-time*.

5   Experimental Results

The FRH case study and its ABS model ($\approx$ 2.000 lines of code[6]) forms the basis of our experimental results. We focus on the following metric, which is part of the SLA negotiated between Fredhopper and its customers (the exact percentages are not fixed, they can be negotiated by customers):

---

[6] The source code for the FRH model is at http://github.com/abstools/habs-frh.

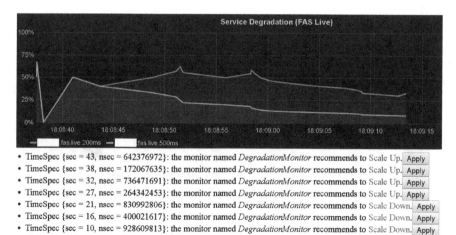

- TimeSpec {sec = 43, nsec = 642376972}: the monitor named *DegradationMonitor* recommends to Scale Up. Apply
- TimeSpec {sec = 38, nsec = 172067635}: the monitor named *DegradationMonitor* recommends to Scale Up. Apply
- TimeSpec {sec = 32, nsec = 736471691}: the monitor named *DegradationMonitor* recommends to Scale Up. Apply
- TimeSpec {sec = 27, nsec = 264342453}: the monitor named *DegradationMonitor* recommends to Scale Up. Apply
- TimeSpec {sec = 21, nsec = 830992806}: the monitor named *DegradationMonitor* recommends to Scale Down. Apply
- TimeSpec {sec = 16, nsec = 400021617}: the monitor named *DegradationMonitor* recommends to Scale Down. Apply
- TimeSpec {sec = 10, nsec = 928609813}: the monitor named *DegradationMonitor* recommends to Scale Down. Apply
- TimeSpec {sec = 5, nsec = 453975631}: the monitor named *DegradationMonitor* recommends to Scale Up. Apply

Fig. 5. The GUI of the HITL framework intended for training Cloud Engineers.

"Services must maintain 95% of the queries with less than 200 ms of processing time, and 99% with less than 500 ms, subtracting the 2% slowest queries."

Initially, our experiments were focused on the FRH case study behavior when simulating its model (expressed in ABS) without any human intervention. A provisioning script generated by SmartDeployer automatically instantiated all services of the Cloud Architecture (Fig. 2), requested suitable VMs from the `CloudProvider` and deployed the various kinds of Service instances shown in the diagram on it. For the `QueryService`, a minimal setup was used with a single instance (co-located with a `DeploymentService` instance) deployed to an Amazon `m4.large` VM. The input to the simulation was a real-world log file of a particular customer with length of 4 min and 30 s, coming from a single production VM (of type `m4.large`). Figure 6a visualizes the Service Degradation of that log file (customer names are anonymized); We then proceeded with simulating the FRH system on the Haskell and Erlang backends of ABS, inputted with the same exact log and using the same deployment scenario.

The simulation of the FRH model on the Haskell-ABS backend took 4 min and 30 s to complete, which matches the log's length and encourages us to believe that the simulation is done in real-time. The output of the simulation on the Haskell backend is shown in Fig. 6b. There is a deviation that can be seen when comparing it to the original graph of Fig. 6a: the Haskell output reports higher degradation than what would be expected from the real-world log. This can be attributed to three causes; first, there is the overhead of processing the log file itself (network communicating to the logreplay tool). Secondly, the simulation of the real-time measurements of the log file involves *sleep* system calls, which as explained in Sect. 2, dictates that any "sleeping" thread will be re-activated

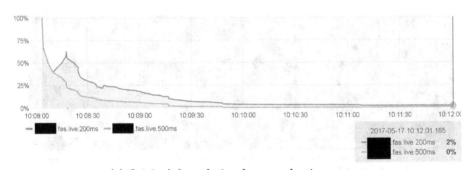

(a) Original degradation from production system

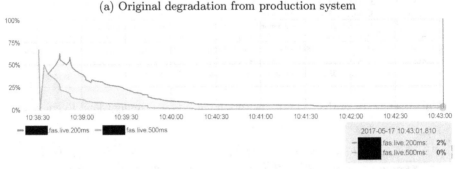

(b) Haskell simulation of the degradation when simulating the original log

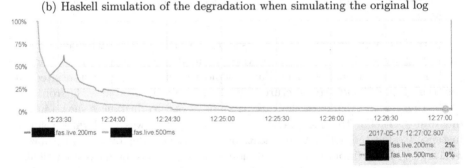

(c) Erlang simulation of the degradation when simulating the original log

Fig. 6. Degradation in the production system and as simulated on different backends

no sooner than the specified time, but most likely later than prescribed, which depends on factors such as backend implementation, hardware configuration, or the workload of the particular model. Fortunately none of these had great effect on the models we tested, and the reported degradation is negligibly affected by this. The last cause which however has a larger effect on the degradation is that the log file contains a certain number of concurrent requests (requests on a single machine that were served concurrently in time). The recorded processing time of the requests are translated into *Cost* annotations (taking into account the resource capacities of the machine that has processed the request), and therefore the concurrent execution of such requests in the simulation as described in Fig. 1

will further increase the *simulated* processing time of the individual requests. In general, the recorded processing time of the individual requests includes the overhead of time sharing and as such do not specify their "intrinsic" processing time. In practice we think one can obtain a "correct" model by approximating these intrinsic processing time of the individual requests by averaging over different log files and different deployment scenarios.

Moving on to the Erlang symbolic-time simulation, we observe slight inaccuracies of the output (Fig. 6c) compared to the original graph. These inaccuracies can be attributed to two reasons: first, the monitors act autonomously (`while (True){await duration(1,1);...}`), so they may uncontrollably advance the symbolic time by themselves between REST calls of the logreplay tool; as a result the graph is slightly "stretched" because of extra erroneous time advancements. We propose two ways to mitigate this at the ABS language level: (a) having a statement `every(intExp()){body};` which will register the body as a callback to be executed with the period given or (b) a statement `await until(t);` which will resume the process only after the specific time given. In either case the two statements do not advance the time by themselves. The other reason which leads to inacccuracies is that the concurrent requests of the log are processed sequentially (as opposed to Haskell) because of practical difficulties of synchronizing an external tool that uses the real-world clock (logreplay) and the Erlang-ABS runtime which uses the symbolic clock. Since, as mentioned before part of the requests in the log happen to be concurrent, the resulted degradation of the Erlang simulation may differ from the expected original.

The Erlang-ABS backend took 15 min and 30 s to complete the simulation of real-world 4 min and 30 s of the log. This may be attributed to the fact that the granularity of the request timestamps is per *ms* (as given in the log file). We could speed it up by having a more coarse-grained (less accurate) timestamps. Furthermore, the Erlang backend does not use a (parallel) Discrete-Event simulation runtime (called also as-fast-as-possible computer simulation) but a timed-automata inspired runtime for the advancement of the clock, which requires a computationally-heavier continuous global administration of the simulation. Given the reasons above, the code for the monitors `while (True){await duration(1,1);...}` affects the execution speed. A way to mitigate this is again to have a coarser periodicity for the monitors. Based on these experimental findings, we believe in general simulation frameworks based on symbolic time are not suited for HITL simulations of Cloud applications.

To evaluate the HITL simulation of FRH case study, a training exercise was carried out for the Cloud Engineers. Using our framework, we first visualized the Service Degradation of a different real-world log file, but include the same Service Degradation metric from the SLA as above. The deployment configuration used for that customer was the initial default configuration used by the Cloud Ops team, which provisions the minimum number of VM's, and each VM has as few resources as needed by the services running on the VM. In particular, aside from the Service instances shared between different customers, such as the `PlatformService` and `LoadbalancerService`, the non-shared initial default

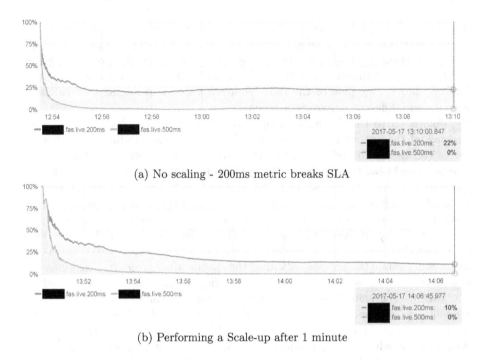

(a) No scaling - 200ms metric breaks SLA

(b) Performing a Scale-up after 1 minute

Fig. 7. No-scaling versus scaling during the haskell simulation

per-customer setup consisted of 1 query service instance and a corresponding deployment service instance in every availability zone (in the region of the customer), and those were deployed on an Amazon VM with instance type m4.large.

Figure 7a shows the resulting Service Degradation for that customer on this deployment configuration. The graph shows that in the beginning, performance is low (and Service Degradation is high). This is caused by the fact that after a service is started, an initialization phase is triggered, and performance is (as expected) low during this phase. After a few minutes, initialization finishes and the service degradation metrics stabilize to around 20% queries slower than 200 ms and 0% queries slower than 500 ms (subtracting the two percent slowest queries). This means that while the target QoS as agreed in the SLA for the category "slower than 500 ms" is achieved, this is (by far) not the case for the category "slower than 200 ms".

After establishing that the initial default deployment configuration was not sufficient to satisfy the SLA as agreed with that customer (on that real-world query log file), the training exercise continued. The Cloud Ops were tasked with selecting and executing appropriate scaling actions to mitigate the situation. The scaling actions could be selected through the ABS REST API, or in a very simple front-end (Fig. 5).

During the training exercise, several different scenarios were trained; Fig. 7b shows one scenario of the effect on the Service Degradation after the engineer decided to scale up with 2 query services instances (and corresponding deployment service instance) in two zones on a (simulated) Amazon m4.xlarge instance after 1 min (13:51) into the simulation. At time 13:54 the new machines have finished initializing, and the services deployed on them have been started. After that time, the 200 ms metric quickly improves , and after about 25 min reaches the target ≤ 5% degradation.

The integrated tool suite described in Sect. 4 considerably simplified the task of the Cloud Engineers in managing the day-to-day operation of the Cloud services. In particular:

- The support for real-time simulation was critical in providing a realistic training experience for the cloud engineers. It allowed the Ops to evaluate and view metrics of the system and apply corrective actions to the system *at the same speed as they do in the production environment.*
- The high abstraction level of the metrics captured by the ABS monitoring framework enables *SLA-based scaling*, simplifying the decision process of the Cloud ops in selecting the appropriate corrective scaling actions. Still, domain knowledge of the Cloud operator is crucial to properly "translate" their interpretation of multiple (possibly conflicting) metrics over time into corrective actions. The direct relation of the metrics to SLAs and business KPIs in our tool suite eliminated the burden on the Cloud ops to manually interpret how traditional lower-level metrics (such as CPU usage, memory consumption) relate to the higher-level SLA/KPI metrics.
- By suggesting to the Cloud ops only a limited number of possible corrective actions (synthesized by SmartDeployer), the number of choices the Cloud Op has to take in real-time (i.e.: which and how many services to deploy, how to link them, on what kind of VM to deploy them, etc.) was reduced substantially. Since the SmartDeployer actions are synthesized based on the deployment requirements and Smartdeployer generates a corresponding provisioning script, the numerous deployment requirements are satisfied automatically "by construction". However, the quality of the suggestions (actions) proposed by the framework should be improved.

In principle, the suggested SmartDeployer scaling actions could be exploited for a full auto-scaling approach, without any human intervention. We carried out initial experiments, but it turned out to be very complex how to deal with different monitors from heterogeneous sources that give conflicting scaling suggestions, taking into account machine booting time, upcoming promotions from web-shops where peaks in demand are expected, historic data, etc. Thus keeping the human in the loop - the cloud engineers with their domain knowledge - still is crucial to optimize the day-to-day management of services.

6   Conclusion

Our initial experimental results on the use of the presented tool suite provides clear evidence for the viability of HITL simulation of Cloud services for training purposes. The training sessions themselves can further be used to provide feedback to the underlying ABS models of the Cloud services and the monitors. Ultimately, the resulting fine-tuning of these models may reach a level of maturity and confidence that allows their deployment in the real-time monitoring and management of the actual service instances.

In general, we believe that HITL simulation of Cloud services provides a variety of interesting and challenging research problems, for example mining the log files to calculate an approximation of the "intrinsic" processing time of the individual service requests, cancelling the effect of time sharing.

References

1. Albert, E., de Boer, F.S., Hähnle, R., Johnsen, E.B., Schlatte, R., Tarifa, S.L.T., Wong, P.Y.H.: Formal modeling and analysis of resource management for cloud architectures: an industrial case study using real-time ABS. Serv. Oriented Comput. Appl. **8**(4), 323–339 (2014)
2. Bezirgiannis, N., de Boer, F.: ABS: a high-level modeling language for cloud-aware programming. In: Freivalds, R.M., Engels, G., Catania, B. (eds.) SOFSEM 2016. LNCS, vol. 9587, pp. 433–444. Springer, Heidelberg (2016). doi:10.1007/978-3-662-49192-8_35
3. de Boer, F.S., de Gouw, S.: Combining monitoring with run-time assertion checking. In: Bernardo, M., Damiani, F., Hähnle, R., Johnsen, E.B., Schaefer, I. (eds.) SFM 2014. LNCS, vol. 8483, pp. 217–262. Springer, Cham (2014). doi:10.1007/978-3-319-07317-0_6
4. Calheiros, R.N., Ranjan, R., Beloglazov, A., De Rose, C.A.F., Buyya, R.: Cloudsim: A toolkit for modeling and simulation of cloud computing environments and evaluation of resource provisioning algorithms. Softw. Pract. Exp. **41**(1), 23–50 (2011)
5. Giachino, E., de Gouw, S., Laneve, C., Nobakht, B.: Statically and dynamically verifiable SLA metrics. In: Theory and Practice of Formal Methods - Essays Dedicated to Frank de Boer on the Occasion of His 60th Birthday, pp. 211–225 (2016)
6. de Gouw, S., Mauro, J., Nobakht, B., Zavattaro, G.: Declarative elasticity in ABS. In: Aiello, M., Johnsen, E.B., Dustdar, S., Georgievski, I. (eds.) ESOCC 2016. LNCS, vol. 9846, pp. 118–134. Springer, Cham (2016). doi:10.1007/978-3-319-44482-6_8
7. Johnsen, E.B.: Separating cost and capacity for load balancing in ABS deployment models. In: Giachino, E., Hähnle, R., Boer, F.S., Bonsangue, M.M. (eds.) FMCO 2012. LNCS, vol. 7866, pp. 145–167. Springer, Heidelberg (2013). doi:10.1007/978-3-642-40615-7_5
8. Johnsen, E.B., Schlatte, R., Tapia Tarifa, S.L.T.: Modeling resource-aware virtualized applications for the cloud in real-time ABS. In: Aoki, T., Taguchi, K. (eds.) ICFEM 2012. LNCS, vol. 7635, pp. 71–86. Springer, Heidelberg (2012). doi:10.1007/978-3-642-34281-3_8
9. Kliazovich, D., Bouvry, P., Audzevich, Y., Khan, S.U.: Greencloud: a packet-level simulator of energy-aware cloud computing data centers. In: 2010 IEEE Global Telecommunications Conference GLOBECOM 2010, pp. 1–5, December 2010
10. Núñez, A., Vázquez-Poletti, J.L., Caminero, A.C., Castañé, G.G., Carretero, J., Llorente, I.M.: iCanCloud: a flexible and scalable cloud infrastructure simulator. J. Grid Comput. **10**(1), 185–209 (2012)

Toward Automatic Semantic API Descriptions to Support Services Composition

Marco Cremaschi$^{(\boxtimes)}$ and Flavio De Paoli

Department of Informatics, Systems and Communication,
University of Milan - Bicocca, Viale Sarca 336/14, Milan, Italy
{cremaschi,depaoli}@disco.unimib.it

Abstract. The ability to provide appropriate and complete API descriptions to let users discover services that satisfy a set of requirements and compose them to fulfil more complex users' needs is critical for the success of any modern ICT solution. Composition suffers from the lack of semantic matching between properties included in published API descriptions. The work presented in this paper addresses this issue by discussing the current formats and tools to build API descriptions, and presenting a method for extracting and associating semantic to properties. Such method relies on a revised version of Table Interpretation techniques to support semantic annotations of API properties. The objectives are to enrich the popular OpenAPI Specification format with semantic annotations, and add the functionality of semantic annotation and composition to the associated editor.

1 Introduction

The ability to provide appropriate and complete API descriptions to let users discover services that satisfy a set of requirements and compose them to fulfil more complex users' needs is critical for the success of any modern ICT solution. Extensive researches have been conducted with the vision to create automatic integration of Web Services and APIs. Most of these approaches face the problem to make candidate APIs communicate each others due to the lack of semantic matching between input and output data. Although implementing APIs has become common practice, meta-level API definition and implementation have yet to be settled to widely-accepted standards [14]. To automate the interactions between APIs a semantics description of the exchanged data is needed. Approaches to achieve the goal are: creating API descriptions in a logic-based language (e.g., RDF), or linking existing descriptions to shared domain vocabularies or ontologies (e.g., DBpedia). As the former needs expertise in logic-based languages, its adoption has demonstrated to be curtailed; the latter is more approachable, and enriching existing descriptions reduces the effort required.

The work presented in this paper has been partially supported by the EU H2020 project EW-Shopp - Supporting Event and Weather-based Data Analytics and Marketing along the Shopper Journey - Grant n. 732590.

F. De Paoli et al. (Eds.): ESOCC 2017, LNCS 10465, pp. 159–167, 2017.
DOI: 10.1007/978-3-319-67262-5_12

There are many active initiatives to promote the creation and publication of descriptions associated with APIs (see Sect. 2). A shortcoming is the lack of support to add detailed information that qualifies the properties of an API (e.g., classification of input and response data). As a result, these formats are suitable to complete simple tasks, but inefficient in automatic API discovery and composition due to the lack of machine processable semantics [16]. A critical aspect is the capability of including metadata, which can be interpreted by machine agents in a bottom up way (i.e., information structure should be in pieces to whole) [17]. In the real world, a developer may need to compose APIs that refer, for example, to location information. He or she may search directories such as Programmable Web[1], collect descriptions, and understand the meaning of involved terms, e.g., understand that *address* refers to *city* and *street*, and *latitude/longitude* refer to a geographic *area*; but a machine agent is unable to understand those links without a shared representation of property semantics. The use of links to concepts in shared vocabularies allows machine agents to address the issue.

The goal of our project is to (semi)automatically create semantic descriptions that correlate properties at semantic level to enhance interoperability and composition by machine. The adopted methodology is: (i) evaluate the current approaches to create API descriptions to identify a reference format; (ii) develop a Table Interpretation method to collect sample data from existing APIs and associate them to appropriate concepts from shared vocabularies; and finally (iii) develop methods to support automatic composition. In this paper we concentrate on the first two steps to describe the approach and outline the tools under development. This work roots and extends the one presented in [10] by proposing a more effective Table Interpretation technique, and an initial set of composition rules.

Section 2 discusses the different approaches to API descriptions and motivate the choice of addressing OpenAPI Specification as the reference standard. Section 3 illustrates the methods to extract information and associate them with semantic concepts. Section 4 outlines composition techniques and shortly describe the ongoing works on tools development and testing, and finally Sect. 5 illustrates conclusions and future work.

2   Service Descriptions: State of the Art

Descriptions have been classified into functional, dealing with provided APIs and exchanged parameters to state what a service provide and how to access it, and non-functional, dealing with meta information that allow potential users to understand how a given service provides its service [9]. A further classification splits descriptions in syntactic and semantic. The former dealing with the format of calls and exchanged messages, and the latter adding a meaning to the description terms.

---

[1] http://www.programmableweb.com.

The most popular syntactic description model is WSDL 2.0 (Web Services Description Language) [3], which defines an XML format for describing Web services by separating the abstract functionality offered by a service from concrete details such as "how" and "where" that functionality is offered. Although it supports descriptions of both SOAP-based services, and REST/API services, it is the de-facto standard for the former, but is rarely adopted for the latter. The Web Application Description Language (WADL) [6] is a machine-readable XML format that was explicitly proposed for API services. WADL was also proposed for standardisation, but there was no follow-up.

More recently, *user-friendly* and *easy-to-use* metadata formats have been introduced, along with editors to support developers in the creation of descriptions for REST APIs. Among others, popular description formats are the Open API Specification (OAS)[2] (also known as Swagger specification), which provides human-readable API descriptions based on YAML and JSON. RAML is a YAML-based language for describing RESTful APIs. API Blueprint is a documentation-oriented web API description language, which provides a set of semantic assumptions laid on top of the Markdown syntax. The Hydra specification, which is currently under heavy development, tries to enrich current web APIs with tools and techniques from the semantic web area.

The OAS is the most promising choice at the moment [15], since (i) a simple format to specify descriptions, and (ii) a large set of vendor-neutral API tools, supported by a very large community of active users, are provided. Such tools provide great support to almost every modern programming languages to create and test APIs. Moreover, the Open API Initiative is an open source project sustained by relevant stakeholders, such as Google, IBM, Microsoft and PayPal[3].

The description formats discussed so far are mainly syntactic, which means that little support to automate operations such as services discovery and composition, and verification of coherence to given interaction and building patterns is provided. Although there are many approaches proposed to enrich services descriptions with semantics, the manual work required to create descriptions, and the lack of interoperability standards limited their adoption. The initial approach proposed by the semantic web community was to define a global ontology to include model, definitions and descriptions in a coherent system that can be used to make discovery and automatic composition. The most popular proposals are OWL-S (Ontology Web Language for Services) [11] and WSMO (Web Service Modelling Ontology) [13]. The major problem with these approaches is the expertise required to build and manage such descriptions. The result is that nobody actually use them. Anyway, the knowledge gained with these semantic studies has led to the definition of simpler and easier models that marries the annotation approach introduced by hRESTS and RDFa.

Table 1 illustrates the characteristics of API description models with respect to the supported type of services (SOAP and/or REST), the capability of hosting semantic annotations, the serialisation language to publish the descriptions,

---

[2] https://www.openapis.org/specification/repo.
[3] https://www.openapis.org/membership/members.

Table 1. Comparison of API description standards.

Description	Service type	Semantics		Serialization	Tool	Human readable
		Yes/No	Format			
WSDL [3]	v1.1 SOAP v2.0 REST	No	-	XML	Yes	No
WADL [6]	REST	No	-	XML	Yes	No
hREST [7]	REST	No	-	Microformat	No	Yes
RDFa [1]	REST	No	-	HTML+RDF	No	Yes
OpenAPI Specification	REST	No	-	YAML, JSON	Yes	Yes
RAML	REST	No	-	YAML	Yes	Yes
API Blueprint	REST	No	-	Markdown	Yes	Yes
OWL-S [11]	SOAP REST	Yes	OWL	OWL	No	No
WSMO [13]	SOAP REST	Yes	MOF^a	MOF	No	No
SA-WSDL [8]	v1.1 SOAP v2.0 REST	Yes	RDF	XML	No	No
Micro WSMO [7]	REST	Yes	RDF	RDF	No	Yes
SA-REST [5]	REST	Yes	RDF, OWL	RDF	No	Yes

^{a} Meta-Object Facility

Table 2. Comparison of API description models.

Detail/Model		API blueprint	RAML	WADL	OpenAPI spec
Format		Markdown	YAML	XML	YAML, JSON
Licence		MIT	ASL2.0	Sun	ASL 2.0
Available		Github	Github	www.w3c.org	Github
Sponsored by		Apiary	Mulesoft	Sun	Reverb
Version		Format 1A revision 7	1.0	31 August 2009	2.0
Initial commit		Apr 2013	Sep 2013	Nov 2006	Jul 2011
Pricing plan		Yes	Yes	No	No
StackOverflow questions	2015	75	37	156	732
	2017	921	644	1,075	8,954
Github stars	2015	1,819	1,058	N/A	2,459
	2017	5,390	2,735		6,360

the availability of supporting tools, and finally the human readability of the descriptions. Table 2 is an adapted and updated version of the one presented in [15] to compare the number of questions posed in Stack Overflow and the number of stars (showing appreciation to a project) received by the four description models under study. The numbers give evidence of increasing interests in the use of description models. The presence of a comprehensive set of tools that support the creation, publication, use and maintenance of service descriptions is one of the most relevant elements that state the success of a description model. The most popular model is OAS, which we consider as reference format for our research that aims at delivering semantic-enabled tools for describing and discovering first, and then compose API services.

3   An Approach to Semantic Description Building

The task of building descriptions has been recognised as a critical activity mainly for the effort needed to actually write such descriptions, and the expertise required to deliver semantic enriched descriptions. The use of tools that (semi)automatically extract information to enrich existing descriptions should be the right approach to incrementally build effective descriptions. In this project we adopt the best practices proposed by the OAS model, which have been already implemented in the Swagger editor[4], and extend them to add semantic annotations. The extension consists in the definition of new elements in the description format to host semantics, and a technique to identify such annotations by collecting actual responses of services. The process of annotating an API description consists of three steps: (i) building a table with the results collected from actual executions of the service; (ii) annotate the table by a Table Interpretation technique; and finally (iii) include the annotations in the API description.

The execution of a set of calls on the bases of the *input parameters*[5] in the existing descriptions allows for collecting responses to create a table with *properties*[6] populating the header row and responses data populating the columns. The Table Interpretation technique [18] allows for extracting semantic information from a table, which means give an interpretation to the values in structured data sources.

An algorithm analyses the table content and associates the semantic concepts (or classes, types) extracted from ontologies in the Linked Open Data Cloud (LOD), which represents the knowledge in a certain domain. In this way API's properties and values can be "understood" by a computer. Based on the state of the art [12,18], given a well-formed relational table and reference sets of concepts (e.g., DBpedia classes), datatypes (e.g., DBpedia datatypes), named entities (e.g., DBpedia resources) and relations (e.g., DBpedia objectProperty and datatypeProperty), a Table Interpretation process is composed of these tasks:

1. classify columns as a "literal column" (Literal column) if contains generic data (e.g., strings, numbers, dates) or as a "named entities columns" (NE-column) if contains instances of a concept (e.g., dbr:Milan is a dbo:City);
2. annotate column headers with concepts if they contain entity mentions (NE-column) (e.g., the header *city* can be mapped to dbo:City), or properties of concepts if they contain literals (Literal column) (e.g., the header *latLng* can be mapped to *geo:location*);
3. disambiguate entity mentions in "content cells" (or simply cells) by linking them to the existing reference entities (e.g., *Milan* and *London* can be mapped to *dbr:Milan* and *dbr:London*);

---

[4] https://swagger.io/swagger-editor/.
[5] https://github.com/OAI/OpenAPI-Specification/blob/master/versions/2.0.md#parameters-definitions-object.
[6] https://github.com/OAI/OpenAPI-Specification/blob/master/versions/2.0.md#schema-object.

4. identify the relations between columns (e.g., set a relation between columns *city* and *country* using *dbo:country*). The type of relationship can be an object property if it connects two semantic concepts (from NE-column to a NE-column), or a data-type property if it links a concept to its specific property (from the NE-column to a literal column).

Once the annotation has been identified, the API description we propose to enrich a OpenAPI Specification adding two new properties: (i) *classAnnotation* to hold the annotations relating to the type of the columns, (ii) *propertyAnnotation* to hold the annotations that represent the relationships between columns. Semantic annotations included in the description take the form of URIs that uniquely identifies the concepts and relations in the reference ontologies.

Inputs need a different approach since the input parameters cannot populate a table. Natural Language Processing (NLP) techniques [4] can help to extract entities from the textual description associated with the API. Such entities will be sought after in reference ontologies, and the user needs to validate or modify the candidate annotations.

Listing 1.1 show an example of an OpenAPI description augmented with semantic annotation. This API provides a list of spots (places to practice surf) in the specified city. Listing shows how the input parameter "city" has been annotated with the class *City* and "name" with the class *Place* of DBpedia (*classAnnotation*). Similarly, classes have been identified for the other properties. In addition, "address" and "country" have been annotated with *propertyAnnotations* to qualify them as related to "name", which has been identified as a main property, through the relations *dbo:address* and *dbo:country*, respectively.

4   Composition Rules

As noted above, the annotations can enable the composition of services, which mainly takes the form of "mashup" of API responses. Let's proceed with an example to clarify what we mean by API composition. Assume that a professional surfer wants to find the best location (spot) to practise. The sportsman want to choose the spot, based on personal preferences and/or the context (e.g., weather and sea conditions, spot facilities, accessibility, etc.). Unfortunately, he has to invoke different services (e.g., weather forecast, spot list) to collect data before making an informed decision. The surfer saves time and effort if all data are available in an aggregated way; for example the list of spots returned by the previous API can be composed with an API that provide information about weather[7] or sea condition[8], or with a list of surf schools[9].

Two kind of composition patterns can be identified: *flow composition*, which means that all or part of the output of an API is used as input of another API; and *parallel composition* (or mashup of outputs).

---

[7] https://www.wunderground.com/weather/api.

[8] https://developer.worldweatheronline.com/api/marine-weather-api.aspx.

[9] http://www.surfline.com/home/index.cfm.

In the former, if inputs and outputs are not of the same type, an additional API that allows conversion or integration of data is needed. In the example, to compose the API regarding sea condition and spot list, a third API that convert the address of a spot into latitude and longitude (e.g., Google Maps API) is required. This two new parameters can be used to invoke sea-condition API. The second pattern foresees that the responses from an API will be filtered out with the responses from another API. The user can define what are the discriminating properties for the composition. The user can also define the metrics that will be used in the composition of the responses. These metrics are: strings similarity metrics that are used for text fields; and, definition of ranges, used for properties with numeric values. Regarding the example, the spot list can be merged with the list of surf schools.

The described compositions can be performed automatically by exploiting semantic descriptions by applying the following rules:

Annotations referring to a single ontology, same concepts. If the properties of two APIs refer to the same concepts in an ontology, the composition is straightforward.

Annotations referring to a single ontology, different concepts. If the involved concepts are related to rdfs:subClassOf or rdfs:subPropertyOf, as defined by the RDF Schema [2], to indicate respectively the sub-class relationship, in which all instances of the class are also instances of the class indicated by the object, and the sub-property relationship, that is, a defined property as a specialization of another property, the composition can be performed by considering the parent classes.

Annotation referring to different ontologies. If the involved concepts belongs to different ontologies, the composition becomes straightforward if the ontologies are *aligned* (e.g., relations of type owl:sameAs exist between the two ontologies).

The algorithms discussed in the previous sections have been implemented by extending the Swagger editor that can now support both the annotation of API descriptions and composition of API. According to the test-first principle, a set of API descriptions have been created. They are realistic since they derive from real ones identified in Programmable Web, include all relevant property types, and address possible composition patterns. The test phase is still ongoing, but the initial results are encouraging since about 70% of the tested patterns was successfully accomplished. The compositions that failed involved semantic descriptions that included hierarchical concepts, which will trigger a further refinement of the algorithm.

5   Conclusions and Future Work

The work presented in this paper is part of the EW-Shopp H2020 project that aims to provide real-time responsive services to integrate consumer and market data with weather and event data in the digital marketing domain. The semantic annotation of such services is crucial to prepare the data to support analytics and decision making. It can be accomplished by linking properties and associated values of services to concepts in shared ontologies. Such knowledge can be extracted by techniques like Table Interpretation that has been introduced and exploited to populate OAS descriptions. The current activity deals with testing to perform an initial validation and tune up of the table annotation and annotation techniques against a set of selected artificial and real services. Future work will deal with extensive validation activities against the large set of real-world APIs developed within EW-Shopp to evaluate usability (the goal is to build effective tools for developers with little experience on semantic techniques), and effectiveness (the challenge is to be able to augment and compose generic APIs as well as generic data sources published in marketplaces) of the tools.

Listing 1.1. Example of API description following OAS with annotation of input parameter and properties.

```
1   prefix dbo: <http://dbpedia.org/ontology/>
    prefix dbp:  <http://dbpedia.org/property/>
3   prefix rdfs: <http://www.w3.org/2000/01/rdf-schema#>
    [...]
5   paths:
      /spots:
7       get:
          tags:
9         -"Spot"
          description: "Returns the spots in the specified city"
11        produces:
          - "application/json"
13        parameters:
          - name: "city"
15          description: "Name of the city"
            type: "string"
17          classAnnotation: "dbo:City"
          responses:
19          200:
              schema:
21              $ref:  "#/definitions/Spot"
                [...]
23  definitions:
      Spot:
25      type: "object"
        properties:
27        name:
            type: "string"
29          classAnnotation: "dbo:Place"
          address:
31          type: "string"
            propertyAnnotation: "dbo:address"
33          classAnnotation:  "rdfs:Literal"
          country:
35          type: "string"
            propertyAnnotation: "dbp:country"
37          classAnnotation: "dbo:country"
            [...]
```

References

1. Adida, B., Birbeck, M., McCarron, S., Pemberton, S.: RDFa in XHTML: syntax and processing. Recommendation **W3C**, 7 (2008)
2. Brickley, D., Guha, R.V., McBride, B.: RDF schema 1.1. W3C recommendation 25, 2004–2014 (2014)
3. Chinnici, R., Moreau, J.J., Ryman, A., Weerawarana, S.: Web services description language (WSDL) version 2.0 part 1: core language. W3C recommendation 26, 19 (2007)
4. Chowdhury, G.G.: Natural language processing. Annu. Rev. Inf. Sci. Technol. **37**(1), 51–89 (2003)
5. Gomadam, K., Ranabahu, A., Sheth, A.: SA-REST: semantic annotation of web resources. W3C Member Submiss. **5**, 52 (2010)
6. Hadley, M.J.: Web Application Description Language (WADL). Technical report, Mountain View, CA, USA (2006)
7. Kopeckỳ, J., Vitvar, T., Fensel, D., Gomadam, K.: hRESTS and MicroWSMO. Technical report, STI International (2009)
8. Lausen, H., Farrell, J.: Semantic annotations for WSDL and XML schema. W3C recommendation, W3C, p. 69 (2007)
9. Li, P., Comerio, M., Maurino, A., De Paoli, F.: An approach to non-functional property evaluation of web services. In: Proceedings of IEEE International Conference on Web Services, ICWS 2009, pp. 1004–1005 (2009)
10. Lucky, M.N., Cremaschi, M., Lodigiani, B., Menolascina, A., De Paoli, F.: Enriching API descriptions by adding API profiles through semantic annotation. In: Sheng, Q.Z., Stroulia, E., Tata, S., Bhiri, S. (eds.) ICSOC 2016. LNCS, vol. 9936, pp. 780–794. Springer, Cham (2016). doi:10.1007/978-3-319-46295-0_55
11. Martin, D., Burstein, M., Hobbs, J., Lassila, O., McDermott, D., McIlraith, S., Narayanan, S., Paolucci, M., Parsia, B., Payne, T., et al.: OWL-S: semantic markup for web services. W3C member submission 22, 2007–04 (2004)
12. Ramnandan, S.K., Mittal, A., Knoblock, C.A., Szekely, P.: Assigning semantic labels to data sources. In: Gandon, F., Sabou, M., Sack, H., d'Amato, C., Cudré-Mauroux, P., Zimmermann, A. (eds.) ESWC 2015. LNCS, vol. 9088, pp. 403–417. Springer, Cham (2015). doi:10.1007/978-3-319-18818-8_25
13. Roman, D., Kopeckỳ, J., Vitvar, T., Domingue, J., Fensel, D.: WSMO-Lite and hRESTS: lightweight semantic annotations for web services and RESTful APIs. Web Semant. Sci. Serv. Agents World Wide Web **31**, 39–58 (2015)
14. Sheng, Q.Z., Qiao, X., Vasilakos, A.V., Szabo, C., Bourne, S., Xu, X.: Web services composition: a decades overview. Inf. Sci. **280**, 218–238 (2014)
15. Tsouroplis, R., Petychakis, M., Alvertis, I., Biliri, E., Lampathaki, F., Askounis, D.: Community-based API builder to manage APIs and their connections with cloud-based services. In: CAiSE Forum (2015)
16. Verborgh, R., Harth, A., Maleshkova, M., Stadtmüller, S., Steiner, T., Taheriyan, M., Van de Walle, R.: Survey of semantic description of rest APIs. In: Pautasso, C., Wilde, E., Alarcon, R. (eds.) REST: Advanced Research Topics and Practical Applications, pp. 69–89. Springer, New York (2014). doi:10.1007/978-1-4614-9299-3_5
17. Verborgh, R., Mannnens, E., Van de Walle, R.: Bottom-up web APIs with self-descriptive responses. In: Proceedings of the First Karlsruhe Service Summit Workshop-Advances in Service Research, p. 143. KIT Scientific Publishing (2015)
18. Zhang, Z.: Start small, build complete: effective and efficient semantic table interpretation using tableminer. Under Transparent Rev. Seman. Web J. (2014)

On Abstraction-Based Deadlock-Analysis in Service-Oriented Systems with Recursion

Mandy Weißbach$^{(\boxtimes)}$ and Wolf Zimmermann

Institute of Computer Science, Martin Luther University Halle-Wittenberg,
Von-Seckendorff-Platz 1, 06120 Halle, Germany
{mandy.weissbach,wolf.zimmermann}@informatik.uni-halle.de

Abstract. We examine deadlock analysis for service-oriented systems with unbound concurrency and unbound recursion. In particular, abstraction-based approaches are considered, i.e., abstract behavior models are derived from service implementations and composed according to the architecture of service-oriented systems. It turns out that there are some limitations of Petri-net-based approaches, e.g., such as workflow nets if deadlocks are analyzed. We show an example that ends in a deadlock if recursion is considered but on a Petri-net-based abstraction, it may regularly end.

Keywords: Process rewrite systems · Deadlock · Workflow nets

1 Introduction

To reduce the risk of unintended behavior (e.g., deadlocks or livelocks [14]) of service-oriented systems due to composition, many approaches are proposed, e.g., protocol conformance checking [2,10,11] or deadlock analysis [13].

In this paper we focus on an abstraction-based approach for deadlock analysis of service-oriented systems including concurrency and recursion.

Approaches, e.g., van der Aalst's workflow nets [13] are Petri-net-based and used to analyze deadlocks. They do not consider recursion, recursive callbacks and synchronization. These approaches are refinement-based, i.e., the behavior of a service is modeled as a workflow net and then refined to the service implementation. Workflow nets are used to check for the absence of deadlocks. In contrast, we provide an abstraction-based approach, i.e., the behavior is automatically abstracted from the service's implementation using classical compiler technologies [1] covering all kinds of programming concepts (synchronous and asynchronous procedure calls, synchronization, cf. Table 1). Motivation for an abstraction-based approach is that there are many services not developed according to a refinement-based approach. Furthermore, even if they have been developed initially by a refinement-based approach, it is unlikely that programmers consistently maintain the implementation and its abstraction.

F. De Paoli et al. (Eds.): ESOCC 2017, LNCS 10465, pp. 168–176, 2017.
DOI: 10.1007/978-3-319-67262-5_13

In [15] it was shown that abstraction from recursion may lead to false positives for protocol conformance checking. In this work, we examine the same question for deadlock analysis. We compare Petri-net-based abstractions with abstractions including recursion. The behavior of recursive procedures and synchronous procedure calls corresponds to the LIFO principle and requires therefore a stack [8] to trace the calling context. Process rewrite systems (PRSs) are an extension of Petri nets by stacks [9] and therefore PRS allow to model the behavior of (recursive) procedure calls, concurrency (fork), synchronization and exception handling [6].

Furthermore, [6] shows that there is a correspondence between process algebraic expressions defined by an abstraction based on process-algebras and cactus stacks (introduced as tree of stacks by [4]). Therefore, we focus on PRSs which include pushdown systems as well as Petri nets. Checking reachability and deadlocks remains decidable in process rewrite systems [9].

Our main results are:

- Each trace of a process rewrite system based abstraction corresponds step by step to a trace of the corresponding Petri-net-based abstraction.
- A (reachable) deadlock in the process rewrite system based abstraction does not necessarily correspond to a deadlock in the corresponding Petri-net-based abstraction.

This paper is organized as follows: In Sect. 2 we introduce service-oriented systems, Mayr's process rewrite systems according to [9] and we show the abstraction and composition process of a service-oriented system including unbound concurrency and unbound recursion. Section 3 discusses the correspondence between Petri net and process rewrite system abstractions. Furthermore, it shows that reachable deadlocks in the process rewrite system based abstraction do not correspond to deadlocks in the corresponding Petri-net-based abstraction. Section 4 discusses the related work and Sect. 5 concludes with a short overview of the results and gives an outlook.

2 Foundations

2.1 Services and Service-Oriented Systems

A service-oriented system is composed by two or more services which communicate over a required and provided interface, cf. Fig. 1. We assume that a service A is an implementation with a provided interfaces I_A, where an interface is a set of procedure signatures. The required interface R_s of service S is the set of procedures of other services called by S, cf. Fig. 1. It is possible that a service calls a procedure of other services, e.g., service S calls the required procedure a of service A provided by the provided interface I_A.

Procedures of an interface can be either called synchronously (procedure a of interface I_A) or asynchronously (procedure b of interface I_B). If a synchronous procedure is called, it blocks the caller until the callee has been completed. If an

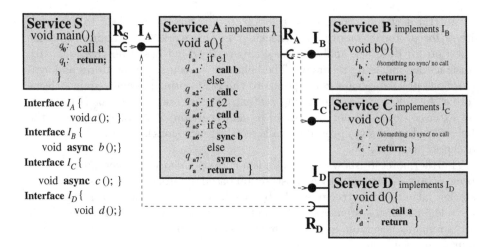

Fig. 1. A service-oriented system with services S, A, B, C and D. Service S acts as a client. Procedure b, c are asynchronous and a, d synchronous procedures.

$$\frac{e \rightarrow e'}{e \Rightarrow e'} \text{ (R)} \qquad \frac{e \Rightarrow e'}{e.s \Rightarrow e'.s} \text{ (S)} \qquad \frac{e \Rightarrow e' \quad e' \Rightarrow e''}{e \Rightarrow e''} \text{ (T)}$$

$$\frac{e \Rightarrow e'}{e \parallel s \Rightarrow e' \parallel s} \text{ (P1)} \qquad \frac{e \Rightarrow e'}{e \parallel s \Rightarrow e' \parallel s} \text{ (P2)} \qquad \frac{}{u \Rightarrow u} \text{ (L)}$$

$$e, e', e'', s \in PEX(Q)$$

Fig. 2. Inference rules for the definition of the derivation relation in a PRS

asynchronous procedure is called then the callee and the caller continue their execution in parallel. They are either synchronized by an explicit statement (**sync**, program point q_{a6} of service A) on the caller site or when both, caller and callee reach their return statement, cf. Fig. 1 r_a of service A.

2.2 Process Rewrite Systems

Mayr presented a unified view of Petri nets and several simple process algebras by representing them as subclasses of the general rewriting formalism *Process Rewrite Systems* [9]. It is based on rewrite rules on process-algebraic expressions. The set $PEX(Q)$ of process-algebraic expressions over a finite set Q (*atomic processes*) is the smallest set satisfying:

(i) $Q \subseteq PEX(Q)$,
(ii) If $e, e' \in PEX(Q)$, then $e.e' \in PEX(Q)$ and $e \parallel e' \in PEX(Q)$
     (*sequential* and *parallel composition*, respectively).

The parallel composition is associative and commutative. The sequential composition is associative but not commutative.

Table 1. Control-flow abstractions to (G,G)-PRS and (P,P)-PRS

Control Structure	Abstraction	Control Structure	Abstraction
q_i : *assignment*; q_j : $\cdots$	**(G,G)** $q_i \rightarrow q_j$ **(P,P)** $q_i \rightarrow q_j$	Synchronization q_i : **sync** b; q_{i+1} : $\cdots$ $b\{$ $\ldots$ q_j : **return**}	**(G,G)** $q_i \parallel q_j \rightarrow q_{i+1}$ **(P,P)** $q_i \parallel q_j \rightarrow q_{i+1}$
q_i : **while** $e\{$ q_j : $\cdots$ } q_k : $\cdots$	**(G,G)** $q_i \rightarrow q_j$ $q_i \rightarrow q_k$ **(P,P)** $q_i \rightarrow q_j$ $q_i \rightarrow q_k$	Synchronous procedure a q_i : **call** a; q_{i+1} : $\cdots$ $a\{q_j$: $\cdots$ q_k : **return**}	**(G,G)** $q_i \rightarrow q_j \cdot q_{i+1}$ $q_k \cdot q_{i+1} \rightarrow q_{i+1}$ **(P,P)** $q_i \rightarrow q_j$ $q_k \rightarrow q_{i+1}$
q_i **if** $e\{$ q_j $\cdots$ q_k *last program point*} **else**{ q_l $\cdots$ q_m *last program point*} q_n $\cdots$	**(G,G)** $q_i \rightarrow q_j$ $q_i \rightarrow q_l$ $q_k \rightarrow q_n$ $q_m \rightarrow q_n$ **(P,P)** $q_i \rightarrow q_j$ $q_i \rightarrow q_l$ $q_k \rightarrow q_n$ $q_m \rightarrow q_n$	Asynchronous procedure b $a\{$ $\cdots$ q_i **call** b; q_{i+1} $\cdots$ q_j **return** $\}$ $\cdots$ $b\{$ $\cdots$ q_k : $\cdots$ q_l : **return**}	**(G,G)** q_i $\rightarrow q_{i+1} \parallel q_k$ $q_j \parallel q_l \rightarrow q_j$ **(P,P)** q_i $\rightarrow q_{i+1} \parallel q_k$ $q_j \parallel q_l \rightarrow q_j$

Definition 1 (Process Rewrite Systems). *A* process rewrite system *(short: PRS) is a tuple* $\Pi \triangleq (Q, q_0, \rightarrow, F)$ *where*

(i) Q *is a finite set (*atomic processes*),*
(ii) $q_0 \in Q$ *(the* initial state, *an atomic process),*
(iii) $\rightarrow \subseteq PEX(Q) \times PEX(Q)$ *is a set of* process-rewrite rules,
(iv) $F \subseteq Q$ *(the set of* final processes*).*

   The PRS Π defines a derivation relation $\Rightarrow \subseteq PEX(Q) \times PEX(Q)$ by the inference rules in Fig. 2.

PRSs where no rule contains a sequential composition operator ((P,P)-PRS) are equivalent to Petri nets [9]. Hence, the following definition applies to general process rewrite systems ((G,G)-PRS) as well as to Petri nets.

Definition 2. *Let $\Pi = (Q, q_0, \rightarrow, F)$ be a PRS. A* process algebraic expression *$e \in PEX(Q)$ is* reachable *iff $q_0 \Rightarrow e$. A reachable $e \in PEX(Q)$ is a* deadlock *iff there exists no $e' \in PEX(Q) \setminus F$, $e' \neq e$ such that $e \Rightarrow e'$.*

2.3   Abstraction and Composition Process

Table 1 shows different control structures and their abstraction to (P,P)-PRS and (G,G)-PRS. The main principle is that each statement corresponds to a program point (which refers to a statement). The most important control structures are contained in Table 1, atomic statements, e.g., assignments, conditionals, synchronous and asynchronous procedure calls and synchronizations. Loops

Source Code of Fig. 1	(G,G)-PRS	(P,P)-PRS
main{ q_0 : **call** a q_1 : **return**; }	$q_0 \rightarrow i_a.q_1$	$q_0 \rightarrow i_a$

a{i_a :   **if** e_1
    q_{a1} :   **call** b
       else
    q_{a2} :   **call** c
    q_{a3} : **if** e_2
    q_{a4} :   **call** d
    q_{a5} : **if** e_3
    q_{a6} :   **sync** b
       else
    q_{a7} :   **sync** c
    r_a : **return**}
	$i_a \quad\rightarrow q_{a1}, \quad i_a \quad\rightarrow q_{a2}$
	$q_{a1} \quad\rightarrow q_{a3} \parallel i_b$
	$r_a \parallel r_b \rightarrow r_a$
	$q_{a2} \quad\rightarrow q_{a3} \parallel i_c$
	$r_a \parallel r_c \rightarrow r_a$
	$q_{a3} \quad\rightarrow q_{a4}, \quad q_{a3} \rightarrow q_{a5}$
	$q_{a4} \quad\rightarrow i_d.q_{a3}$
	$r_d.q_{a5} \rightarrow q_{a5}$
	$q_{a5} \quad\rightarrow q_{a6}, \quad q_{a5} \rightarrow q_{a7}$
	$q_{a6} \parallel r_b \rightarrow r_a$
	$q_{a7} \parallel r_c \rightarrow r_a$
	$r_a.q_1 \quad\rightarrow q_1, \quad r_a.r_d \rightarrow r_d$
		$i_a \quad\rightarrow q_{a1} \quad i_a \rightarrow q_{a2}$
		$q_{a1} \quad\rightarrow q_{a3} \parallel i_b$
		$r_a \parallel r_b \rightarrow r_a$
		$q_{a2} \quad\rightarrow q_{a3} \parallel i_c$
		$r_a \parallel r_c \rightarrow r_a$
		$q_{a3} \quad\rightarrow q_{a4}, \quad q_{a3} \rightarrow q_{a5}$
		$q_{a4} \quad\rightarrow i_d$
		$r_d \quad\rightarrow q_{a5}$
		$q_{a5} \quad\rightarrow q_{a6}, \quad q_{a5} \rightarrow q_{a7}$
		$q_{a6} \parallel r_b \rightarrow r_a$
		$q_{a7} \parallel r_c \rightarrow r_a$
		$r_a \quad\rightarrow q_1, \quad r_a \rightarrow r_d$

b{ i_b : calc(no call/sync) r_b : **return**}	$i_b \rightarrow r_b$	$i_b \rightarrow r_b$
c{ i_c : calc(no call/sync) r_c : **return**}	$i_c \rightarrow r_c$	$i_c \rightarrow r_c$
d{ i_d : **call** a r_d : **return**}	$i_d \rightarrow i_a.r_d$	$i_d \rightarrow i_a$

Fig. 3. Abstractions of the service-oriented system in Fig. 1

and case statements are abstracted similarly to conditionals. For service-oriented abstractions, the control-flow abstraction rules can be applied to every services. The main difference is that entry and exit points are n eeded for the first program point and the return statement of the procedure of a required interface of a service. These entry and exit points are identified upon composition with the corresponding services implementing the required interface. This combination yields to a PRS modeling an abstract behavior of the service-oriented system, cf. [2]. An analogous idea is used in [13] for combining workflow nets to Petri nets representing the behavior of the composed service-oriented system.

Example 1 (A Service-Oriented System and its Abstractions). The example in Fig. 1 was introduced in Subsect. 2.1. Figure 3 shows the abstraction of the single services using the entry points i_a, i_b, i_c, i_d and the exit points r_a, r_b, r_c, r_d for the initial program points and the program points of the return statements of a, b, c, d, respectively. The final state of the PRS is q_1. Figure 3 shows the resulting abstractions for (G,G)-PRS and (P,P)-PRS, respectively.

3   Correspondence Between (G,G)-PRS and (P,P)-PRS Abstractions

A *run* of process rewrite system $\Pi = (Q, q_0, \rightarrow, F)$ is a sequence $e_0, \dots, e_n$ of process-algebraic expressions such that $e_i \Rightarrow e_{i+1}$, $i = 0, \dots, n-1$ where $e_i \Rightarrow e_{i+1}$ can be proven without using rules (T) and (L). Intuitively, this means that exactly one PRS-rule is being applied in $e_i \Rightarrow e_{i+1}$ and the sequence $e_0, \dots, e_n$ represents a step-wise execution of Π. Let S be a service-oriented system, $\Pi_S \triangleq (Q, q_0, \rightarrow_\Pi, F)$ be the (G,G)-PRS abstraction of S and $\Pi'_S \triangleq (Q, q_0, \rightarrow_{\Pi'}, F)$ the (P,P)-PRS abstraction of S, cf. Table 1. Note that the set of atomic processes

| (G,G)-PRS | (P,P)-PRS | applied rules (cf. Fig. 3) | |
		(G,G)-PRS	(P ,P)-PRS
q_0	q_0		
$i_a.q_1$	i_a	$q_0 \rightarrow i_a.q_1$	$q_0 \rightarrow i_a$
$q_{a1}.q_1$	q_{a1}	$i_a \rightarrow q_{a1}$	$i_a \rightarrow q_{a1}$
$(q_{a3} \parallel i_b).q_1$	$q_{a3} \parallel i_b$	$q_{a1} \rightarrow q_{a3} \parallel i_b$	$q_{a1} \rightarrow q_{a3} \parallel i_b$
$(q_{a4} \parallel i_b).q_1$	$q_{a4} \parallel i_b$	$q_{a3} \rightarrow q_{a4}$	$q_{a3} \rightarrow q_{a4}$
$(q_{a4} \parallel r_b).q_1$	$q_{a4} \parallel r_b$	$i_b \rightarrow r_b$	$i_b \rightarrow r_b$
$((i_d.q_{a5}) \parallel q_{12}).q_1$	$i_d \parallel r_b$	$q_{a4} \rightarrow i_d.q_{a5}$	$q_{a4} \rightarrow i_d$
$((i_a.r_d.q_{a5}) \parallel r_b).q_1$	$i_a \parallel r_b$	$i_d \rightarrow i_a.q_{16}$	$i_d \rightarrow i_a$
$((q_{a2}.r_d.q_{a5}) \parallel r_b).q_1$	$q_{a2} \parallel r_b$	$i_a \rightarrow q_{a2}$	$i_a \rightarrow q_{a2}$
$(((q_{a3} \parallel i_c).r_d.q_{a5}) \parallel r_b).q_1$	$q_{a3} \parallel i_c \parallel r_b$	$q_{a2} \rightarrow q_{a3} \parallel i_c$	$q_{a2} \rightarrow q_{a3} \parallel i_c$
$(((q_{a3} \parallel r_c).r_d.q_{a5}) \parallel r_b).q_1$	$q_{a3} \parallel r_c \parallel r_b$	$i_c \rightarrow r_c$	$i_c \rightarrow r_c$
$(((q_{a5} \parallel r_c).r_d.q_{a5}) \parallel r_b).q_1$	$q_{a5} \parallel r_c \parallel r_b$	$q_{a3} \rightarrow q_{a5}$	$q_{a3} \rightarrow q_{a5}$
$(((q_{a6} \parallel r_c).r_d.q_{a5}) \parallel r_b).q_1$	$q_{a6} \parallel r_c \parallel r_b$	$q_{a5} \rightarrow q_{a6}$	$q_{a5} \rightarrow q_{a6}$

Fig. 4. Runs in the (G,G)-PRS and (P,P)-PRS abstractions of Fig. 3

and the initial state is by construction the same in both (G,G)- and (P,P)-PRS. We show that each run of Π_S corresponds to a run in $\Pi_{S'}$.

For this, we need to define an abstraction function α for process-algebraic expressions of Π_S and Π'_S. Since the PRS rules $\rightarrow_{\Pi'}$ do not contain the sequential operator the same holds for all reachable expressions. Therefore, the abstraction function $\alpha : PEX(Q) \rightarrow PEX(Q)$ forgets the sequential composition, i.e., α is inductively defined by

(i) $\alpha(q) \triangleq q$ for $q \in Q \cup \{\varepsilon\}$
(ii) $\alpha(e_1 \parallel e_2) \triangleq \alpha(e_1) \parallel \alpha(e_2)$ for $e_1, e_2 \in PEX(Q)$
(iii) $\alpha(e_1.e_2) \triangleq \alpha(e_1)$ for $e_1, e_2 \in PEX(Q)$

Example 2 (Runs and Abstractions). The first two columns of Fig. 4 shows a run of the (G,G)-PRS abstraction $\Pi_S = (Q, q_0, \rightarrow_\Pi, F)$ and a corresponding run of the (P,P)-PRS abstraction $\Pi'_S = (Q, q_0, \rightarrow_{\Pi'}, F)$ of the service-oriented system S in Example 1 (cf. Figs. 1 and 3). The process algebraic expressions in each row corresponds, i.e., $e'_i = \alpha(e_i)$ where e_i is the first expression (contained in the run in Π_S) of the i-th row and e'_i is second expression (contained in the run in Π'_S) of the i-th row. Furthermore, it holds $\rightarrow_{\Pi'} = \{\alpha(e_1) \rightarrow_{\Pi'} \alpha(e_2) : e_1 \rightarrow_\Pi e_2\}$

Remark 1. A look at Table 1 shows that in general, $\rightarrow_{\Pi'} = \{\alpha(e_1) \rightarrow_{\Pi'} \alpha(e_2) : e_1 \rightarrow_\Pi e_2\}$, i.e., the rewrite rules of the (P,P)-PRS can be obtained from the rewrite rules of the (G,G)-PRS by forgetting about the sequential composition.

Theorem 1 (Correspondence between Abstractions to (G,G)-PRS and (P,P)-PRS). *Let S be a service-oriented system, $\Pi_S = (Q, q_0, \rightarrow_\Pi, F)$ be the abstraction of S to (G,G)-PRS according to Table 1, and $\Pi'_S = (Q, q_0, \rightarrow_{\Pi'}, F)$ be the abstraction of S to (P,P)-PRS according to Table 1. If $e \Rightarrow_\Pi e'$ then $\alpha(e) \Rightarrow \alpha(e')$.*

Proof. The proof is by induction on the number of applications of the inference rules. Suppose $e \Rightarrow_\Pi e'$.

Case 1: Rule (R) is being applied. Then $e \rightarrow_\Pi e'$ according to Remark 1 it is $\alpha(e) \rightarrow_{\Pi'} \alpha(e')$.

Case 2: Rule (S) has been applied. Then, $e = e''.s$ and $e' = \bar{e}.s$ for some $e'', \bar{e}, s \in PEX(Q)$, and $e'' \Rightarrow_\Pi \bar{e}$. By induction hypothesis, it holds $\alpha(e'') \Rightarrow_{\Pi'} \alpha(\bar{e})$. Now, rule (S) can be applied to obtain $\alpha(e'').s \Rightarrow_{\Pi'} \alpha(\bar{e}).s$. Thus $\alpha(e) \Rightarrow_{\Pi'} \alpha(e')$ using property (iii) of the definition of α.

The cases where rules (P1), (P2), and (T) are applied are proven analogously to Case 2.

Corollary 1. *For each run $e_0, \ldots, e_n$ of Π_S, the sequence $\alpha(e_0), \ldots, \alpha(e_n)$ is a run of Π'_S.*

Hence, each run in the PRS-abstraction corresponds to a run in the (P,P)-PRS abstraction (which is equivalent to the Petri nets). Thus, the workflow nets [13] lead to a coarser abstraction than using general PRS [6].

Now, we examine the deadlock situations. Expression $e \triangleq (((q_{a6} \parallel r_c).r_d.q_{a5}) \parallel r_b).q_1$ is a deadlock because no PRS rule is applicable, cf. Fig. 4. However, the corresponding (P,P)-PRS expression $\alpha(e) = q_{a6} \parallel r_c \parallel r_b$ is not a deadlock. Since $\parallel$ is associative and commutative, it holds

$$q_{a6} \parallel r_c \parallel r_b \overset{\text{ass. and com. } \parallel}{\Longrightarrow} q_{a6} \parallel r_b \parallel r_c \overset{q_{a6} \parallel r_b \rightarrow r_a}{\Longrightarrow} r_a \parallel r_c \overset{r_a \rightarrow r_d}{\Longrightarrow} r_d \parallel r_c \overset{r_d \rightarrow q_{a5}}{\Longrightarrow}$$

$$q_{a5} \parallel r_c \overset{q_{a5} \rightarrow q_{a7}}{\Longrightarrow} q_{a7} \parallel r_c \overset{q_{a7} \parallel r_c \rightarrow r_a}{\Longrightarrow} r_a \overset{r_a \rightarrow q_1}{\Longrightarrow} q_1$$

Thus, the final state q_1 is reached. However, there are alternatives leading to a deadlock. For example the rules $r_a \rightarrow r_d$ and $r_d \rightarrow q_{a5}$ could be applied to the derivation r_a. This can lead to the deadlock q_{a7}.

4   Related Work

Van der Aalst [13] uses Petri-net-based analysis tool to verify business process workflows. Recursion, e.g., recursive callbacks, is not considered.

In [12] recursive Petri nets (rPNs) are used to model the planning of autonomous agents which transport goods form location A to B. The model of rPNs is used to model dynamic processes (e.g., agent's request). Recursion in our sense is not considered. Deadlocks can only arise when interactions between agents (e.g., shared attributes) invalidates preconditions. Another refinement based approach is described in [7]. Hicheur models healthcare processes based on algebraic and recursive Petri nets [5]. Recursive Petri nets are used to model by the main process called subprocesses. All these approaches use the ability of rPNs to prune subtrees.

Bouajjani et al. [3] work is the closest to ours. They discuss the abstraction-based analysis of recursive parallel programs based on recursive vector addition systems. They explore decidability of reachability for recursively parallel programs. It seems that their model is slightly more general as there are situations where the reachability problem becomes undecidable.

To our knowledge, abstraction-based deadlock analysis in service-oriented systems including synchronous and asynchronous procedure calls (forking), recursion and recursive callbacks and synchronization in the context of service-oriented systems was not investigated before.

5 Conclusion

We examined two different abstractions from service-oriented systems S to general (G,G)-PRS Π_S and to (P,P)-PRS Π' (which are equivalent to Petri nets). We have shown that Π' is more abstract than Π (Theorem 1). However, there is a reachable deadlock e in Π_S where the corresponding situation e' in Π'_S is not necessarily a deadlock although each run $q_0 \rightarrow_{\Pi_S} e_1 \rightarrow_{\Pi_S} \cdots \rightarrow_{\Pi_S} e_n$ in the PRS Π_S has a corresponding run $q_0 \rightarrow_{\Pi'_S} e'_1 \rightarrow_{\Pi'_S} \cdots \rightarrow_{\Pi'_S} e'_n$. To the best of our knowledge, we are not aware on studies on abstraction-based deadlock analysis of service-oriented systems taking into account unbound recursion and unbound concurrency with synchronization.

The main result shows that the Petri net abstraction is too coarse. Furthermore, the example requires recursion. However, in our example the Petri net abstraction Π'_S the final state as well as a deadlock situation is reachable from e'. Therefore, the example doesn't provide a false positive (i.e., it erroneously classifies the service-oriented system S deadlock-free) in the classical sense. Our hypothesis, is that in the context of the paper, if a deadlock situation e in the PRS abstraction Π_S of a service-oriented system S is reachable, then a deadlock situation e'' is reachable from the corresponding situation e' in the Petri net abstraction Π'_S. It is an open question whether this hypothesis is true. However, even it is true, the trace leading to a deadlock situation e'' cannot be obtained by execution of S. This may erroneously lead to classify the deadlock e'' as a false alarm.

References

1. Aho, A.V., Lam, M.S., Sethi, R., Ullman, J.D.: Compilers: Principles, Techniques, and Tools, 2nd edn. Addison-Wesley Longman Publishing Co. Inc., Boston (2006)
2. Both, A., Zimmermann, W.: Automatic protocol conformance checking of recursive and parallel component-based systems. In: Chaudron, M.R.V., Szyperski, C., Reussner, R. (eds.) CBSE 2008. LNCS, vol. 5282, pp. 163–179. Springer, Heidelberg (2008). doi:10.1007/978-3-540-87891-9_11
3. Bouajjani, A., Emmi, M.: Analysis of recursively parallel programs. In: ACM SIGPLAN Notices, vol. 47, pp. 203–214. ACM (2012)
4. Dahl, O.J., Nygaard, K.: Simula: an algol-based simulation language. Commun. ACM 9, 671–678 (1966)
5. Haddad, S., Poitrenaud, D.: Modelling and analyzing systems with recursive petri nets. In: Boel, R., Stremersch, G. (eds.) Discrete Event Systems. The Springer International Series in Engineering and Computer Science, vol. 569, pp. 449–458. Springer, Boston (2000)

6. Heike, C., Zimmermann, W., Both, A.: On expanding protocol conformance checking to exception handling. Serv. Oriented Comput. Appl. **8**(4), 299–322 (2014)
7. Hicheur, A., Ben Dhieb, A., Barkaoui, K.: Modelling and analysis of flexible healthcare processes based on algebraic and recursive petri nets. In: Weber, J., Perseil, I. (eds.) FHIES 2012. LNCS, vol. 7789, pp. 1–18. Springer, Heidelberg (2013). doi:10.1007/978-3-642-39088-3_1
8. Hopcroft, J.E., Motwani, R., Ullman, J.D.: Introduction to automata theory, languages, and computation, 2nd edn. SIGACT News **32**(1), 60–65 (2001). http://doi.acm.org/10.1145/568438.568455
9. Mayr, R.: Process rewrite systems. Inf. Comput. **156**(1–2), 264–286 (2000)
10. Parizek, P., Plasil, F.: Modeling of component environment in presence of callbacks and autonomous activities. In: Paige, R.F., Meyer, B. (eds.) TOOLS EUROPE 2008. LNBIP, vol. 11, pp. 2–21. Springer, Heidelberg (2008). doi:10.1007/978-3-540-69824-1_2
11. Schmidt, H.W., Krämer, B.J., Poernomo, I., Reussner, R.: Predictable component architectures using dependent finite state machines. In: Wirsing, M., Knapp, A., Balsamo, S. (eds.) RISSEF 2002. LNCS, vol. 2941, pp. 310–324. Springer, Heidelberg (2004). doi:10.1007/978-3-540-24626-8_22
12. Seghrouchni, A.E.F., Haddad, S.: A recursive model for distributed planning. In: Proceedings of the 2nd International Conference on Multi-Agent Systems (ICMAS 1996), pp. 307–314 (1996)
13. Van Der Aalst, W.M.P.: Workflow verification: finding control-flow errors using petri-net-based techniques. In: van der Aalst, W., Desel, J., Oberweis, A. (eds.) Business Process Management. LNCS, vol. 1806, pp. 161–183. Springer, Heidelberg (2000). doi:10.1007/3-540-45594-9_11
14. Weißbach, M., Zimmermann, W.: Termination analysis of business process workflows. In: Proceedings of the 5th International Workshop on Enhanced Web Service Technologies, pp. 18–25, WEWST 2010, NY, USA (2010). http://doi.acm.org/10.1145/1883133.1883137
15. Zimmermann, W., Schaarschmidt, M.: Automatic checking of component protocols in component-based systems. In: Löwe, W., Südholt, M. (eds.) SC 2006. LNCS, vol. 4089, pp. 1–17. Springer, Heidelberg (2006). doi:10.1007/11821946_1

Internet of Things and Data Streams

IoT-Based Compliance Checking of Multi-party Business Processes Modeled with Commitments

Marco Montali[1] and Pierluigi Plebani[2(✉)]

[1] Free University of Bozen-Bolzano, Bolzano, Italy
montali@inf.unibz.it
[2] Politecnico di Milano, Milan, Italy
pierluigi.plebani@polimi.it

Abstract. In a multi-party business process, the choreography defines the conversational protocol among the parties, so that the visibility of the parties' private processes is limited to the set of operations required to respect such a protocol. Especially in scenarios where physical resources are exchanged, knowing how a resource owned by a party is managed in the premises of another party is not possible. Thus, possible misalignments can be detected too late. At the same time, IoT is increasingly adopted to enact business processes in many domains: e.g., logistics, manufacturing, healthcare. As, with IoT, smart devices can physically flow through the different parties involved in a process, their sensing capabilities can be exploited to improve the process compliance checking. With this work we propose an approach for compliance checking that mixes commitments and smart devices. Commitments, declaratively defining mutual contractual relationships between parties, drive the configuration of smart devices that, flowing along with the process flow, check their satisfaction and, in case of misalignment, timely inform the involved parties.

Keywords: Multi-party process compliance · Timed commitments · BPMN choreography model · IoT

1 Introduction

In a multi-party business process, to properly achieve the final common goal, the involved participants agree on a process choreography which must be respected when the process is being executed. This requires that the participants enforce their services with respect to the agreed protocol [10]. To this aim, IoT is attracting more and more interest of researchers and practitioners as it can improve the service monitoring capabilities. Indeed, *smart devices* are currently adopted in organizations to analyze the environment in which the service is operating, by equipping them with sensors able to measure some physical phenomenon (e.g., temperature, presence) accurately and continuously to reduce the time-to-repair in case of error. As long as the objective of monitoring is related to its internal

© IFIP International Federation for Information Processing 2017
Published by Springer International Publishing AG 2017. All Rights Reserved
F. De Paoli et al. (Eds.): ESOCC 2017, LNCS 10465, pp. 179–195, 2017.
DOI: 10.1007/978-3-319-67262-5_14

activities, a participant has total control over it. Conversely, in multi-party business processes, an interaction with the other participants means to consume a service offered by an external party and the visibility of what is happening inside the boundary of such external partners is limited to the information that partner offers. This is typical, for instance, in the logistic domain: e.g., a manufacturer gives their products to a courier that promises to deliver them to the final customer but the information about the status of the goods is usually limited to the position with a very coarse-grained (e.g., the city of the last deposit).

Based on this scenario, to improve the compliance checking of a multi-party business process, in this work we assume to couple smart devices to all the physical resources transferred among the different participants. In this way, as the smart device could embed several sensors, the owner of the resources can have a finer-grained data about the status regardless of the participant who is managing them.[1] To support this envisioned scenario, the goal of this work is to propose an approach to improve the definition and the monitoring of requirements that holds between participants in multi-party business processes. The design of the process takes advantage of an extended *BPMN choreography meta-model* able to embed *social commitments*. The resulting choreographies make explicit which conditions/properties shall be brought during their execution. Moreover, commitments explicitly account for the mutual promises/obligations arising when multiple parties interact. The explicit definition of a timed commitment lifecycle proposed in this paper that, to the best of our knowledge, has never being analysed in the literature, allows the commitments to be directly incorporated into a smart device. Thus, it is possible to track of the progression of the system and to check the compliance between occurring events affecting the state of the commitments of interest and the expected lifecycle.

The rest of the paper is organized as follows. Section 2, using a motivating example taken from the logistic domain, discusses the characteristics and the challenges in monitoring a multi-party business processes. Section 3 introduces the approach describing how the commitments are adopted and extended, as well as integrated in a BPMN choreography model. Section 4 provides the formalization of the commitments and their lifecycle validated by some example taken from our running case study. Finally, Sect. 5 discusses the related work, while Sect. 6 conclude the paper outlining possible future work.

2   Motivation

To better motivate the proposed approach, the choreography diagram referring to the logistic domain is reported in Fig. 1. This sample process is enacted by *Sea.Co.*, a seafood company. Every time a *customer* submits an order, which consists of a list of fishes where the quantity for each item and the delivery date are specified. A negotiation phase with the customer checks the feasibility of the delivery date, possibly shifting it to a date where the delivery can be

---

[1] Due to the technical nature of the proposed solution, the economical aspects are not yet considered in this paper.

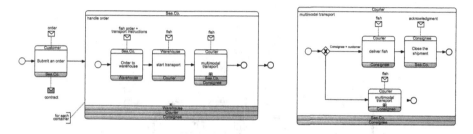

Fig. 1. Running example: BPMN Choreography diagram.

guaranteed, and a contract is finally signed by the two parties. At this point, the Sea.Co. organizes the actual delivery, in particular: *(i)* selecting the fish warehouses (among the various that have the required food units), *(ii)* from each *warehouses* a package is shipped to the customer, *(iii)* splitting the delivery of each package into phases each of them managed by a *courier*, *(iv)* determining which transportation modes are involved, *(v)* ultimately defining a timetable, compatible with the expected delivery date.

Based on this information, several shipments will leave from the selected warehouses to the customer and, according to the defined plan, each delivery could consist of several steps, possibly involving different couriers. Yet, each courier is responsible for a specific phase of the shipment that lasts from the courier premises to the consignee premises. When the consignee corresponds to the final customer, the shipment of the related portion of the order can be considered concluded and an acknowledgment is sent to Sea.Co. Conversely, when the consignee refers to the courier which has to perform the next step in the chain, the same process is recursively repeated. On this basis, each shipment corresponds to different process instances that could differ in terms of activities performed, resources (e.g., trucks) involved, operating actors (e.g., couriers).

As the compliance checking for these internal processes has been extensively studied in the literature [10], the goal of this work is to check the compliance of the choreography: i.e., to check if all the actors operate correctly with respect to the other actors. In fact, due to the complexity of the delivery, deviations to the plan may occur. For example, in case of unexpected traffic, some phase might be dynamically rearranged (e.g., changing the route and/or the transportation mode). This, in turn, may create a ripple effect, requiring to consequently rearrange one or more consequent phases, so as to guarantee that the final delivery date is respected. On the other hand, the contract established between the Sea.Co. and the customer fixes a series of constraints (or, to be more precise, *commitments*) that the involved parties have to, or should, honor no matter how the process is dynamically rearranged. Now, the question is: "how can the Sea.Co. and the customer check the compliance of the process that is being executed?". Generally speaking, this question can be reformulated as: "how can every actor involved in a multi-party business process be enabled to check if the other actors are behaving correctly with respect to the initial agreement?"

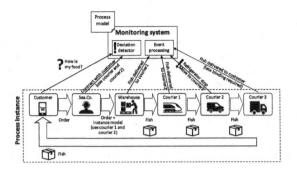

Fig. 2. Centralized monitoring

To address this question, centralized solutions [14] are available (see Fig. 2). In addition to the infrastructure enabling the execution of the process based on the exchange of messages, a central monitoring node is responsible to receive all the updates and to inform about the *process instance* execution, as well as to identify possible deviations with respect to the expected behavior (defined by the *process model*). Although the deviation detection can be not that complex to implement as all the needed information are known, the central node needs to know in advance which will be the entity that will publish or subscribe to the information about the status of the process. Moreover, each entity needs to support the protocols adopted for the communication and if a new entity will be included in the process to manage a deviation, it must adhere to these protocols. For instance, when *Courier2* realizes the refrigerator on the van has broken, it decides to involve *Courier3* to deliver the fish a safe-mode and, to make the centralized approach working, late binding mechanisms are required to make this new actor connected to the monitoring system.

The approach presented in this paper aims to overcome to this limitation extending the usage of smart devices not only to monitor how the tasks operating on a resource are behaving, but also which are the status of the resources. As the resources should move among the participants following what modeled in the choreography, monitoring if the status of the resources give some clue on how the process choreography evolves (see Fig. 3). The adoption of this approach gives two types of advantages. On the one side, instead of leaving to the involved parties the burden of communicating the status of the process instance, autonomic systems implemented on smart devices are paired to the shipping goods to continuously monitor them and, when requested, to inform about the status of the package. Such smart devices are configured by the owner of the goods, i.e., the Sea.Co. company in our realistic scenario, before leaving the warehouses.

Moreover, smart devices are responsible not only to sense the environment in which they are immersed, but they are also configured to host portions of the process model which include the *commitments* stating how, when, and where the smart device should be managed. This, in turn, allows to timely identify possible deviations and establish new, compensating commitments to handle

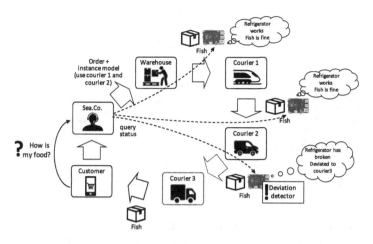

Fig. 3. IoT-based monitoring architecture.

which mutual obligations shall be fulfilled when a deviation is detected. In this way, the knowledge about the status of the process should not be a privilege only of the owner of the smart device, but it can be made available to all the parties[2].

3   Commitments in Multi-party Business Processes

In our approach we advocate the use of (social) commitments [4, 5, 16] as a way for specifying the conditions under which the multi-party business process should be executed. This section briefly introduces commitments and their lifecycle (also called commitment machine in the literature), and then provides an informal description of how commitments are used in our approach; a more formal definition of commitments, and how they can be managed, is introduced in the next section. The modeled commitments will be used to configure the smart devices, so as to make them able to check if actual instantiations of those commitments are indeed satisfied or not. To informally describe what is a commitment and how it can be useful for our purposes, we adopt the graphical notation introduced in [16] (see Fig. 4). More specifically, a commitment involves two actors: the *debtor*, who is willing to offer a service under certain circumstances, and a *creditor*, who takes advantage of this service. *Antecedent* and *consequent* are two logic expressions which define under which conditions the service must be provided and consumed. Focusing on the lifecycle, a commitment is initially *null* and needs to be created. Once created, if the antecedent does holds it goes to a *detached* state, otherwise in the *conditional* one. The latter represents a state in which the commitment exists but is not yet active, as the antecedent still needs

---

[2] For the sake of simplicity, this paper does not address privacy issues. These are aspects that definitely need to be investigated in future work.

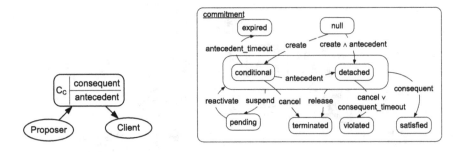

Fig. 4. Commitment notation (left) and lifecycle (right) [16].

to become true and consequently trigger the actual obligation of the debtor to make the consequent true as well. This is what happens in the detached state. When the consequent holds, then the commitment is declared as *satisfied*; it also might happen that the commitment is released or – only if it is in the conditional state – canceled. The operations are under the responsibility of the creditor and debtor of the commitment, and may be employed to flexibly evolve the multi-party interaction. Such a flexibility distinguishes social commitments from normative (in particular, deontic) approaches where obligations are considered in a rigid, immutable way. Timeouts can be also attached to the antecedent and consequent to force their validity for a period of time. Indeed, if the antecedent timeout expires then also the commitment is declared as *expired*. Conversely, if the consequent timeout expires then the commitment is declared as *violated* as the debtor was not able to perform what it has been promised although the pre-condition for its fulfillment (i.e., the antecedent) were holding.

3.1   Commitment Templates

As well-exemplified in this survey [15], commitments are typically used to declaratively capture (business) interactions, abstracting away from control-flow details. In this light, commitment-based approaches are usually considered complementary to activity-/flow-centric ones. The first distinctive feature of our contribution is to establish a synergy between these two paradigms. To do so, we propose an extension of commitments to make them attachable to BPMN choreography models, and in particular to choreography activities. In this way, the choreography takes care of the flow-related constraints, whereas commitments focus on the contractual nature of the collaboration. Specifically, a choreography activity provides the context of existence for certain commitments. This means that, at runtime, whenever an instance for such an activity is executed, corresponding instances for those commitments are created and evolved in accordance with the course of execution. In other words, the lifecycle of choreography activities becomes connected to that of its attached commitments. More details on this aspect, which to the best of our knowledge has never been explored in the past, are given in Sect. 4.1.

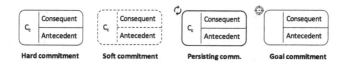

Fig. 5. Types of commitments.

In particular, we introduce four types of commitments classified along two orthogonal dimensions (related shapes are shown in Fig. 5):

- *Importance:* we distinguish between *hard* (solid line) and *soft* commitments (dashed lines). In the former case the consequent must be valid to consider the commitment fulfilled. In the latter case, the creditor is expecting that the debtor will do its best to fulfill the commitment. This distinction provides the basis for a fine-grained handling of commitment violations and corresponding compensations.
- *Time of validity:* the linkage between commitments and choreography activities calls for a distinction between *persisting* (cycle icon decoration) and *goal* commitment (target icon decoration). In the former case, the consequent must be valid *during* the execution of its target activity, possibly even spanning its entire execution. In the latter case, the consequent must become valid when the activity completes.

To discuss our extension more formally, we introduce the concept of *commitment template*: a schema for a multitude of "ground" commitments reflecting the same contractual relationship, but instantiated on different activity instances, that is, possibly different actual participants and/or timestamps and/or targeted objects. This reflects the dual nature of commitments: at design time, as modeling abstractions to capture "types" of business relationships, and at runtime, as computational abstractions to track the evolution of "instances" of such relationships. The importance of this duality has been increasingly recognized in the literature, constituting an interesting point of departure from standard logical approaches to commitments [4,6,12].

In our setting, the notion of commitment template is used to extend the standard BPMN choreography meta-model, as depicted in Fig. 6. Concretizing

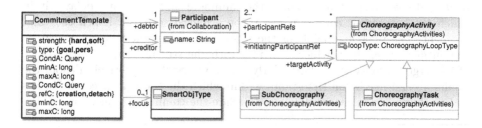

Fig. 6. Commitment-aware extension of the BPMN choreography metamodel

what discussed above, the entity type `CommitmentTemplate` captures a commitment template by declaring its target `ChoreographyActivity`. Among the `Participant` (types) referenced by the choreography activity, two are selected as debtor and creditor of the commitment template. This induces the constraint that, at runtime, each instance of the commitment template will relate a debtor d and a creditor c, with the constraint that d and c participates to the activity playing the corresponding roles attached to the commitment template. Consider, e.g., a template established between a `Warehouse` and a `Courier` in the context of the choreography activity `start transport`. At runtime, commitment instances for that template will be created and evolved by relating actual couriers and warehouses, in turn involved in the execution of instances of `start transport`. Alongside `CommitmentTemplate`, we also extend the choreography meta-model with the notion of `SmartObjType`, which models a type of smart object that may exist in the system. It is then possible to (optionally) declare the focus of a commitment template, relating it to a smart object type. This association has a twofold nature: on the one hand, it explicitly tracks whether the reason/subject of a commitment corresponds to a physical (smart) object; on the other hand, it provides a context for querying the characteristics/data of such an object. This, in turn, provides the basis for defining the antecedent and consequent of the commitment template. Additionally, a commitment template comes with a number of attributes (cf. Fig. 6). We review them one by one. The `strength` of a commitment template indicates whether the commitment is hard or soft, whereas the `type` indicates whether the template has a goal or persistence nature. Such two attributes determine the graphical appearance of commitment templates, as specified in Fig. 5. The two attributes `CondA` and `CondC` respectively identify the antecedent and consequent conditions of the commitment template. Such conditions may be concretely specified in different query languages, possibly expressed over the attributes/properties of a smart object type. Such query languages may range from standard SQL when commitments insist over relational data (such as, e.g., in the case of [6,12]), to query languages over dynamically evolving data such as the CQL continuous query language or proprietary languages to query sensor data provided by smart objects. For the sake of generality, we abstract away from the specific query language at hand. The remaining attributes are used to express quantitative temporal constraints on the commitment template. These are used to refine the representation of the antecedent and consequent, defining relative temporal windows within which they are checked. Specifically, `minA` and `maxA` respectively denote the minimum and maximum delay within which the antecedent condition has to be achieved so as to detach the commitment. The reference point for these two extremes is the time at which the commitment is created, which coincides with the starting time of an instance of its target activity starts.[3] Similarly, `minC` and `maxC` respectively denote the minimum and maximum timestamp within which the consequent condition has to be achieved or maintained so as to declare the commitment as satisfied. For

---

[3] Absolute temporal constraints can be seamlessly realized as syntactic sugar, scheduling the execution of the target activity at a fixed time.

the `minC-maxC` time window, two reference points may be selected: the creation time or the detach time. This is specified through the `refC` attribute. The latter choice is particularly relevant when the time window associated to the consequent has to be determined depending on the exact moment when the commitment was detached, i.e., the moment where a "conditional" obligation turned into an actual one. In the spirit of [13], for goal commitments `minC` represents the minimal delay at which the goal has to be achieved, while `maxC` captures the deadline of the goal; for persistence commitments, instead, the time window delimited by `minC` and `maxC` is the interval within which the consequent is expected to hold. Differently from [13], though, the achievement/maintenance of the commitment consequent are bound to that of its target activity. In this light, goal commitments implicitly impose temporal constraints on when an activity is expected to end, whereas persistence commitments may be released by the completion of an activity.

3.2 Modeling Commitments

The proposed extension of the BPMN choreography metamodel enables the decoration choreography activities with commitments. Thus, a process designer can specify not only the conversation among the parties, but also which are the contractual obligations and their characteristics. By connecting the commitments to a BPMN Choreography model we link the lifecycle of commitments to the lifecycle of the activities. Referring to the example shown in Fig. 7, there is a goal commitment in which the Sea.co. is the debtor, while the consignee is the creditor. As the commitment is attached to the whole activity, and no explicit antecedent is included in the commitment, then the commitment becomes immediately detached when the activity starts. This shows one of the benefits obtained through the commitment-activity linkage. Being a goal commitment, we are expecting that the consequent becomes true when the activity ends. In more details, the diagram is stating that the fish has to be delivered within 25 days. This can be obtained by setting $minC = 0$ and $maxC = 25d$ for the commitment template, with reference point the detach time (which, in this case, coincides with the creation time). As said, in this case the antecedent is implicitly linked to when the activity starts. Similarly, the validity of the commitment is related to the termination of the activity. Thus, if the commitment consequent (i.e., fish delivery) is achieved when the activity ends, then it will be considered as satisfied, otherwise it will be considered violated. This implicitly sets a deadline on the **handle order** activity, since whenever it takes more than 25 days, then the commitment becomes violated.

In the same process, the warehouse and the first courier agrees on another commitment. In this case, being a soft commitment, the *start transport* activity should possibly be executed in 5 days. Similarly to the previous case, this goal commitment moves to the *detached* state when the fish is ready to leave the warehouse, while it can be considered satisfied if the consequent is verified, i.e., when the food is on board of the first courier. This latter condition can be specified by querying

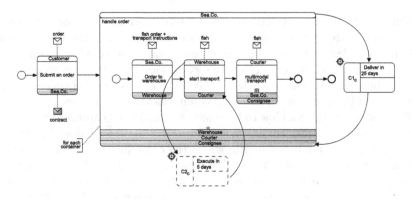

Fig. 7. Example of hard/goal and soft/goal of commitments.

a positioning sensor for the smart device attached to the food container, or by simply checking when the start transport activity completes.

When the antecedent is specified, like the case in Fig. 8, the activation of the commitment occurs when the activity starts and the antecedent becomes true (maybe at a later time). In our running example, this occurs when the courier responsible of a transportation phase signals that the refrigerator used to transport the fish is broken. If multiple couriers are involved in the SeaCo-to-customer transportation, each one will be attached to an instance of the *multimodal transport* activity, and in turn to an instance of such a commitment template. When the refrigerator of a courier gets broken, a corresponding instance of such a commitment is detached and, contrarily from the previous cases, starts monitoring the maintenance of a property related to the fish temperature, being a persisting commitment. In particular, the consequent in this case is not expected to hold when the multimodal transport activity ends, but for the whole time window that spans from detach moment, to that marking the completion of the activity. This means that, while the multimodal transport activity is under execution,

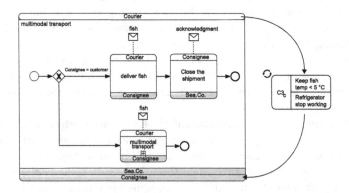

Fig. 8. Example of hard, persisting commitment.

as soon as the fish temperature reaches $5\,^{\circ}\mathrm{C}$, the commitment instance will become violated. Also in the case, we may declare that the commitment template focuses on a type of smart object that is attached to a fish container, and is equipped with a sensor providing timely information about the fish temperature.

4   Tracking Commitments

When the commitments are applied to a physical resource that is exchanged among the parties, we propose to use smart devices to monitor if the resource is managed according to the defined commitments. When doing this, we need to be sure that the smart device is able to understand if the actors that are managing the resources are respecting the defined obligations. Before entering into the details of the timed-commitment lifecycle which puts the formal basis for managing the evolution of a commitment (that has been informally introduced in the previous section), it is fundamental to clarify how, starting from a BPMN Choreography model extended with commitments, is possible to derive the associations between smart devices and commitments to be tracked. Assuming that for each resource to be monitored one smart device is used, the configuration of the smart device D^R related to a resource R requires to perform the following steps:

- *Identification of relevant activities:* being A the set of Choreography Activity, $A^R \in A$ corresponds the subset of ChoreographyActivity for which the resource is either the receiving or the sending message.
- *Identification of relevant commitments:* being C the set of Commitment Template, $C^R \in C$ corresponds to the subset CommitmentTemplate for which the debtor or the creditor refers to one of the Participant in A^R.

Being C^R the commitments to be tracked by the smart devices D^R, we assume that the smart device supports the needed capabilities to check the antecedent and the consequent of these commitments: e.g., the smart device monitoring a fish package will have a sensor for temperature on-board, and it is able to recognize (manually or automatically) when an activity starts or ends. Once deployed on a smart device, the tracking of a commitment is possible by considering the evolution of a commitment template as expressed by the timed commitment lifecycle formalized in the next section.

4.1   Timed Commitment Lifecycle

Consider a specific commitment template, indicating its target activity and debtor/creditor types, and providing values for its various attributes. At a given time, an instance of such a commitment can be in one of the states depicted in its commitment lifecycle (cf. Fig. 4). We now formally ground this abstract lifecycle, indicating when, and how, a transition between states occur. More

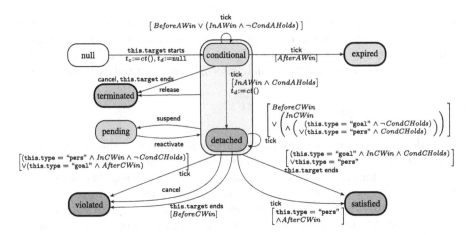

Fig. 9. Formalization of the timed commitment lifecycle with a target activity; *tick* denotes an arbitrary event, just used to inform the commitment machine about the current time.

specifically, a transition occurs in response to events, possibly depending on the validity of the commitment antecedent/consequent. We consider three types of events. First, we have *activity-related events*, i.e., the start and end of (an instance of) the choreography activity targeted by the commitment. Second, we have *explicit commitment manipulation events*, used to suspend, release, reactivate, or cancel a commitment instance. Interestingly, such events may actually be automatically generated in response to events issued on the activity lifecycle. For example, the designer may decide that whenever a choreography activity instance is suspended, then all commitment instances attached to it will be suspended, too. This is just an example of the benefits of our approach. Third, *Tick events*, represents the current time flowing. These events are useful to communicate the new current time to the commitment lifecycle, and in turn evaluate the quantitative temporal conditions attached to it [4]. Ticks may be internally generated, or communicated from the external environment, based on who is aware of the flow of time.

With these events at hand, we devise the timed commitment lifecycle of Fig. 9, where the keyword this refers to the specific commitment template of interest, function $ct()$ returns the time associated to the currently processed event, while t_c and t_d get respectively assigned the time at which the commitment is created or detached. Our approach formalizes the abstract diagram of Fig. 4 with concrete, testable transitions, employing the following macros[4]:

---

[4] The commitment machine we propose enriches standard commitment machines from the literature, adding temporal conditions on transitions. It is worth noting that, as usual in the commitment literature, the interpretation of such different states, and the corresponding set up of reactions, sanctions, and countermeasures, has to be handled in a domain-specific way on top of the commitment machine, not within the machine itself.

- *BeforeAWin* $= ct() \leq t_c + $ `this.minA` checks that the current time is before the antecedent time window.
- *InAWin* $= ct() > t_c + $ `this.minA` $\wedge\ ct() \leq t_c + $ `this.maxA` checks that the current time falls within the antecedent time window.
- *AfterAWin* $= ct() \geq t_c + $ `this.maxA` checks that the current time is after the antecedent time window.
- *BeforeCWin*, *InCWin* and *AfterCWin* reconstruct the previous three macros for the consequent time window. The additional complication, here, is that the reference point depends on the `this.refC` attribute. E.g., *InCWin* is formalized as:

$$\begin{cases} ct() > t_c + \texttt{this.minC} \wedge ct() \leq t_c + \texttt{this.maxC} & \text{if this.refC} = \text{creation} \\ ct() > t_d + \texttt{this.minC} \wedge ct() \leq t_d + \texttt{this.maxC} & \text{if this.refC} = \text{detach and } t_d \neq \text{null} \end{cases}$$

- *CondAHolds* and *CondCHolds* are respectively true if `this.condA` and `this.condC` hold at time $ct()$.

We briefly comment on the formalization. Call *active* a commitment (instance) that is either *conditional* or *detached*. A commitment instance becomes active when an instance of its target activity starts. Specifically, the commitment instance becomes conditional or detached depending on whether its antecedent condition evaluates to true at the creation time, and its antecedent time window has a minimum displacement of 0 (`minA` $= 0$). A *conditional* commitment instance becomes:

- *Expired* as soon as the deadline of its antecedent time window, calculated w.r.t. its creation time, is over.
- *Terminated* if its target activity instance ends (marking the fact that the commitment instance never required an actual obligation to be fulfilled).
- *Detached* when, within its associated antecedent time window (calculated w.r.t. the creation time), its antecedent condition evaluates to true.

The explicit cancellation of an active commitment instance has the effect of terminating or violating the commitment instance, depending on whether it has been detached or not. The other transitions of an active commitment instance depend on whether it has a goal or persistence nature. In the first case, it becomes:

- *Violated* as soon as the consequent time window (calculated w.r.t. the creation or detach time depending on the `refC` attribute) expires, witnessing that the target activity instance has not completed on time. If the commitment instance is detached, also a premature completion of the activity instance leads to violation.

- *Satisfied* if its corresponding activity instance completes on time, and in a moment in which the consequent condition holds.

  Conversely, in the latter case, it becomes:

- *Violated* when, during the consequent time window, the consequent condition becomes false, thus witnessing that the promised condition has not been maintained.
- *Satisfied* as soon as the consequent time window passes or its corresponding activity instance is completed, witnessing that the consequent condition has been continuously maintained until this time point.

Notice the complementary behavior of goal vs. persistence commitments in Fig. 9, when the commitment is detached. A goal commitment is satisfied if its target activity is completed at a time that falls within the consequent time window, and at which the consequent holds; it is instead violated if the deadline of the consequent time window expires while the commitment is still in the detached state. Contrariwise, a persistence commitment is violated during the consequent time window as soon as the consequent is not maintained anymore, whereas it gets automatically satisfied if the commitment is still detached when the consequent time window expires.

4.2   Implementation

The lifecycle presented in the previous section can be directly used as an actual computational artifact during the system execution, tracking the evolution of commitment instances as new events occur. When the commitment instance resides on a smart object, checking the antecedent/consequent amounts to issue the corresponding query on the data maintained the object, and/or retrieved through its sensors. The actual implementation obviously depends on the specific programming language of choice, and the computational resources available. To show the feasibility of the implementation, we have encoded the different transition rules of the lifecycle in the (Reactive) Event Calculus (REC) [3], a logic-based calculus of events that has been already used to formalize and monitor business constraints [13] and timed commitments [4]. The query language to express commitment conditions is in this case natively provided by REC itself.

The complete formalization in REC, together with the encoding of our case study (cf. Sect. 3.2) and its embedding into a monitoring test application, can be downloaded from http://tinyurl.com/kd8wtre. Figure 10 shows the result produced by REC on a hypothetical partial run of our case study.

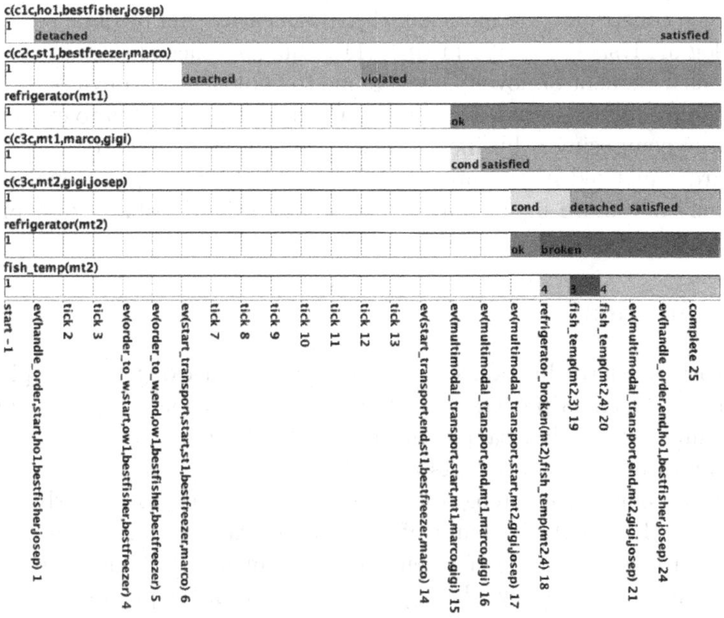

Fig. 10. Monitoring timed commitment instances in REC.

5   Related Work

Checking the compliance of a business process requires to verify that the execution of a process is respecting what has been conceived by the process designer. In the literature, there are several approaches and solutions able to cope with this issue and [10] organizes them in a systematic literature review. Among the dimensions of analysis, the survey discusses the compliance monitoring functionality that a monitoring system should support and in particular the importance of considering time, data, and resources in the constraints. Going towards this direction, and similarly to [2] where collaborative processes modeled with BPMN has been extended to include monitoring instructions, our approach extends the BPMN choreography model to attach commitments where constraints on time, data, and resources are possible to be defined.

Focusing more on the peculiarities of cross-organizational processes, [9] has identified some research challenges among which there is the need to model cross-organizational compliance rules. To this aim, we rely on commitments [15], exploited in [16] to model the interaction among several participants inspired by the agent-based system literature, and translated into automaton as suggested in [7,12]. At the same time, [8] focuses on the way in which the compliance rules are specified and verify if there are not conflicts between them. Even though approaches for monitoring timed extensions of commitments have been already proposed in the past [5,15,16], the explicit definition of a timed commitment lifecycle proposed in this paper, to the best of our knowledge, has never been devised.

Once the constraints are modeled, their verification can be done a-posteriori, through log analysis [1], or at run-time [11]. Our approach is close to the second case and, as a element of novelty, we assume to exploit smart devices to perform the compliance checking. Indeed, smart devices are now adopted to execute some of the tasks composing a business process, as well as to monitor the status of the resources manged in the process [17,18]. As their computational power is getting more and more significant, we investigated the possibility to exploit this capabilities.

6   Conclusions

In this work, we have introduced an approach for checking the compliance of a multi-party business process by extending BPMN choreography model with timed commitments. Classical commitments have been extended in this work to consider hard and soft constraints as well as persisting and goal commitments. The resulting enriched choreography model can be used to properly configure smart devices that will be in charge of checking the validity of those commitments due to the proposed lifecycle of extended commitments. Although this approach is in its infancy, we can now check possible deviations of process instance in a distributed way exploiting smart devices, inheriting the constraints defined at design-time. Nevertheless, there are several limitations that need to be addressed in future work. Firstly, although if the control-flow that can be defined for a choreography model is more simple than what possible to express in a collaboration diagram, how to manage switches and loops is currently an open issue that needs to be investigated. Furthermore, the proposed approach lives on the assumption that the communication is always up, and the smart device is always reachable. We will extend or approach to by considering reliability and communication failures.

Acknowledgments. This work has been partially funded by the Italian Project ITS Italy 2020 under the Technological National Clusters program and by the UNIBZ CRC Project *Planning for WORkflow Management* (PWORM).

References

1. van der Aalst, W.M.P., de Beer, H.T., van Dongen, B.F.: Process mining and verification of properties: an approach based on temporal logic. In: Meersman, R., Tari, Z. (eds.) OTM 2005. LNCS, vol. 3760, pp. 130–147. Springer, Heidelberg (2005). doi:10.1007/11575771_11
2. Baumgraß, A., Herzberg, N., Meyer, A., Weske, M.: BPMN extension for business process monitoring. In: Proceedings of International Workshop on Evolution of Information Systems and their Design Methods (EMISA 2014) (2014)
3. Bragaglia, S., Chesani, F., Mello, P., Montali, M., Torroni, P.: Reactive event calculus for monitoring global computing applications. In: Artikis, A., Craven, R., Kesim Çiçekli, N., Sadighi, B., Stathis, K. (eds.) Logic Programs, Norms and Action. LNCS, vol. 7360, pp. 123–146. Springer, Heidelberg (2012). doi:10.1007/978-3-642-29414-3_8

4. Chesani, F., Mello, P., Montali, M., Torroni, P.: Representing and monitoring social commitments using the event calculus. J. Auton. Agents Multi-agent Syst. **27**(1), 85–130 (2013)

5. Chopra, A.K., Singh, M.P.: Generalized commitment alignment. In: Proceedings of the International Conference on Autonomous Agents and Multiagent Systems (AAMAS 2015)

6. Chopra, A.K., Singh, M.P.: Cupid: commitments in relational algebra. In: Proceedings of the 29th AAAI Conference on Artificial Intelligence. AAAI Press (2015)

7. Ferrario, R., Guarino, N.: Commitment-based modeling of service systems. In: Snene, M. (ed.) IESS 2012. LNBIP, vol. 103, pp. 170–185. Springer, Heidelberg (2012). doi:10.1007/978-3-642-28227-0_13

8. Knuplesch, D., Reichert, M., Fdhila, W., Rinderle-Ma, S.: On enabling compliance of cross-organizational business processes. In: Proceedings of the International Conference on Business Process Management (BPM 2013) (2013)

9. Knuplesch, D., Reichert, M., Mangler, J., Rinderle-Ma, S., Fdhila, W.: Towards compliance of cross-organizational processes and their changes. In: La Rosa, M., Soffer, P. (eds.) BPM 2012. LNBIP, vol. 132, pp. 649–661. Springer, Heidelberg (2013). doi:10.1007/978-3-642-36285-9_65

10. Ly, L.T., Maggi, F.M., Montali, M., Rinderle-Ma, S., van der Aalst, W.M.: Compliance monitoring in business processes: functionalities, application, and tool-support. Inf. Syst. **54**, 209–234 (2015)

11. Maggi, F.M., Montali, M., Westergaard, M., van der Aalst, W.M.P.: Monitoring business constraints with linear temporal logic: an approach based on colored automata. In: Rinderle-Ma, S., Toumani, F., Wolf, K. (eds.) BPM 2011. LNCS, vol. 6896, pp. 132–147. Springer, Heidelberg (2011). doi:10.1007/978-3-642-23059-2_13

12. Montali, M., Calvanese, D., De Giacomo, G.: Verification of data-aware commitment-based multiagent systems. In: Proceedings of the 13th International Conference on Autonomous Agents and Multiagent Systems (AAMAS) (2014)

13. Montali, M., Maggi, F.M., Chesani, F., Mello, P., van der Aalst, W.M.P.: Monitoring business constraints with the event calculus. ACM TIST **5**(1), 17 (2013)

14. Sahai, A., Machiraju, V., Sayal, M., van Moorsel, A., Casati, F.: Automated SLA monitoring for web services. In: Feridun, M., Kropf, P., Babin, G. (eds.) DSOM 2002. LNCS, vol. 2506, pp. 28–41. Springer, Heidelberg (2002). doi:10.1007/3-540-36110-3_6

15. Singh, M.P.: Commitments in multiagent systems: some history, some confusions, some controversies, some prospects. In: The Goals of Cognition: Essays in Honor of Cristiano Castelfranchi, pp. 601–626. College Publications (2012)

16. Telang, P.R., Singh, M.P.: Specifying and verifying cross-organizational business models: an agent-oriented approach. IEEE Trans. Serv. Comput. **5**(3), 305–318 (2012)

17. Thoma, M., Meyer, S., Sperner, K., Meissner, S., Braun, T.: On IoT-services: survey, classification and enterprise integration. In: 2012 IEEE International Conference on Green Computing and Communications (2012)

18. Tranquillini, S., Spieß, P., Daniel, F., Karnouskos, S., Casati, F., Oertel, N., Mottola, L., Oppermann, F.J., Picco, G.P., Römer, K., Voigt, T.: Process-based design and integration of wireless sensor network applications. In: Barros, A., Gal, A., Kindler, E. (eds.) BPM 2012. LNCS, vol. 7481, pp. 134–149. Springer, Heidelberg (2012). doi:10.1007/978-3-642-32885-5_10

Empowering Low-Latency Applications Through a Serverless Edge Computing Architecture

Luciano Baresi, Danilo Filgueira Mendonça, and Martin Garriga[✉]

Dipartimento di Elettronica, Informazione e Bioingegneria, Politecnico di Milano,
Milan, Italy
{luciano.baresi,danilo.filgueira,martin.garriga}@polimi.it

Abstract. The exponential increase of the data generated by pervasive
and mobile devices requires disrupting approaches for the realization of
emerging mobile and IoT applications. Although cloud computing provides virtually unlimited computational resources, low-latency applications cannot afford the high latencies introduced by sending and retrieving data from/to the cloud. In this scenario, edge computing appears as a
promising solution by bringing computation and data near to users and
devices. However, the resource-finite nature of edge servers constrains
the possibility of deploying full applications on them. To cope with these
problems, we propose a serverless architecture at the edge, bringing a
highly scalable, intelligent and cost-effective use of edge infrastructure's
resources with minimal configuration and operation efforts. The feasibility of our approach is shown through an augmented reality use case for
mobile devices, in which we offload computation and data intensive tasks
from the devices to serverless functions at the edge, outperforming the
cloud alternative up to 80% in terms of throughput and latency.

Keywords: Serverless architectures · Edge computing · Mobile Edge
Computing · Low-latency applications

1 Introduction

Mobile data will skyrocket in the coming years, mainly driven by mobile video
streaming and the Internet of Things (IoT). In 2017, data traffic of mobile devices
is expected to exceed 6 Exabytes ($6 * 10^9$ Gb) per month, and when combined
with the traffic generated by laptops and machine-to-machine communications,
the overall demand should reach 11 Exabytes per month [1]. Although cloud
computing appears as a straightforward solution for processing such an amount
of data, in certain scenarios the latency introduced by sending/retrieving heavy
payloads from/to the cloud can be prohibitive [2]. To address data-intensive
and low latency requirements, as well as to avoid the bottlenecks of centralized servers, edge computing proposes to bring computation to the edge of the
network, that is, near to where it is needed by users and devices [3]. Moreover, Mobile Edge Computing (MEC) allows for the use of its services with low

Published by Springer International Publishing AG 2017. All Rights Reserved
F. De Paoli et al. (Eds.): ESOCC 2017, LNCS 10465, pp. 196–210, 2017.
DOI: 10.1007/978-3-319-67262-5_15

latency, location awareness and mobility support to make up for the disadvantages of cloud computing [4].

However, the distributed and resource-finite nature of edge infrastructure also imposes limitations regarding its capability of hosting many diverse applications and/or services, otherwise hosted remotely in the cloud [3], since an overloaded MEC server significantly degrades user experience and negates the advantages of MEC [4]. Thus, such an scenario cannot be simply supported by a straightforward migration of the existing cloud model at the edge, that is, simply adopting *virtualization* and *containerization* technologies [5]. Recently, *Serverless Architectures* [6], also known as *Functions-as-a-Service (FaaS)*, appeared as a disruptive alternative that delegates the management of the execution environment of an application (in the form of stateless functions) to the infrastructure provider [7]. As a consequence, provider-managed containers are used to execute functions, without pre-allocating any computing capability or dealing with scalability and load-balancing burden. This should boost the utility of the edge nodes, allowing one to deploy more functionality given their limited capabilities and resources, while meeting application's low latency requirements.

This paper presents a *serverless edge computing* architecture that enables the offloading of mobile computation with low latency and high throughput. The objective is to allow low-latency mobile applications to minimize the impact on the resources of devices (which are battery and CPU constrained) and satisfy their latency requirement. The feasibility of the proposed architecture is evaluated through a mobile augmented reality application, and compared against a cloud-based solution. Results show that, in data-intensive scenarios, the proposed serverless edge solution outperformed the cloud-based offloading solution up to 80% in terms of throughput and latency.

The rest of the paper is organized as follows. Section 2 defines edge computing and serverless architectures. Section 3 presents a motivating case study: a Mobile Augmented Reality application. Section 4 describes the proposed architecture. Section 5 presents the evaluation we carried out. Section 6 discusses related work. Section 7 concludes the paper.

2   Background

Edge computing is a distributed computing paradigm that aims to cope with the rapid increase in data coming from the plethora of mobile devices. Its main purpose is to boost the potential of the Internet-of-Things and other real-time and data-intensive applications [3,8], by shifting the computation from the center (server) of the system towards a computing infrastructure deployed at the edges of the system (or of the network). The aim is to mitigate the latency and bottlenecks of centralized or coarsely distributed servers.

In contrast to the more general term, Mobile Edge Computing (MEC) focuses on co-locating computing and storage resources at base stations of cellular networks, thus reducing the stress of the network by shifting computational efforts from servers deployed in the Internet to the edges of the mobile network [3,9].

Being co-located at base stations, computing and storage resources of MEC servers are also available in close proximity to mobile users, thus eliminating the need for routing these data through the core network. MEC is seen as a future and promising approach to increase the quality of experience in cellular networks, and a key enabler for the evolution to 5G networks [10]. A distributed PaaS (Platform as a Service) can be deployed within the radio access network to serve low-latency, context-aware applications timely.

A Serverless Architecture is a refined cloud computing model to process requested functionality without pre-allocating any computing capability. Provider-managed containers are used to execute functions (often called lambdas), which are event-triggered and ephemeral (may only last for one invocation) [6]. This approach allows one to write and deploy code without considering the runtime environment, resource allocation, load balancing, and scalability; all these aspects are handled by the provider.

The serverless model represents a further evolution of the pay-per-use computing model: we started allocating virtual machines (e.g., Amazon EC2), then moved to containers (e.g., CS Docker Engine) and now we only allocate the resources (a container shared by several functions) for the time needed to carry out the computation.

The Serverless architecture has many benefits with respect to more traditional, server-based approaches. Functions share the runtime environment (typically a pool of containers), and the code specific to a particular application is small and stateless by design. Hence, the deployment of a pool of shared containers (workers) on a machine (or a cluster of machines) and the execution of some code onto any of them becomes inexpensive and efficient.

Horizontal scaling is completely automatic, elastic, and quick, allowing one to increase the number of workers against sudden spikes of traffic. The serverless model is much more reactive than the typical solutions of scaling virtual machines or spinning up containers against bursts in the workload [11]. Finally, the pay-per-use cost model is fine-grained, down to a 100 ms granularity for all the major vendors, in contrast to the "usual" hour-based billing of virtual machines and containers. This allows companies to drastically reduce the cost of their infrastructures with regard to a typical monolithic architecture or even a microservices architecture [12].

Several cloud providers have developed serverless solutions recently, many of which are still in their explicit or implicit beta testing phase[1]. Table 1 summarizes the main serverless solutions, with AWS Lambda that appeared 1.5 years before the others. All these alternatives provide similar capabilities; IBM Openwhisk is the only open-source solution among the major vendors.

---

[1] https://blog.zhaw.ch/icclab/faas-function-hosting-services-and-their-technical-characteristics.

Table 1. Serverless providers and supported languages

Provider	Languages
AWS Lambda	Node.js, Java, Python
Google Cloud Functions	Node.js
Azure Functions	Node.js, C#
IBM OpenWhisk	Node.js, Swift, Binary (Docker)
Webtask.io	Node.js
OpenLambda	Python

3 Mobile Augmented Reality

Augmented reality (AR) is the combination of a view of the real world and sup-plementary computer-generated information [10]. More recently, Mobile Augmented Reality (MAR) emerged as a fusion of AR and mobile computing. MAR is an example of applications for which low latency and high throughput are key requirements. These applications enrich the interaction of users with the physical world by augmenting their vision of the reality with relevant information (e.g., historical information about buildings and monuments), modifying it (e.g., by translating captured text in a different language), or by adding virtual elements that can mimic interactions with the real world (e.g., virtual objects or creatures from a fantasy game), or helping users fulfill physical tasks (e.g., by highlighting a free parking spot).

Our example MAR application is supposed to help the tourists that visit a city and want to receive relevant information about Points-of-Interest (POIs), such as monuments, buildings, and other architectural elements, by looking at them through their mobile devices (Fig. 1) or special glasses [13].

Based on the approach described by Huang et al. [14], the following steps summarize the sequence of data- and computational-intensive tasks in MAR applications:

1. The reality that must be augmented should be captured by using the device's camera, with a rate between 2 and 6 images per second [15,16].
2. The captured frame must be scanned to extract the features that allow the app to identify the physical objects in the scene.
3. Virtual content, associated with the identified scene and objects, must be retrieved from servers[2] based on the previously extracted features.
4. Finally, the app produces a combined image of the real and virtual contents and displays it on the device screen.

As users can rapidly move and target different portions of the world around them, target scenes must be captured by the device's camera at a fast rate (step 1),

---

[2] This information cannot be usually stored on the device given its size and dynamic nature.

Fig. 1. An example mobile augmented reality app (etips.com).

generating a significant volume of data frequently. Also, the extraction of features from the objects in these frames (step 2) is a computational-intensive task. Prohibitive network traffic and latency can be avoided by letting step 2 be performed locally and delegating only steps 3 and 4 to services in the cloud [14]. However, this kind of approach may fail to meet users' expectations because continuously transferring information to cloud services and interacting with them could be slow, and it can significantly reduce the battery of their devices [17]. Offloading mobile computation to a MEC platform rather than using "traditional" cloud services should bring several advantages: First, it provides the low latency and high throughput required by mobile augmented reality applications; second, it prevents the overloading of mobile devices with computational-intensive tasks; and finally, the MEC platform can adjust provisioned resources on-the-fly and no resources are wasted.

4   Proposed Solution

Figure 2 shows the proposed architecture. Its main physical elements are mobile devices and MEC servers. Mobile devices can be of any type (e.g., tablets, smartphones), running a low-latency application that needs offloading part of its computation to more powerful servers. For this, the devices send the information to be processed to the MEC server through standardized network protocols [18]. A Base Transceiver Station[3] (BTS) bridges mobile devices and MEC servers as a part of the cellular infrastructure and MEC architecture, according to its current specifications [10]. In this scenario, mobile devices and MEC servers are

---

[3] Different generations of wireless mobile networks use distinct names (e.g., eNodeB in 4G).

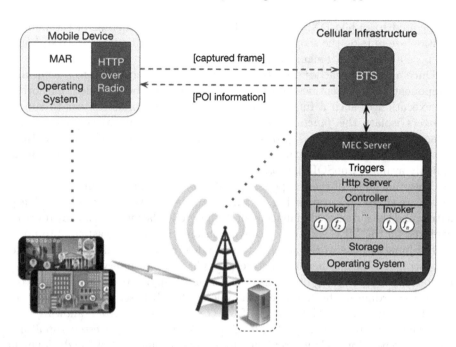

Fig. 2. Proposed architecture: A MAR application running on mobile devices send requests to the MEC server hosted on a cellular infrastructure (shared components of the serverless MEC server are depicted in grey).

at no more than a few hops from each other. MEC servers host the serverless environment, where stateless functions are deployed and executed.

While MEC servers are ideal candidates for offloading the computation to preserve devices' resources and kill latency, these nodes are themselves potentially constrained. Accordingly, the feasibility of hosting dedicated *virtual machines*, *containers*, and *stateful applications* would also be limited, as these nodes cannot scale "infinitely" to host always-running VMs/containers as the cloud itself. To overcome this limitation, we propose to deploy a serverless architecture [6] onto the MEC servers.

Figure 2 also shows the serverless components deployed on the MEC server. The entry points are the *triggers* associated with events: in the MAR application, an event that triggers a function consists of uploading of an image or capturing a frame with the device's camera. These triggers fire requests to an *Http Server* that exposes a Restful API of available functions.

To achieve network transparency, a local Domain Name Server (DNS), deployed on the cellular infrastructure, must distinguish between requests to the RESTful APIs exposed by the MEC server and any other request for an Internet endpoint. The main difference from a regular DNS is locality, as the requests must be handled by the MEC server on the current base station. To this end, the names of edge resources must be resolved locally without being propagated to public DNS servers. Whereas the specific details of the naming solution are outside the scope of this work, we argue that such a feature should not pose a significant technical challenge.

Once a request reaches the MEC server, it is then forwarded to a *controller* component, which identifies and retrieves the function being called, authorizes the execution of such a function and identifies an available invoker to run it. *Invokers* isolate the *functions* in containerized environments, optimized and managed by the serverless provider to reduce overhead and response time. Finally, results and logging information are stored in the *Storage* component, a highly available, noSQL database.

Note that most of the components of the serverless architecture of the MEC server are shared (in grey in Fig. 2) among all the functions. The highly shared nature and the automated management of the whole platform allows any function deployed on the MEC servers to scale up automatically and elastically to unexpected bursts in the workload, and to scale down when it is not used anymore. In contrast with container-based stateful applications, the serverless platform is responsible for allocating functions of one or more applications on a pool of containers according to the resources available at the MEC server. As a result, the use of the computational resources of MEC servers is optimized, allowing both more functions to be deployed and more requests to be processed simultaneously. A conventional cloud provider can always become part of the deployment if needed, but it is not the focus of this paper.

There is no need to follow the common practice of deploying multiple virtual machines or containers to be resilient and responsive against downtime of single instances or bursts of workload. The on-demand execution of functions provides inherent scalability and optimal utilization as the number of running functions always matches the trigger rate. Additionally, the application developer only focuses on the application code and can fully outsource the management of the deployment/execution infrastructure. The serverless approach also provides a fine-grained *pay-per-use* billing model with benefits for both application owners and telecom operators (in charge of the MEC servers).

4.1   Mobile Augmented Reality on MECs

To instantiate the proposed architecture fpr the Mobile Augmented Reality application presented in Sect. 3, the client MAR application must continuously capture frames from the camera and send them together with other parameters (type of POIs of interest, screen size and resolution) to the nearest MEC server. The server is in charge of retrieving the features of the POIs in the scene, match them against a local database, and return the corresponding data (information about monuments, buildings and other points of interest) to the client application, which must merge them with the image on the screen to offer a seamless experience to the user.

Serverless functions deployed on the MEC servers are in charge of: (1) image processing; (2) feature extraction; (3) matching; and (4) information retrieval based on these features. Many of these activities are supported by libraries already integrated in major vendors' serverless frameworks, such as IBM Visual Recognition[4], Azure Visual Cognitive Services[5] and AWS Rekognition[6]. The management of the execution of these functions is optimized by the serverless environment on the MEC server, and different client applications may use the same functions (for instance, those related to image processing and other common use cases).

The MEC architecture further provides the advantage of data locality, which restricts the scope of the feature matching by letting a given MEC server to store data only regarding the POIs within the region covered by its base station (instead of considering the probably wider area covered by the cloud service). Such advantage has two aspects: feature matching against a reduced database becomes less expensive, and substantially reduces data fetching latency [19], and less data must be persisted on each MEC server.

Finally, the creation and update of existing information about the POIs managed by different base stations could be performed by administrators by means of a Web application backed by cloud services. Following this approach, administrators could also request reports about the usage of the MAR application on each base station (e.g., which touristic assets have been most accessed and which advertised services have been most viewed in a given period of time).

5   Experimental Evaluation

We evaluated the proposed architecture in the context of the MAR application (Sect. 3), using two alternative deployments for the serverless functions: at the edge or in the cloud. The main goal of this experiment is not to compare "traditional" cloud services against a serverless solution, but to demonstrate that the proposed serverless edge architecture can outperform a typical serverless cloud provider under certain circumstances and requirements.

The experimental setup is depicted in Fig. 3. Capturing and uploading an image (Steps 0 and 1) is emulated using Postman[7], a JavaScript open source application designed to load test functional behaviors and measure the performance of Web APIs.

A Node.js Http server provides the endpoint for the requests and uploads of the image (Step 2), then triggering different subsequent steps depending on the two different deployments: Steps 3.a, 4.a and 5.a for the edge-based solution, and Steps 3.b, 4.b and 5.b for the cloud one. Additionally, the Node.js server collects the metrics relevant to the experiment, such as latency, throughput and computation time.

The edge node deploys the IBM Openwhisk serverless framework[8] that manages *actions* (the equivalent of functions in openwhisk). Being open-source, openwhisk is (to date) the only serverless alternative among the major vendors that

---

[4] https://console.ng.bluemix.net/catalog/services/watson_vision_combined.

[5] https://azure.microsoft.com/en-us/services/cognitive-services.

[6] https://aws.amazon.com/rekognition/.

[7] https://www.getpostman.com/.

[8] https://developer.ibm.com/openwhisk/.

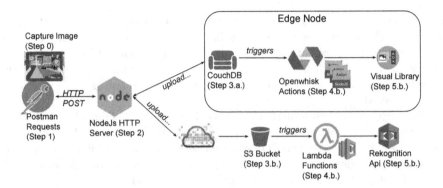

Fig. 3. Experimental setup for the example system.

can be deployed locally or on private clouds. Particularly, openwhisk provides a built-in noSQL database: CouchDB, which is associated with the implemented actions through user-defined triggers and rules. In our experiment, uploading an image to CouchDB (Step 3.a) triggers the action that performs the feature extraction and matching (Step 4.a) with the points-of-interest, supported by a visual recognition library (Step 5.a).

For this experiment, we considered two alternatives for the deployment of the serverless architecture to mimic the behavior of an edge node (Fig. 4). The edge-local alternative is an implementation with openwhisk deployed on a regular laptop, in a virtual machine with 4x CPU, 4x GB of RAM and 40 GB SSD of storage. This deployment allows us to represent an extreme situation where latency is close to zero, but the computational resources are highly constrained. On the other hand, we deployed the serverless architecture on Policloud[9], the private IaaS solution of Politecnico di Milano where the computational resources are less constrained, and still low latency can be achieved due to physical proximity and data locality. This setup runs on a small cluster of 4 virtual machines with 2x CPU, 4x GB of Ram and 100 GB SSD, each running a different component of openwhisk (triggers and storage, Http server, controller, and invokers). Note that in both cases the edge node is deployed in the same LAN that originates the requests, to emulate the few-hop scenario in which devices are directly connected to their corresponding MEC.

The cloud alternative for this experiment uses AWS Lambda[10] and the associated AWS services, as the first-available and most mature serverless solution in the market. Both the functions and the services (S3 storage, image recognition) are hosted in the us-west region, which is enforced by AWS to guarantee a certain degree of data locality. The image is uploaded through an S3 bucket (Step 3.b), a trigger associates it with the corresponding lambda functions (Step 4.b) that

---

[9] http://policloud.polimi.it/.
[10] https://aws.amazon.com/lambda/.

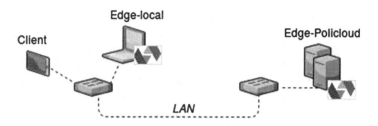

Fig. 4. Deployment alternatives to mimic the behavior and network proximity of edge nodes.

perform the feature extraction and matching supported by the AWS Rekognition service (Step 5.b).

The size of the payload for this experiment was fixed using a sample image of approximately 500 Kb, which is a reasonable size for this use case [20]. The workload was parameterized, ranging from 100 to 1000 requests, considering not only the default maximum for concurrent executions in AWS Lambda[11], but also the limited resources of the local edge node. All functions deployed at the edge and on cloud were configured with a maximum of 256 Mb of RAM per instance.

Results. Figure 5 shows the execution results for 100 and 1000 requests served by the edge-based (locally and on PoliCloud) and cloud-based deployment alternatives. We run five times each experiment and show the average values.

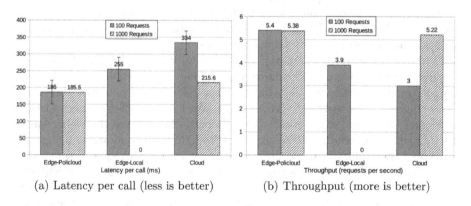

(a) Latency per call (less is better)   (b) Throughput (more is better)

Fig. 5. Experimental results for 100 and 1000 requests in the Edge-based and in the Cloud-based deployments.

The latency is shown in Fig. 5(a), along with the standard deviation, calculated as the average over 100 and 1000 requests, respectively. These results do not consider the actual computation time of the functions, that is, they only consider the overhead of network communication per call. For the 100-request

---

[11] http://docs.aws.amazon.com/lambda/latest/dg/concurrent-executions.html.

scenario, the latency added by the edge-based solution is 80% and 31% less (Policloud and local, respectively) than the latency in the cloud alternative. For 1000 simultaneous requests, Edge-Policloud maintains a latency similar to the previous scenario. It still shows a clear advantage over the Cloud deployment (72% in latency), which features a slight improvement but still higher latency and higher deviation (as shown by the error indicators of top of each bar in Fig. 5(a)). The results for edge-local deployment are not shown since it was not able to serve this heavy workload, thus the openwhisk architecture throttles the execution causing considerable overhead. The throughput is shown in Fig. 5(b) (standard deviation is negligible thus not shown here) where the number of requests served per second is better in the edge-based solutions, 80% (Policloud) and 30% (local) for the 100 requests scenario. Regarding the 1000-request scenario, Edge-Policloud maintains a similar throughput, a 3% better than the Cloud deployment, which improved significantly due to the higher degree of parallelism achieved. Again, the throughput for the Edge-local deployment is not shown since it was not able to serve the workload timely.

Discussion. Obtained results confirm our hypotheses regarding the higher latencies introduced by a cloud solution in the context of data-intensive, low-latency applications. Despite the high degree of parallelism that can be achieved by deploying a serverless solution in the cloud, the throughput decreases when dealing with a heavy workload with images as payload.

In the 100-request scenario, where the cloud solution does not exploit all the parallelism that it can achieve, the Edge solution clearly outstands. Particularly, the Edge-Policloud solution outperformed the Cloud one by a 80% both in latency and throughput. Even the Edge-local solution brings some improvement (30%) despite its strictly constrained resources.

In the heavy workload scenario, the throughput of the Edge-Policloud and Cloud solutions are similar. The naïve edge-local alternative fails on this scenario since it cannot increase its allocated resources, which is a potential shortcoming of too resource-constrained MEC nodes. We foresee that with even heavier workloads, the Cloud solution will certainly outperform, since the higher latencies introduced by sending/retrieving data from/to the Cloud are compensated by its high scalability and parallelism, serving almost all requests simultaneously. However, in a real deployment, we foresee that the edge nodes will also have access to more resources than in our experiment. Although the edge is certainly more resource-constrained than the cloud, several edge nodes would be involved and interconnected in this architecture, allowing one to load-balance the requests among them, and this achieve better throughput and lower latency, as shown in the experiments.

Threats to Validity. First, the CPU power of serverless functions is allocated proportionally to their memory configuration[12]. Thus, for CPU-intensive

---

[12] https://aws.amazon.com/lambda/faqs/#functions.

applications, allocating the maximum memory to cloud functions will certainly outperform the edge alternative (where it is not feasible to over-allocate memory and CPU due to limited resources) because of the shorter processing times, and mitigates the gains in terms of latency. One should test and benchmark the architecture to find the adequate trade-off among the resources allocated to functions, the resources available in the edge nodes, and the overall cost. Second, the connection among nodes in the mimicked edge architecture (local and Policloud) was done through LAN (as depicted in Fig. 4), which may deliver different connection speeds than a cellular network. To make this scenario more accurate, we emulated 4G connection speeds between the Postman requests and the Node.js server (Fig. 3) using network throttling tools[13]. Experiments with real mobile devices and different link quality are very important. Finally, the experiments focused on the latency of the serverless architecture stressed with varying numbers of requests to the same functions. The performance of a serverless solution stressed with heterogeneous functions calls was not part of this work. Nonetheless, the ability of serverless providers [6, 11] to handle the deployment of heterogeneous functions on a limited set of containers is a strong argument in favor of our solution when compared against a "simple" container-based edge solution.

6   Related Work

The work in [3] presents the technical details of the first real-world MEC platform by Nokia Siemens and Intel [21]. In this platform, MEC servers on base stations are equipped with commodity hardware and application deployment is based on virtualization technologies. Applications running on the mobile edge are expected to be event-driven, which is in line with the serverless model discussed in our paper. Besides, the authors present a taxonomy of MEC applications that can profit from MEC deployment. Interestingly, our MAR application (Sect. 3) is representative of two of the most benefited application classes: "Offloading" and "Augmentation".

Ismail et al. [22] evaluated different aspects of the deployment and operation of a container technology locally on edge nodes. In their work, a testbed was setup using a database and three edge nodes interconnected by a company network. Despite the similarity with this work, our proposal moves away from virtualization and containerization of application logic, in favor of serverless computing to optimize the use of edge resources and boost the potential of mobile edge computing.

The work in [4] proposes two different recovery schemes for overloaded or broken MEC servers. One recovery scheme is where an overloaded MEC server offloads its work to available neighbors within transfer range. The other recovery scheme is for situations when there is no available neighboring MEC within transfer range, and uses devices as ad-hoc relay nodes in order to bridge two

---

[13] https://developers.google.com/web/tools/chrome-devtools/network-performance/network-conditions.

MEC servers. In a similar direction, Tärneberg et al. [2] proposed a model that bridges mobile edge computing and the distributed cloud paradigm, as well as an algorithm to solve the resource management challenges that emerge from this integration. In contrast with these works, our approach mitigates the overload in MEC servers by deploying a serverless architecture on them, which provides an effective and efficient usage of available resources. Certainly, the scalability of our proposed architecture could be extended by means of a neighbor offloading strategy as proposed in [4] or by an integration of MEC and cloud resources as proposed in [2].

The first documented efforts for bringing serverless capabilities to the edge are very recent, and come mostly from industry. Lambda@Edge[14] is a new functionality of AWS (in preview at the time of writing this paper) that allows one to explicitly deploy lambda functions to certain edge locations, closer to the user. However, the notion of edge locations in AWS is coarse grained (but finer grained than AWS regions): their edge schema, named CloudFront, consists of approximately 70 edge nodes worldwide. In contrast, we consider that MEC enables fine-grained edge nodes to be deployed closer to the user. In our proposed architecture, MEC servers can be distributed one every km^2 or less. Furthermore, the upcoming small 5G cells and microcells [3] allow us to think of one edge node per block, or even per building in certain vital places, such as government buildings, shopping centers or transport stations.

EdgeScale [23] is another platform that leverages serverless cloud computing to enable storage and processing on a hierarchy of data centers, positioned over the geographic span of a network between the user and traditional wide-area cloud providers. EdgeScale applications are structured as lightweight, stateless functions that can be rapidly instantiated on demand. This approach implements all the functions, storage, routing and additional capabilities from scratch, while we opted for leveraging current open technologies such as Openwhisk, which have broad support from a major vendor (IBM) and an active community. Besides, regarding the expected benefits of the approach, EdgeScale is on an early stage and does not report any empirical evaluation of concrete gains in terms of latency, throughput and bandwidth.

7   Conclusions and Future Work

This paper presents a novel *serverless edge computing* architecture that enables the offloading of mobile computation with low latency and high throughput. MEC servers are ideal candidates for offloading the computation to preserve devices' resources and kill latency, while a serverless model provides inherent scalability and optimal resource utilization as the allocation of functions to containers is handled by the serverless platform itself, and the number of running functions always matches the trigger rate. Additionally, the application developer only focuses on the application code and can fully outsource the management of the deployment/execution infrastructure.

---

[14] http://docs.aws.amazon.com/lambda/latest/dg/lambda-edge.html.

The proposed architecture is instantiated using a Mobile Augmented Reality application, as a good example of a low-latency application in which the latency introduced by transferring heavy payloads from/to the cloud can degrade the user experience. We conducted experiments comparing an edge-based solution with a cloud-based solution in this scenario, with the former outperforming the latter up to 80% in terms of throughput and latency.

Our future work comprises the scenario in which several edge nodes are interconnected and can be involved in serving the requests. This should allow us to achieve better throughput and lower latency, but with the additional complexity of introducing load-balancing and resource-allocation mechanisms [24]. Additionally, the comparison with a traditional (non-serverless) deployment in the cloud should be addressed, to find the right balance among resource consumption, performance, and cost.

References

1. Dehos, C., González, J.L., Domenico, A.D., Kténas, D., Dussopt, L.: Millimeter-wave access and backhauling: the solution to the exponential data traffic increase in 5G mobile communications systems? IEEE Commun. Mag. **52**(9), 88–95 (2014)
2. Tarneberg, W., Mehta, A., Wadbro, E., Tordsson, J., Eker, J., Kihl, M., Elmroth, E.: Dynamic application placement in the mobile cloud network. Future Gener. Comput. Syst. **70**, 163–177 (2017)
3. Beck, M.T., Werner, M., Feld, S., Schimper, S.: Mobile edge computing: a taxonomy. In: Proceedings of the Sixth International Conference on Advances in Future Internet, pp. 48–54 (2014)
4. Satria, D., Park, D., Jo, M.: Recovery for overloaded mobile edge computing. Future Gener. Comput. Syst. **70**, 138–147 (2017)
5. Pahl, C.: Containerization and the PaaS cloud. IEEE Cloud Comput. **2**(3), 24–31 (2015)
6. Roberts, M.: Serverless architectures: what is serverless? (2016). http://martinfowler.com/articles/serverless.html
7. Fromm, K.: Why the future of software and apps is serverless (2012). http://readwrite.com/2012/10/15/why-the-future-of-software-and-apps-is-serverless/
8. Salman, O., Elhajj, I., Kayssi, A., Chehab, A.: Edge computing enabling the Internet of Things. In: IEEE World Forum on Internet of Things (WF-IoT), pp. 603–608, December 2015
9. Ahmed, A., Ahmed, E.: A survey on mobile edge computing. In: 2016 10th International Conference on Intelligent Systems and Control (ISCO), pp. 1–8, January 2016
10. Hu, Y.C., Patel, M., Sabella, D., Sprecher, N., Young, V.: Mobile edge computing: a key technology towards 5G. ETSI White Paper 11 (2015)
11. Hendrickson, S., Sturdevant, S., Harter, T., Venkataramani, V., Arpaci-Dusseau, A.C., Arpaci-Dusseau, R.H.: Serverless computation with openlambda. In: Proceedings of the 8th USENIX Conference on Hot Topics in Cloud Computing, pp. 33–39 (2016)
12. Villamizar, M., Garcés, O., Ochoa, L., Castro, H., Salamanca, L., Verano, M., Casallas, R., Gil, S., Valencia, C., Zambrano, A., Lang, M.: Cost comparison of running web applications in the cloud using monolithic, microservice, and AWS lambda architectures. Serv. Oriented Comput. Appl. **11**(2), 233–247 (2017)

13. Barfield, W.: Fundamentals of Wearable Computers and Augmented Reality. CRC Press, Boca Raton (2015)
14. Huang, B.R., Lin, C.H., Lee, C.H.: Mobile augmented reality based on cloud computing. In: Anti-counterfeiting, Security, and Identification, pp. 1–5, August 2012
15. Wagner, D., Schmalstieg, D., Bischof, H.: Multiple target detection and tracking with guaranteed framerates on mobile phones. In: IEEE International Symposium on Mixed and Augmented Reality (ISMAR), pp. 57–64 (2009)
16. Dollar, P., Wojek, C., Schiele, B., Perona, P.: Pedestrian detection: an evaluation of the state of the art. IEEE Trans. Pattern Anal. Mach. Intell. **34**(4), 743–761 (2012)
17. Baresi, L., Guinea, S., Mendonca, D.F.: A3droid: a framework for developing distributed crowdsensing. In: 2016 IEEE International Conference on Pervasive Computing and Communication Workshops (PerCom Workshops), pp. 1–6, March 2016
18. Sill, A.: Standards at the edge of the cloud. IEEE Cloud Comput. **4**(2), 63–67 (2017)
19. Abase, A.H., Khafagy, M.H., Omara, F.A.: Locality sim: cloud simulator with data locality. Int. J. Cloud Comput. Serv. Archit. (IJCCSA) **6**, 17–31 (2016)
20. Rodriguez-Santana, B.G., Viveros, A.M., Carvajal-Gámez, B.E., Trejo-Osorio, D.C.: Mobile computation offloading architecture for mobile augmented reality, case study: visualization of cetacean skeleton. Int. J. Adv. Comput. Sci. Appl. **1**(7), 665–671 (2016)
21. Nokia Siemens Networks, Intel: Increasing mobile operators' value proposition with edge computing (2013). http://www.intel.co.id/content/dam/www/public/us/en/documents/technology-briefs/edge-computing-tech-brief.pdf
22. Ismail, B.I., Goortani, E.M., Karim, M.B.A., Tat, W.M., Setapa, S., Luke, J.Y., Hoe, O.H.: Evaluation of docker as edge computing platform. In: 2015 IEEE Conference on Open Systems (ICOS), pp. 130–135, August 2015
23. de Lara, E., Gomes, C.S., Langridge, S., Mortazavi, S.H., Roodi, M.: Hierarchical serverless computing for the mobile edge. In: IEEE/ACM Symposium on Edge Computing (SEC), pp. 109–110. IEEE (2016)
24. Baresi, L., Guinea, S., Leva, A., Quattrocchi, G.: A discrete-time feedback controller for containerized cloud applications. In: Proceedings of the 2016 24th ACM SIGSOFT International Symposium on Foundations of Software Engineering, pp. 217–228 (2016)

Industrial Applications of Service and Cloud Computing

uStorage - A Storage Architecture to Provide Block-Level Storage Through Object-Based Storage

Felipe Oliveira Gutierrez[1]([⊠]), Vinicius Cardoso Garcia[1],
Jose Fernando S. Cardoso[1], Thiago Jamir[1], Josino R. Neto[1,2], Rodrigo Assad[3],
and Marcos Barreto[4]

[1] Universidade Federal de Pernambuco (UFPE) - CIn, Recife, PE, Brazil
{fog,vcg,jfsc}@cin.ufpe.br, tjamir@gmail.com
[2] Instituto Federal de Pernambuco (IFPE), Palmares, PE, Brazil
josino.neto@palmares.ifpe.edu.br
[3] Universidade Federal Rural de Pernambuco (UFRPE), Recife, PE, Brazil
assad@deinfo.ufrpe.br
[4] Universidade Federal da Bahia (UFBA), Salvador, BA, Brazil
marcosb@ufba.br

Abstract. Block-level Storage is widely used to support heavy workloads. It can be directly accessed by the operating system, but it faces some durability issues, hardware limitations and performance degradation in geographically distributed systems. Object-based Storage Device (OSD) is a data storage concept widely used to support *write-once-read-many* (WORM) systems. Because OSD contains data, metadata and an unique identifier, it becomes very powerful and customizable. OSDs are ideal for solving the increasing problems of data growth and resilience requirements while mitigating costs. This paper describes a scalable storage architecture that uses *OSD* from a distributed P2P Cloud Storage system and delivers a Block-level Storage layer to the user. This architecture combines the advantages of the replication, reliability, and scalability of a OSD on commodity hardware with the simplicity of raw block for data-intensive workload. We retrieve data from the OSD in a set of blocks called *buckets*, allowing read-ahead operations to improve the performance of the raw block layer. Through this architecture we show the possibility of using OSD on the back end and deliver a storage layer based on raw blocks with better performance to the end user. We evaluated the proposed architecture based on the cache behavior to understand non-functional properties. Experiments were performed with different cache sizes. High throughput performance was measured for heavy workloads at the two storage layers.

Keywords: Software architecture · Cloud computing · Storage as a service · Object-based Storage · Block-level Storage

© IFIP International Federation for Information Processing 2017
Published by Springer International Publishing AG 2017. All Rights Reserved
F. De Paoli et al. (Eds.): ESOCC 2017, LNCS 10465, pp. 213–228, 2017.
DOI: 10.1007/978-3-319-67262-5_16

1   Introduction

The concept for Block-level Storage is almost universally employed for all types of storage [10,17]. It splits files into evenly-sized blocks of data, each with its own address, but with no additional information (metadata) to provide more context about the block. This data storage concept can be directly accessed by the operating systems as a mounted drive volume and it delivers a significant performance improvement compared to others data storage concepts. Beyond a hundred of terabytes, however, it may run into durability issues, hardware limitations, or management overhead. Moreover, performance degrades on geographically distributed systems.

Object-based Storage (OSD) emerged after promising to be more powerful and customizable [6,13]. This data storage concept does not split files into raw blocks of data, but into entire clumps of data stored in objects that contain data, metadata, and an unique identifier. There is no limit on the type or amount of metadata, so objects can include anything (e.g., security classification). OSD is mainly used to solve problems related to data growth due to its scalability properties. Nevertheless, OSD typically does not offer good throughput for the end user.

In this work we attempt to combine the benefits of both data storage concepts. We propose a storage architecture that uses Block-level Storage on its first layer and OSD on its second layer. We created a set of blocks on the first layer and called them buckets. The buckets have metadata that are used to upload and retrieve them from the OSD to a very small and fast device for the Block-level Storage (cache). This storage architecture we call *uStorage*. The OSD layer we call *CSP* (Cloud Storage Platform) and it consists of a low-cost distribute system to store files using P2P networks.

There are several other systems that deliver a Block-level Storage to the end user, but store data in a different architectures. *Ceph* uses POSIX [24], *Panasas* uses a cluster with RAID [14], *IBM Storwize* uses a cluster [9] and *Nexenta* uses a Cloud Storage Service based on Objects [1]. It is very acceptable to use Block-level Storage on the user interface and couple with another storage architecture, as long the back-end Storage architecture addresses non-functional requirements to the Block-level Storage (e.g., reliability, responsiveness, availability). However, it is also crucial to have a good strategy on the first storage layer to handle heavy workloads.

This paper presents *uStorage*, an architecture that can handle heavy workloads on the Block-level Storage and also be coupled to an OSD. We evaluated the architecture based on the cache non-functional properties, using the same methodology adopted by others [3,7]. The buckets that are not used on the cache can be removed, and those that are requested have to be restored from the OSD. The challenge in this architecture is to optimize the bucket and the cache size to avoid performance degradation. This paper presents the uStorage architecture on Sect. 2 and its implementation details on Sect. 3. The evaluation is presented on Sect. 4 followed by some related works on Sect. 5. The final Sect. 6 describes the main conclusions and proposed future work.

2   uStorage Architecture

The *uStorage* architecture delivers raw block interface to the users through the iSCSI components presented on the Fig. 1. All the components on the *CSP* [4,5] module are used as a OSD storage. The *CSP* is a module of the *uStorage* that is responsible for saving all buckets on the *DataPeers* with its metadata on the *Metadata Storage*. The *CSP* also provides high availability for the buckets because there are at least two copies of them in different *DataPeers*. Each *DataPeer* is a commodity hardware where the buckets are stored. The horizontal scalability property is achieved by adding more *DataPeers* on the *Data Storage*.

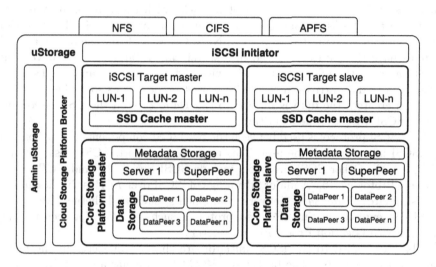

Fig. 1. *uStorage* architecture components: *CSP* (Cloud Storage Platform) contains a *Metadata Storage*, *Server* and *SuperPeer* to manage all buckets on the *DataPeers*. The iSCSI Target cache is located in a SSD drive. The admin layer uses the broker layer to manage the whole *uStorage* platform.

Block-level Storage devices are usually designed to be the first storage layer because it can be directly accessed by the operating system as a mounted drive volume. Meanwhile, OSD cannot do so without significant performance degradation. The OSD storage does not split files up into raw blocks of data. Instead, entire clumps of data are stored in an object that contains the data, metadata, and an unique identifier. There is no limit on the type or amount of metadata, which makes OSD powerful and customizable. In the enterprise data center, OSD is used for these same types of storage needs, where the data needs to be highly available and durable [4,5]. This type of system has certain characteristics that would be impossible to achieve if only one of these types of storage architectures were used. *uStorage* achieves through this architecture the following properties:

– *unlimited* storage space as much the *CSP* module can offer. This is achieved through the *DataPeers* that can be added dynamically.
– It does not use the user's computer as a cache stage or replication of files as *CSP* uses, but still guarantee the scalability and reliability of the *CSP*.
– It reaches an acceptable performance compared to other storage system.
– It provides all these features using a coupled architecture of raw blocks and OSD.

2.1   uStorage Components

uStorage delivers a virtual disk with large capacity using block-level virtualization. This virtual disk delivered to the user is on the master mode. The slave mode achieves the reliability feature of this storage architecture. The architecture uses an iSCSI Target component as cache with the *CSP* as back end to store objects. The users connect to the *uStorage* through the iSCSI initiator or by any interfaces connected to it (e.g., NFS, CIFS, APFS). The original iSCSI systems have the data centralized in a server called Target [18]. However, the iSCSI Target at the *uStorage* is a cache with high performance and small storage capacity. The data arrives in the iSCSI Target cache and as soon the metadata has been created, the data is flushed to the *DataPeers* on the *CSP*, according to the iSCSI Target cache algorithm.

The iSCSI protocol is used between the two iSCSI components and to connect the iSCSI initiator with the user. This protocol transports SCSI messages over TCP/IP [23]. Other SCSI protocols include SCSI Serial [22] and *FCP* (Fibre Channel Protocol) [15]. A major advantage of iSCSI over *FCP* is that it can run over standard *off-the-shelf* network components, such as Ethernet. Moreover, iSCSI can exploit existing IP-based protocols such as *IPSec* for security and *SLP* (Service Location Protocol) for discovery.

The files copied to the iSCSI initiator are sharded in pieces in the iSCSI Target cache (buckets). The bucket size is 2 MB and it has a set of raw blocks. Once the buckets are request by the iSCSI initiator, the iSCSI Target cache has the role of restore them from the *CSP* if they are not in the cache. If the buckets are less used by the iSCSI initiator, the iSCSI Target cache keep them only in the *CSP*. Only the frequently used buckets remain in the cache. The others will stay in the *CSP* to be requested on demand. These buckets are replicated in different *DataPeers* with the minimum quorum of two. Although the *uStorage* architecture does not use RAID as other storages architectures to replicate data [1,14], the *DataPeers* contain replicated buckets.

The cache on the iSCSI Target is a possible spot of failure that has to be always available to the iSCSI initiator. *uStorage* provides a master and slave architecture for the iSCSI Target cache on a second server. The slave server has an iSCSI Target configured with the same IP address of the master server. Its network interface is enabled only when the master goes down. All the buckets are replicated from the master *CSP* to the slave *CSP* through a process running on the *Server*. All the buckets on the master are independent from the slave server. The buckets frequently used on the master iSCSI Target cache are also updated on the slave iSCSI Target cache.

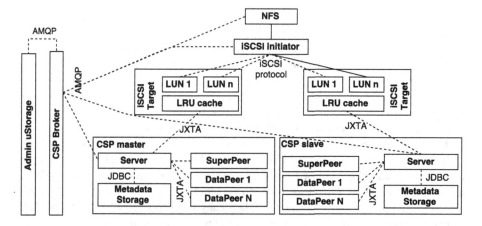

Fig. 2. Physical or deployment architectural view of the *uStorage* according to *architectural model 4+1* [11]. The users can mount the NFS drive or direct connect to the iSCSI initiator. The iSCSI Target manages all buckets on the cache and it uses an improved JXTA protocol to transfer them to the *CSP*. The user can mount the iSCSI drive and manage to add or remove *DataPeers* on the Admin through *AMQP* messages.

The iSCSI Target capacity is limited by the filesystem (i.e., ext4, xfs, NTFS) because it is virtualized. The bucket size (2 MB) allows read ahead on the files and the iSCSI Target cache spares restore operations on the *CSP*. The size of the buckets is a trade-off approach because, if they are too small it is necessary to do a lot of restore operations. Nevertheless, if they are too big the write operation lacks performance on the iSCSI protocol. Figure 2 presents the physical architecture model of the iSCSI Target connected to the *CSP*. The iSCSI Target can contain multiple instances of *LUNs* (Logic Unit Number). These instances can share the same cache space. It is better to have several iSCSI virtual disks of 8 TB capacity connected to the NFS instead of having just one very large iSCSI virtual disk of 128 TB connected. Because the iSCSI Target virtualise its size based on the *CSP* module, it can deliver a very large disk to the iSCSI initiator.

2.2 CSP (Cloud Storage Platform)

The distribute storage module *CSP* (Cloud Storage Platform) [4,5] consists of a low-cost architecture to store files as objects using P2P networks. The files are split and stored in pieces of predefined size (buckets) and recorded on several computers (network nodes) connected to the P2P network. The bucket replication is done by a running algorithm on the *Server* component. The *CSP* module can be used to store large amounts of data (greater than 1 PBytes). Figure 2 presents the communication among all components.

Superpeer is responsible to manage the *Server* and the *DataPeers* connected on the *CSP* through a P2P network. It works as a proxy that has a list of services, managing their availability. The *Server* manages the services used on the P2P network: authentication, bucket management, peers availability, *DataPeer* and bucket lookup. *Metadata Storage* stores the buckets metadata, that we use a relational database. The *Data Storage* is composed by *DataPeers* to store buckets. Buckets are files and its name start with letters that correspond to the *DataPeer* and directory that they located. The algorithm that chooses the location to store each bucket is on the *Server* component. The communication among the *CSP* components is done by a improved *JXTA* protocol, an open source P2P protocol specification created by Sun Microsystems [8].

CSP enables *unlimited* storage space reachable through large levels of horizontal scalability by simply adding new *DataPeers*. The availability feature is done by ensuring the level of bucket replication greater than one. The buckets are built on the iSCSI Target as a set of raw blocks. The *CSP* can sharded them, however this operation is not efficient when they need to be restored. The bucket represents the OSD objects because it is a file with a set of attributes that define various aspects of itself on the metadata (i.e., size, host and filesystem locality, deduplication version). This simplifies the task of the storage architecture and increases its flexibility by distributing the management of the data with the data itself.

After saving the buckets on the *CSP*, they can be removed from the iSCSI Target Cache when they are not being frequently accessed, according to the cache algorithm. The access control of these buckets is done by a read and write cache algorithm, which may have its size configured on the iSCSI Target. The cache size is usually 10 GB less the size of the SSD drive, where the iSCSI Target cache is configured (safety approach in case of the overloaded cache). The cache accelerates the read and write access to the iSCSI Target like some RAID controllers use cache with the same propose.

2.3   Providing Block-Level Storage Through Object-Based Storage

The *uStorage* architecture uses raw block (iSCSI) on the first layer and OSD on the second layer (*CSP*). The capacity of the iSCSI Target cache is virtualized to the OSD layer, that has much more scalability provision through the *DataPeers*. This strategy makes possible to have more space on the iSCSI initiator virtual disk than it is available on the iSCSI Target. Through the raw blocks on the first layer, the I/O operations are faster than OSD [6,13]. Moreover, to achieve scalability the OSD architecture is more recommended [12]. As a result, we deliver a fast interface to the user through the iSCSI initiator and scale horizontally the OSD.

The iSCSI Target cache is the main component that improves the performance of the whole storage architecture. It is possible to create different *LUN's* on this component and connect them on the same iSCSI initiator. So we can have different users sharing the same iSCSI Target cache. The *Server* is responsible to replicate all the buckets on the iSCSI Target master to the slave. All the buckets state are saved on the *Metadata Storage*, so it is possible to know which buckets were on the iSCSI Target cache master fail over.

3   uStorage Architecture Implementation

Given the *uStorage* architecture described before, the implementation of the iSCSI Target cache has the following requirements:

R.1 which clean policy must be used on the iSCSI Target cache?
R.2 when the clean policy must be executed?
R.3 how many buckets must be removed on the policy execution?
R.4 which buckets must be removed from the iSCSI Target cache?

Most of the cache policies use *LRU* (Least Recently Used) algorithm [3, 7]. Moreover, it makes more sense to leave the frequently used buckets on the cache and remove the buckets not used (R.1). The policy must be executed on the same pace that the buckets are accessed in a real scenario. So, if any file (on the raw block layer) is accessed, the policy will execute and the cache is going to have the same buckets that it had before (R.2). For this calibration we set the policy execution schedule between five and seven seconds, based on the evaluation demonstrated at Sect. 4.

It is necessary to make room for the new buckets by removing an amount of buckets that can be written between each policy execution or when the cache is almost full (90%). When the stored buckets amount exceeds 90% of the cache size, the buckets less accessed and already recorded on the *CSP* can be removed from the iSCSI Target cache. When these buckets are required to read or write, they are restored from the *CSP*. In another view, 10% of the cache free space must be enough to have a high write throughput to store new buckets and remove the ones already stored on the *CSP* (R.3), as we demonstrated on Sect. 4.

The *Least Recently Used* on the iSCSI Target cache queue must be removed. This module also knows which buckets have higher probability to contain *inodes*[1]. The metadata of the bucket has two status: *INDEX* or *DATA*. If the status is set to *INDEX*, even if it is not recently used, the bucket will not be removed. The *INDEX* buckets are set during the disk format. All other buckets after the disk formatting are set as *DATA* status. They are eligible to be removed by the policy even if they have *inodes* (R.4), because they are not crucial to open the disk and then can be found through the *inodes chain* [16].

3.1   iSCSI Target Cache Algorithm

Figure 3 shows the sequence diagram of the iSCSI Target cache algorithm, with write and read operations, according to the *architectural model 4+1* [11]. The process can be split into six components. The iSCSI components are the initiator and the Target cache modules of the *uStorage*. It receives *read* and *write* operations from the initiator and the communication is through the iSCSI protocol [18].

---

[1] An *inode* is the primary structure used in many UNIX file systems. It contains file attributes such as access time, size, and group and user information.

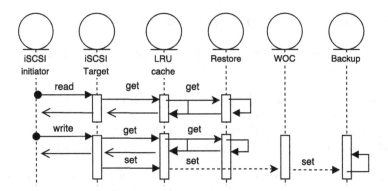

Fig. 3. Sequence diagram of the *uStorage* architecture according to *architectural model 4+1* [11]. The iSCSI's components read and write all buckets from the *LRU cache*. The *get* messages are synchronous and do not use the *WOC* component. When a bucket has to be send to the *Backup* component it is an asynchronous message and it uses the *WOC* component to make sure it is not being edited while it is being send to the *CSP*.

The *LRU cache* component is the *Least Recently Used* algorithm implemented to increase the performance on the iSCSI Target cache. The cache is allocated on a SSD hard drive with 100 GB size, which I/O responses are 250 MB/s, while the HDD are 70 MB/s. If the iSCSI Target receives a *read* operation and the bucket is in the cache, it is not necessary to restore it from the *CSP*, otherwise the process goes to the *Restore* component in a synchronous way to get the bucket. The *write* operation get the bucket from the *LRU Cache* if it is present, otherwise get it from *CSP* through the *Restore* component in a synchronous process. While this operation is writing on the *LRU Cache*, it also set a time on the *WOC* component (*policy write-on-close*) to save this bucket on the *CSP* in an asynchronous process. We decided to allocate the *Metadata Storage* component on the SSD drive to improve the cache performance.

The *WOC* component guarantees the backup process (saving buckets into the *CSP*) more efficient in an asynchronous process. This is based on the *policy write-on-close* for filesystem [20]. This strategy ensures that the bucket will only be sent to the *CSP* when it is no longer receiving bytes and also after 10 s without write access (also configurable). If the bucket contains several *inodes*, it will be changed a lot in less then 10 s and the cache algorithm will not send it to the *CSP*. If the bucket contains only data and no *inodes*, it will be written and not accessed afterwards. After 10 s with out receiving *write* I/O operations it will be sent to the *CSP* in an asynchronous process.

3.2   FSM (Finite-State Machine) for Bucket Management

Figure 4 depicts the usage control flow of buckets within the uStorage architecture. These states are persisted on the *Metadata Storage* component, as was presented at the Fig. 2. A given bucket can be in one of four states:

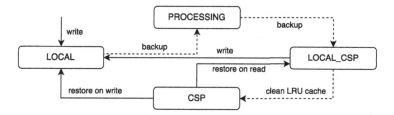

Fig. 4. Buckets metadata Finite-State Machine applied to bucket management within the *uStorage* architecture. The dotted line are asynchronous operations and the continuous lines are synchronous operations. The buckets can have four states (LOCAL, LOCAL_CSP, CSP, PROCESSING).

S.1 *LOCAL*: the bucket is only on the iSCSI Target cache and *CSP* has an old version.

S.2 *LOCAL_CSP*: the bucket has the same version on the iSCSI Target cache and *CSP*.

S.3 *CPS*: the bucket is only on *CSP* and not on the iSCSI Target cache.

S.4 *PROCESS*: the bucket is on backup process to the *CSP* and it is locked to edition.

Five operations can be performed over the buckets:

O.1 *write*: this operation always modify the buckets state to *LOCAL* and the bucket version on *CSP* became old.

O.2 *restore on write*: this operation modifies the bucket state to *LOCAL*, since it is also a *write* operation. It happens when the bucket is only on *CSP*. The bucket needs to be restored before its content is modified. If the restore operation fail the file can be corrupted.

O.3 *restore on read*: this operation doesn't modify the bucket content, however, it happens when the bucket is only on the *CSP*. The bucket state is modified to *LOCAL_CSP*.

O.4 *backup*: this operation is asynchronous (dotted line), so it does not decrease the *uStorage* architecture performance. It happens in two steps. First the buckets are changed to *PROCESS* state and when the backup is successful, its state is changed to *LOCAL_CSP*. These two steps ensure the same version on the iSCSI Target cache and *CSP*.

O.5 *clean LRU cache*: this operation is also asynchronous and it is executed by the *LRU* algorithm. The less accessed buckets and the buckets with the *LOCAL_CSP* state can be deleted from iSCSI Target cache and their state are changed to *CSP*.

3.3   Architecture Calibrations

Since the *uStorage* writing operation should be performed immediately when it is starting, a batch was created to periodically reserve space on the cache. The

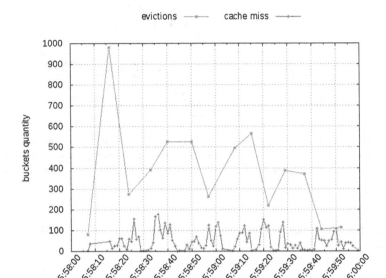

Fig. 5. *uStorage* iSCSI Target cache configured to 20 GB and set of files with 20 GB in total. The cache has the same size of the set of files we are storing. All *eviction* (bucket remove) operations are mostly due to create *inodes*. We have few *Cache Miss* (restore) operations and the *eviction* operations don't need to work often.

cache algorithm will not remove buckets until it reaches 90% of its usage, so we guarantee that 90 GB of buckets are in use. We judge to always keep 10% of the cache space free to receive new buckets and if the *CSP* is off. This space will always be available if there is any recording buckets on the iSCSI Target [19, 20]. It is hard recommended to always have a reserve free space on the iSCSI Target cache to write buckets and avoid performance degradation. This space was estimated according to calibrations and tests with the system explained on the Figs. 5 and 6.

The restore operation had to be implemented to lock the bucket for any possible write. Otherwise it is a big chance to lose the file we are accessing or even lose the whole filesystem. This situation was avoid by making sure that there is always one thread restoring the bucket requested by the iSCSI Target cache. After the restore operation is completed, read and write threads operations can be done concurrently, because the came from the iSCSI protocol. In our scenarios, the restore operations took less than 0.5 s. Considering we are using a 2 MB bucket size, the read-ahead operation gains performance just in this restore process.

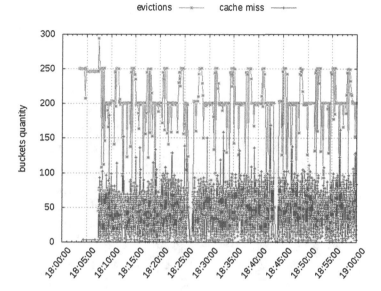

Fig. 6. *uStorage* iSCSI Target cache configured to 5 GB and set of files with 20 GB in total. The cache is four times fewer than the files we are storing. The algorithm is always making space on the cache with the *eviction* (bucket remove) operation and all the *Cache Miss* (restore) operations never overlaps the quantity of *evictions*.

4   uStorage Architecture Evaluation

We used three methodologies to evaluate the *uStorage* architecture. The purpose of each methodology was to simulate the max performance that the iSCSI Target cache can deliver to the user. The first methodology we evaluate the cache using the same concept used by *Amazon ElastiCache* to measure and take the best performance of the iSCSI Target cache [3]. The main factor of an effective cache strategy is to enable systems to have good scalability. *Amazon ElastiCache* has two major operations that are available on its cache. The *eviction* operation has the same semantics of the bucket remove operation of the iSCSI Target cache. Its objective is make place for new buckets that are arriving in the cache. The *Cache Miss* operation has the same semantic of the bucket restore operation of the iSCSI Target cache. When the bucket is not found in the iSCSI Target cache it is necessary to restore it.

A large number of *eviction* operations (bucket remove) can be a sign that the space on the cache is overloaded. If a *Cache Miss* (restore) operation is stable there is nothing to worry. However, if the combination of a large number of *Cache Miss* with a large number of *eviction* operation is happening, it is a sign that the cache is failing due a lack of memory. Figure 5 presents a 20 GB cache size and how many buckets have been processed by the *eviction* (remove) operation and by the *Cache Miss* (restore) operation. Figure 6 presents the same metrics but with a 5 GB cache. Both evaluation we used a file of 20 GB size. Through

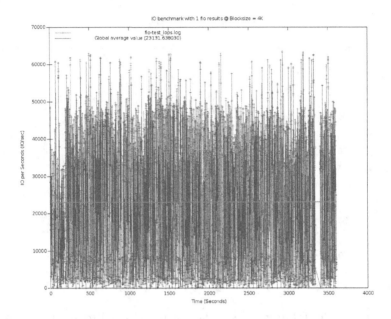

Fig. 7. Benchmark FIO of *uStorage* with 20 GB file and cache of 5 GB. Avg: 23131 IOPs.

these two metrics we can see the good behavior of the cache because the number of *Cache Miss* never exceed the number of the *eviction*. Even in a very small cache of 5 GB size and with files four times its size (20 GB size) the *eviction* and *Cache Miss* operations are more concentrated.

The second evaluation we used *FIO* benchmark [2] to test how many IOPs the iSCSI Target cache could reach. *FIO* is a popular tool to measure IOPs on Linux storage servers. We configured the cache for 5 GB size and the *FIO* benchmark to work with a set of 20 GB files. Through this configuration we could achieve 75% of *Cache Miss* (restore) and *eviction* (bucket remove) operations on the cache. Figure 7 shows that the *uStorage* reaches 63 K IOPs on its peak and an average of 23 K IOPs.

The third evaluation on the iSCSI Target cache we used the methodology proposed by [21]. The *uStorage* was set to work with different number of *LUNs* in each measure and different size of buckets as well. We variated the bucket size from 1 KB to 1 MB and took the average of the results. Then we took 10 metrics for each *LUN* quantity that we configured for the same iSCSI Target cache (1 until 4). Table 1 shows the results for writes on the same iSCSI Target cache using the *dd* command pointed to */dev/random* with a 10 GB file. The write process was in parallel as we add more *LUNs*, and we calculated the average of all results. *uStorage* could reach more IOPs comparing to a *SATA* disk, also when we add more *LUNs* on its cache to do parallel writing. The number of the threads on the *uStorage* didn't grow on the same pace of the number of *LUNs*. The same behavior can be said for the memory and cpu usage.

Table 1. Parallel write comparison on only one *SATA* hard disk and different number of *LUNs* on the same iSCSI Target cache.

SATA	IOPs	LUNs	Target cache	IOPs	Threads	Mem GB	CPU%
10 m 30 s	62.6	1	11 m 21 s	168.5	642	2.3	26.1
23 m 30 s	59.1	2	17 m 26 s	207.2	881	3.4	46.5
39 m 46 s	54.2	3	33 m 45 s	203.6	1127	3.6	59.4
58 m 10 s	81.3	4	41 m 35 s	217.2	1254	4.5	69.4

5   Related Work

This section describes some related works to the *uStorage* architecture, which therefore involve cloud storage and the closest possible to the *SAN* architectures.

NexentaStor [1] is a storage system with access levels to I/Os for files (NFS) and blocks (iSCSI). Its architecture provides techniques for spreading I/O workload over multiple domains (local and remote), while at the same time increasing operational mobility and data redundancy. File and block level I/O access are addressed. *NexentaStor* uses metadata for blocks, the domains are physical, and it has characteristics of horizontal scaling. It has a method for resolving a single server bottleneck performing one or more of the following operations: splitting a filesystem into two or more parts; extending a filesystem residing on a given storage server with its new filesystem part in a certain specified I/O domain; migrating or replicating one or more of those parts into separate I/O domains; merging some or all of the filesystem parts to create a single combined filesystem, and then redirecting the filesystem clients to use the resulting filesystem spanning multiple I/O domains. *NexentaStor* uses File-based Storage and Block-level Storage while uStorage architecture uses also OSD to reach scalability on the second storage layer.

IBM Storwize [9] has an architecture to create, read and write compressed data for utilization with a block mode access storage. The compressed data are packed into plurality of compressed units and stored in a storage *LU* (Logical Unit). One or more corresponding compressed units may be read or updated with no need of restoring the entire storage *LU* while maintaining de-fragmented *LU* structure. *IBM Storwize* specially works with cluster. The blocks are compressed and decompressed from nodes, due to save time for many restore operations and space on the entire cluster. The main goal of the *IBM Storwize* is to use less restore operations as possible, by compressing the data in blocks. The *uStorage* architecture does have similar goal and it is achieved by grouping a set of blocks in buckets, that we are configured to 2 MB size. The larger the bucket is, less restore operations are need. We tested the compress and decompress operations with set of buckets, but it waste a lot of cpu process and compete with the iSCSI PDU process.

Ceph [24] maximizes the separation between data and metadata management by replacing allocation tables with a pseudo-random data distribution function

(*CRUSH*) designed for heterogeneous and dynamic clusters of unreliable OSDs. Its device has intelligence of distributing data replication, failure detection and recovery to semi-autonomous OSDs running on a specialized local object filesystem. The design goals of *Ceph* are a POSIX filesystem (as much as close) that is scalable, reliable, and has very good performance. However, probably the most fundamental core assumption in the design of *Ceph* is that large-scale storage systems are dynamic and there are guaranteed to be failures. Therefore, the storage hardware is added and removed and the workloads on the system are changing. It is presumed there will be hardware failures and the filesystem needs to adaptable and resilient. *Ceph* uses its own filesystem based on OSD, while *uStorage* architecture uses Linux filesystem to deliver raw blocks on the primary storage layer. As result both architectures can provide a reliable storage layer to save contents with heterogeneous and dynamic cluster, but they use different ways to achieve it.

Panasas [14] is a company that builds object storage systems and took over the Extended Object FS (exofs) project, previously called *osdfs* (OSD file system). The exofs is a traditional Linux filesystem built on an object storage system with the origin of the ext2 filesystem. The *Panasas Storage Cluster* architecture is a Block-level Storage interface to OSD. This filesystem is partitioned between clients and manager, and uses RAID to strip data across OSDs. The *Panasas ActiveScale Storage Cluster* core is a decoupling of the datapath (read, write) from the control path (metadata). This separation provides a method for allowing clients direct and parallel access to the storage devices, providing high bandwidth to individual clients and to workstation clusters. It also distributes the system metadata allowing shared file access without a central bottleneck. Metadata is managed in a metadata server, a computing node separate from the OSDs, but residing on the same physical network. While *Panasas* uses RAID to make the data reliable, *uStorage* uses the *DataPeers* to store buckets.

6   Conclusion

This paper presented a storage architecture that uses Object-based Storage Device (OSD) on the back-end and delivers a Block-level Storage interface to the user. The motivation to use these two data storage concepts is because raw blocks handle heavy workloads and the OSD can easily scale horizontally with great reliability. The cache algorithm was evaluated by three methodologies. First we analyzed the health of the cache based on *Amazon ElastiCache* parameters [3]. Second we used the *FIO* benchmark to see how much IOPs the iSCSI Target cache achieves when it is configured in a very small size. Third we instantiated several *LUNs* on the same iSCSI Target cache and took metrics with different buckets size. When multiple users are connected to the *uStorage* the architecture uses less resources than multiple iSCSI Target on the same architecture.

Some considerations of future work on this architecture can be spread to its components. The iSCSI Target cache algorithm can be improved using *blackbox* model for storage system [25]. The *Metadata Storage* can use a different database to improve its performance, but it is still necessary to guarantee the ACID properties.

Acknowledgment. This work was supported by Ustore(http://www.usto.re) and partially supported by the National Institute of Science and Technology for Software Engineering (INES 2.0(http://www.ines.org.br)) grants 465614/2014-0, funded by CNPq(http://www.cnpq.br) grants 573964/2008-4 and FACEPE(http://www.facepe.br) grants APQ-1037-1.03/08.

References

1. Aizman, A.: Location independent scalable file and block storage. Google Patents (2012). https://www.google.com/patents/US20120011176, uS Patent App. 12/874,978
2. Axboe, J.: Fio-flexible i/o tester synthetic benchmark (2005). https://github.com/axboe/fio. Accessed 13 June 2015
3. Chiu, D., Agrawal, G.: Evaluating caching and storage options on the amazon web services cloud. In: 2010 11th IEEE/ACM International Conference on Grid Computing (GRID), pp. 17–24. IEEE (2010)
4. Duarte, M.P., Assad, R.E., Ferraz, F.S., Ferreira, L.P., de Lemos Meira, S.R.: An availability algorithm for backup systems using secure p2p platform. In: 2010 Fifth International Conference on Software Engineering Advances (ICSEA), pp. 477–481. IEEE (2010)
5. Durão, F., Assad, R., Fonseca, A., Fernando, J., Garcia, V., Trinta, F.: USTO.RE: a private cloud storage software system. In: Daniel, F., Dolog, P., Li, Q. (eds.) ICWE 2013. LNCS, vol. 7977, pp. 452–466. Springer, Heidelberg (2013). doi:10.1007/978-3-642-39200-9_38
6. Factor, M., Meth, K., Naor, D., Rodeh, O., Satran, J.: Object storage: the future building block for storage systems. In: 2005 IEEE International Symposium on Mass Storage Systems and Technology, pp. 119–123, June 2005
7. Fitzpatrick, B.: Distributed caching with memcached. Linux J. **2004**(124), 5 (2004)
8. Gong, L.: Jxta: a network programming environment. IEEE Internet Comput. **5**(3), 88–95 (2001)
9. Kedem, N., Amit, Y., Amit, N.: Method and system for compression of data for block mode access storage, 9 September 2008. https://www.google.com/patents/US7424482, uS Patent 7,424,482
10. Khattar, R.K., Murphy, M.S., Tarella, G.J., Nystrom, K.E.: Introduction to Storage Area Network, SAN. IBM Corporation, International Technical Support Organization (1999)
11. Kruchten, P.B.: The 4+1 view model of architecture. IEEE Softw. **12**(6), 42–50 (1995)
12. Martin, B.E., Pedersen, C.H., Bedford-Roberts, J.: An object-based taxonomy for distributed computing systems. Computer **24**(8), 17–27 (1991). doi:10.1109/2.84873
13. Mesnier, M., Ganger, G.R., Riedel, E.: Object-based storage. IEEE Commun. Mag. **41**(8), 84–90 (2003)
14. Nagle, D., Serenyi, D., Matthews, A.: The panasas activescale storage cluster: delivering scalable high bandwidth storage. In: Proceedings of the 2004 ACM/IEEE Conference on Supercomputing, SC 2004, p. 53. IEEE Computer Society, Washington (2004). 10.1109/SC.2004.57

15. Neto, A.J., da Fonseca, N.L.: Um estudo comparativo do desempenho dos protocolos iscsi e fibre channel. IEEE Latin Am. Trans. **5**(3), 151–157 (2007)
16. Rosenblum, M., Ousterhout, J.K.: The design and implementation of a log-structured file system. ACM Trans. Comput. Syst. (TOCS) **10**(1), 26–52 (1992)
17. Ruemmler, C., Wilkes, J.: An introduction to disk drive modeling. Computer **27**(3), 17–28 (1994)
18. Satran, J., Meth, K., Sapuntzakis, C., Chadalapaka, M., Zeidner, E.: Ietf rfc 3720: internet small computer systems interface (iscsi), April 2004. http://www.ietf.org/rfc/rfc3720.txt
19. Gnanasundaram, S., Shrivastava, A. (eds.): Information Storage and Management: Storing, Managing, and Protecting Digital Information in Classic, Virtualized, and Cloud Environments. EBL-Schweitzer, Wiley, Hoboken (2012). https://books.google.com.br/books?id=PU7gkW9ArxIC
20. Silberschatz, A., Galvin, P.B., Gagne, G.: Sistemas Operacionais com Java. Elsevier, Rio de Janeiro (2004)
21. Performance Test Specification: Solid state storage performance test specification enterprise. Citeseer (2013)
22. Steinberg, D., Birk, Y.: An empirical analysis of the ieee-1394 serial bus protocol. IEEE Micro **20**(1), 58–65 (2000)
23. Troppens, U., Erkens, R., Mueller-Friedt, W., Wolafka, R., Haustein, N.: Storage networks explained: basics and application of fibre channel SAN, NAS, iSCSI, infiniband and FCoE. John Wiley & Sons (2011)
24. Weil, S.A., Brandt, S.A., Miller, E.L., Long, D.D.E., Maltzahn, C.: Ceph: a scalable, high-performance distributed file system. In: Proceedings of the 7th Symposium on Operating Systems Design and Implementation. pp. 307–320, OSDI 2006, USENIX Association, Berkeley, CA, USA (2006). http://dl.acm.org/citation.cfm?id=1298455.1298485
25. Yin, L., Uttamchandani, S., Katz, R.: An empirical exploration of black-box performance models for storage systems. In: 14th IEEE International Symposium on Modeling, Analysis, and Simulation of Computer and Telecommunication Systems, MASCOTS 2006, pp. 433–440. IEEE (2006)

Heart Disorder Detection with Menard Algorithm on Apache Spark

Lorenzo Carnevale[1,3(✉)], Antonio Celesti[2], Maria Fazio[1], Placido Bramanti[3], and Massimo Villari[1,3]

[1] Department of Engineering, University of Messina, Messina, Italy
{lcarnevale,mfazio,mvillari}@unime.it
[2] Scientific Research Organisational Unit, University of Messina, Messina, Italy
acelesti@unime.it
[3] IRCCS Centro Neurolesi "Bonino Pulejo", Messina, Italy
{lcarnevale,pbramanti,mvillari}@irccsme.it

Abstract. Nowadays, healthcare is facing Big Data processing in order to support medical staff by means of decision making tools. In this context, a challenging topic is the storing and analysis of data in the cardiology field. Electrocardiogram produces signals about the heart health that need to be processed in order to detect a possible disorder. In this paper, we discuss an Apache Spark based tool and that uses the Menard algorithm. In order to validate our solution, we performed experiments on a use case in which the algorithm has been implemented in order to detect heart disorder. Experiments prove the goodness of our approach in terms of performance.

Keywords: Big Data · Healthcare · Cardiology · Heart · ECG · Arrhythmia

1 Introduction

Currently, the healthcare industry is looking at the adoption of Big Data due to the volume, velocity and variety properties of health data. Big Data solutions have been adopted so far in different healthcare fields including biotechnology [1], clinical analysis [2], and so on. Therefore, a careful study of clinical data performed by means of decision making tools helps doctors to make diagnosis.

In this regard, hospital facilities are relying on external providers or internal staff to manage and analyze clinical data. Apache Spark is a licensed framework designed to support distributed applications for creating batch applications, interactive queries and stream processing. Spark adopts the MapReduce software framework, created by Google to support distributed data computing on cluster.

In this scientific work, we used Apache Spark in order to analyze electrocardiogram (ECG) signals. Specifically, goal of our analysis was to detect heart disorder. To this end, we planned to use the Menard algorithm.

© IFIP International Federation for Information Processing 2017
Published by Springer International Publishing AG 2017. All Rights Reserved
F. De Paoli et al. (Eds.): ESOCC 2017, LNCS 10465, pp. 229–237, 2017.
DOI: 10.1007/978-3-319-67262-5_17

The rest of the paper is organized as follows. Related work are summarized in Sect. 2. An overview about heart physiognomy and functionality and ECG is presented in Sects. 3 and 4, whereas a Menard algorithm description and its Spark implementation for hearbeat peaks detection are presented in Sect. 5. Experiments and evaluation results are presented in Sect. 6. In the end, conclusion and lights to the future are summarized in Sect. 7.

2   Related Work

The scientific community has proposed several scientific works on heart disorder analysis in order to improve the accuracy, prevent diseases and reduce mortality. In the following, we report some of these works.

Many scientific works combine ECG signal analysis with the most famous Big Data framework: Apache Hadoop. A tele-ECG system has been proposed in [3]. The authors aimed to process Big Data in order to detect and monitor heart diseases. They proposed a cluster which takes advantage of Apache Spark framework. Specifically, this system classifies data using decision tree and random forest.

An analysis of arrhythmias has ben proposed in [4], in which the authors proposed an automatic detection of P-wave in an ECG. More specifically, they worked a improved method based on local distance transform, such as horizontal segments and rising or declining segment. As result, they proved the simplicity and efficiency of the algorithms for transplanting to wearable medical devices whose processing ability is weak.

In order to facilitate the data migration from medical devices to Cloud storage, we mention the work proposed in [5]. The authors described the first step of an architecture able to manage the Big Data Acquisition and Integration workflow for storing health data coming from several medical instrumentations. This scientific work has proved the goodness of the method used in terms of time performance.

A Cardiovascular Disease (CVD) detection algorithm was proposed in [6]. The algorithm uses patient demographic data as input, along with several ECG signal features automatically extracted through signal processing techniques. The algorithm has been integrated into a web based system that can be used at anytime by patients to check their heart health status. Signals are sent from the ECG sensor attached on the patient's body to the detection algorithm via an Android device. Cross-validation results showed the 98.29% accuracy.

We aim to enrich the scientific literature by proposing a work that uses the Menard algorithm to perform the distributed calculation of an ECG signal through the Apache Spark framework, in order to detect the most common heart diseases.

3   The Heart. How Does It Work?

The heart is passively filled with blood that comes from veins and actively pushes blood through the body. A complete contraction and relaxation sequence

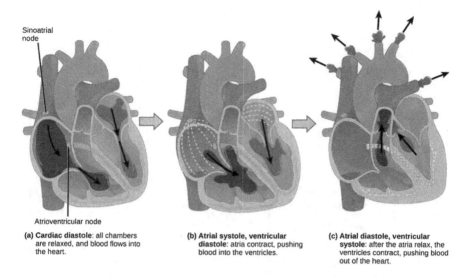

(a) **Cardiac diastole**: all chambers are relaxed, and blood flows into the heart.

(b) **Atrial systole, ventricular diastole**: atria contract, pushing blood into the ventricles.

(c) **Atrial diastole, ventricular systole**: after the atria relax, the ventricles contract, pushing blood out of the heart.

Fig. 1. The heart cycle (The mammalian heart & cardiac cycle)

represents the heart cycle, which normally is repeated about 75 times per minute. The Fig. 1 shows this cycle.

Specifically, in the first phase (diastole) the heart is completely relaxed and blood flows into its four cavities because of the atriovascular valves opening. The second phase (systole) begins with a short limbs contraction that completely fills ventricles with blood. Afterwards, the ventricles will contract for about 0.3 s. The force of their contraction closes the atrioventricular valves, opens the semilunar valves and pumps blood into the large arteries. During the last phase, blood flows into the atrioventriculars.

4   Heart Medical Instrumentation: The ECG

The electrocardiogram (ECG) is an instrumental diagnostic test that graphically records the rhythm and electrical activity of the heart. This allows the cardiologist to detect health disorder such as the presence of heart arrhythmias, ischemia, myocardial infarction or outcomes of a previous heart attack.

Indeed, heart pathological phenomena creates abnormal conditions in the muscle fibrocells, generating a different pattern from the standard. However, a standard pattern does not represent a proper heart condition, and vice versa, healthy people can have abnormal ECG outcomes. In these conditions, medical opinion is always mandatory.

The ECG test produces positive and negative waves, according to the signal position compared to the baseline, called isoelectric. Each wave is the graphic representation of an electric phenomenon that occurred in the heart. In particular, we can distinguish five signal period as reported in the Fig. 2. For our

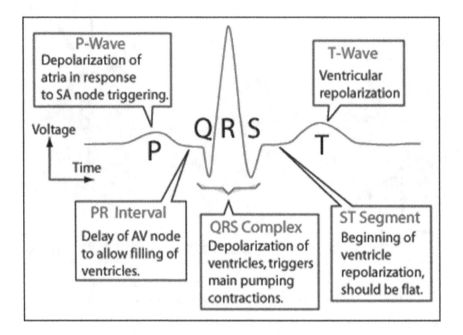

Fig. 2. ECG outcomes (hyperphysics.phy-astr.gsu.edu)

purpose, here we specify the QRS complex as the stimulus propagation to the ventricular muscle.

5   Application Design

Over the years, many algorithms have been developed for recognizing the QRS complex, which can be classified according to their complexity and performance. Specifically, most efficient and complex algorithms are based on appropriate techniques for filtering and processing ECG signals, whereas less complex algorithms are based on statistical thresholds. In the following, we are going to focus on a specific algorithm based on ECG signal derivation: the Menard algorithm [7]. This is calculated using the following equation:

$$Y(n) = -2X(n-2) - X(n-1) + X(n+1) + 2X(n+2) \qquad (1)$$

Afterwards, a ζ threshold of 70% of the maximum $Y(n)$ value is chosen:

$$\zeta = 0.7 * max[Y(n)] \qquad (2)$$

Finally, the algorithm adopts the following decision rule to detect the QRS complex:

$$Y(i) > \zeta \Rightarrow QRS \qquad (3)$$

In this scientific work, the Menard algorithm has been used for calculating the QRS complex thorugh the utilization of Apache Spark. The dataset used for the following experiments comes from the Physionet.org European ST-T Database. It includes a signal acquired by a digitizer with sampling rate equal to $f_s = 250\,Hz$. In order to process it, the file must be properly formatted. For this purpose, two preliminary steps were needed.

Primarily, having to act on multiple samples at the same time, we needed to organize an appropriate set of samples on one file line because Apache Spark treates each of them as a strings RDD. Moreover, Spark distributes workload in tasks, which involves multiple lines processement of the RDD. Nevertheless, the Menard algorithm implementation performs the derivation through the formula 1, which shows how a continuous set of data is needed. Indeed, in order to determine the nth element of the derivative, we needed to know the two previous and subsequent elements of the nth ECG signal. Thus, we overlap content introducing row by row redundancy (except the last one). This avoids the information losing during the cluster distribution phase. Moreover, during the source file formatting process, each line is indexed for tracking the reference samples.

However, how many samples should form an RDD element? How many values should be placed on a row of the file? Let's consider that an electrocardiogram typically oscillates between -20 mv and 20 mv, the calculation of the Menard algorithm threshold may not take into account these variations using a signal large portion. Therefore, it may not correctly detect heartbeat peaks. The proposed solution was to implement a version of the algorithm with an adaptive threshold, which is calculated differently for each sample block.

Thus, our implementation uses a set of samples with a duration equal to 10 s. To this end, if we indicate with f_s the sampling frequency of the ECG signal, all the file lines (except the last one) have $n = (f_s * 10) + 4$, where 4 is due to the abovementioned overlap.

The only information required for calculating the QRS complex is represented by the detected peak index because, multiplying it by the sampling frequency reciprocal, it is useful to trace the beat time. Moreover, we had to determine which peak signals above the threshold may be considered a heartbeat. Indeed, these values are more than one around a QRS complex. In order to simplify it, we chose the first value above the threshold. The Fig. 3 shows the peak signals of an ECG derivative.

In order to distribute the RDD to the cluster's nodes and create a elements list on the driver, it is necessary to use the *collect()* method. It is the first action performed by the application. Indeed, until now, we have only talked about transformations. Therefore, the *saveAsTextFile()* method examines all the peaks' RDD trasformations in order to save it on a file.

What if the threshold values of a ECG signal section were between two blocks (or between two nodes)? Both the first index above the threshold of the first block and the first index above the threshold of the second block would be selected as peaks. The proposed solution requires that application knows the values found, and recognizes the extremely close peaks.

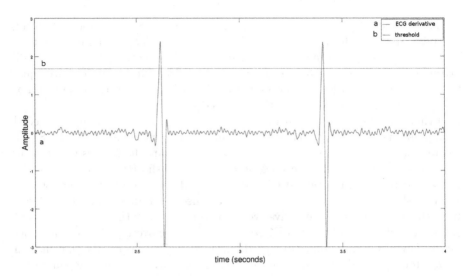

Fig. 3. ECG derivative and threshold

6 Experiments

The testbed for performing our experiments was configured into a three nodes (1 master, 2 slaves) docker distributed environment with the following hardware specifications: Quad-Core and RAM 8 GB. Each node was configured with Ubuntu 14.04, OpenJDK 7, Spark 1.6.1 and Scala 2.11.8. Moreover, the Apache Spark framework used its scheduling process, without relying on third party cluster manager, such as YARN. Specifically, using a 5 GB input file, Spark distributes the workload in 157 tasks among cluster's nodes.

The test included a hour ECG signal with sampling rate equal to 360 Hz. With reference to Sect. 5, actions carried out by the Spark application are *collect* and *saveAsTextFile*. In this regard, we show the *collect* tests outcomes in the Fig. 4.

The temporal outcomes are quite similar, as highlighted by the small confidence interval. The *collect* average time value is about 23 s.

Now consider the case of the *saveAsTextFile* action, shown in the Fig. 5. Again, the input size increasing causes a nonlinear increasing of the action execution time. Specifically, the average execution time is about 5.6 s. In this specific context, the *collect* benefits more from parallelization than *saveAsTextFile*.

The analyses carried out are related to a specific ECG signal. Clearly, each ECG differs from others in terms of peaks and abnormalities, therefore these outcomes are not considered indicative for generic ECG signal.

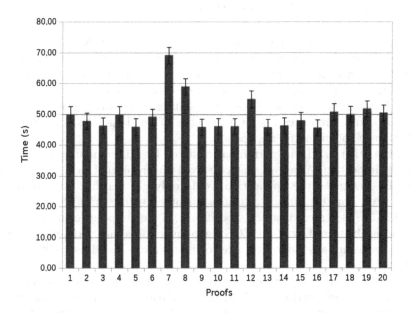

Fig. 4. *collect* action for 5 GB file. 20 proofs average and confidence interval equal to 95%

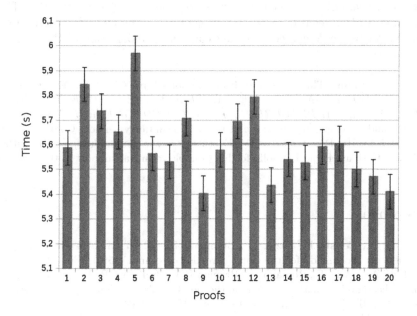

Fig. 5. *saveAsTextFile* action for 5 GB file. 20 proofs average and confidence interval equal to 95%

7   Conclusion and Future Work

This scientific work has addressed the problem of the ECG signals distributed processing. Specifically, the algorithm implemented for the determination of heartbeats and arrhythmias required a preprocessing phase. Each Big Data framework bases its computing philosophy on task independence, wherefore this context is not in the ideal conditions for exploiting distributed processing. To this end, a local files preprocessing must be made. Thus, large files could represent the bottleneck of the entire application.

On the other hand, the performance offered by this computing paradigm is definitely important. As a conseguence, solved the problem of local preprocessing of the ECG signals, the application would only get benefits from processing on a cluster. For this purpose, an idea might be to use an ad hoc device for recording the electrocardiogram. Specifically, if we suppose to make a device that during the recording of the ECG signal introduces the overlapping required for the algorithm, any limitation due to the nature of the data itself would be eliminated.

From the algorithm point of view, the ECG signal analysis was performed based on the heart rhythm obtained by calculating the R-R intervals. Indeed, more complex operations could be implemented by making elaborations based on the shape of the waves that make up a heartbeat. Thus, exploiting the compute parallelization, it would be possible to implement computationally highly costly algorithms by obtaining relevant performance by processing on a cluster.

Finally, Spark Streaming could be used to perform continuous and Real Time processing. In this regard, an ad-hoc device for sending electrocardiogram sections should be implemented, allowing continuous monitoring of the patient's health status.

Acknowledgment. This work has been supported by Cloud for Europe (C4E) Tender: *REALIZATION OF A RESEARCH AND DEVELOPMENT PROJECT (PRE-COMMERCIAL PROCUREMENT) ON "CLOUD FOR EUROPE"*, Italy-Rome: Research and development services and related consultancy services Contract notice: 2014/S 241-424518. Directive: 2004/18/EC (http://www.cloudforeurope.eu/). Authors would like to thank Fabio Pandolfo for his valuable technical support in this scientific work.

References

1. Celesti, A., Celesti, F., Fazio, M., Bramanti, P., Villari, M.: Are next-generation sequencing tools ready for the cloud? Trends Biotechnol. **35**(6), 486–489 (2017)
2. Celesti, A., Maria, F., Romano, A., Bramanti, A., Bramanti, P., Villari, M.: An oais-based hospital information system on the cloud: analysis of a nosql column-oriented approach. IEEE J. Biomed. Health Inform. **PP**(99), 1 (2017)
3. Ma'sum, M.A., Jatmiko, W., Suhartanto, H.: Enhanced tele ECG system using hadoop framework to deal with big data processing. In: 2016 International Workshop on Big Data and Information Security (IWBIS). IEEE, October 2016

4. Wang, Y., Wang, L., Chen, X., Zhu, W.: P wave detection and delineation based on distances transform. In: 2016 IEEE Trustcom/BigDataSE/ISPA. IEEE, August 2016

5. Carnevale, L., Celesti, A., Fazio, M., Bramanti, P., Villari, M.: How to enable clinical workflows to integrate big healthcare data. In: 2017 IEEE Symposium on Computers and Communications (ISCC) (ISCC 2017). Heraklion, Greece, July 2017

6. Alshraideh, H., Otoom, M., Al-Araida, A., Bawaneh, H., Bravo, J.: A web based cardiovascular disease detection system. J. Med. Syst. **39**(10), 122 (2015)

7. Menrad, A. (ed.): Dual microprocessor system for cardiovascular data acquisition, processing and recording. In: Inr. Con5 Industrial Elect. Contr. Instrument. IEEE (1981)

Author Index

Printed in the United States
By Bookmasters